The Eleven Commandments of Wildly Successful Women

Pamela Gilberd

Dear Marilyn—
Thank you for sharing your
words of wisdom to make this
book possible.
Enjoy—
Pam

Macmillan Spectrum • USA

Library of Congress Catalog Card Number: 96-068537

International Standard Book Number: 0-02-861174-8

98 97 96   9 8 7 6 5 4 3 2 1

Interpretation of the printing code: the rightmost number of the first series of numbers is the year of the book's printing; the rightmost number of the second series of numbers is the number of the book's printing. For example, a printing code of 96-1 shows that the first printing occurred in 1996.

Printed in the United States of America

Design by Amy Peppler Adams—designLab, Seattle

About three months into this project, my then-fifteen-year-old son Tyler came to the door of my converted bedroom office and watched me at my desk. "You're really doing this, aren't you, Mom?" he observed in his matter-of-fact way. It was a statement. Not even my own desire to make this happen exceeded my will to make it happen for him. Not to prove to him that his mom could do what she set out to do, but to offer him the hope that if he wanted something and was willing to put in the time, accept the rejections, and face some embarrassment at the inevitable limitations to be overcome, he could make it. I wanted to affirm that people should never limit their thinking. They should dream and then go for their dreams, no matter how unlikely it might seem at the time that they would ever materialize. Tyler became my immediate focus as he stood in the doorway, but this desire is for all of our children.

To Fred, my husband and best friend,
and all of our wonderful children—
Tyler and Tauni Swenson,
Sam, Randall, Peter, and Adam Gilberd

Table of Contents

Foreword

From the founder of the children's retail chain Gymboree to the publisher of the best seller *Random Acts of Kindness* and the construction-company CEO who lives down the street, women across America are enjoying—and creating—wild

"Wildly successful women..." three words that definitely go together!

success in economic sectors from computer technology to wine making. Women offer new visions of what *can be* in business and new means for achieving traditional goals. The list of women creating products, providing jobs, and making new rules for American business is a long one.

So if women already are wildly successful, why do we need this book?

Women's economic creativity is one of the best-kept secrets in business today. Consider this. Nearly eight million U.S. businesses are woman-owned. Women are starting businesses at twice the rate of men. One of every four U.S. workers is employed by a woman-owned business. Yet a recent survey of newspaper business sections showed that only 14 percent of front-page references were to women.

It's time to acknowledge the truth—that working women have the tools to create wild success for ourselves and others and that we use those tools every day. The economic achievement of women *is* the untold business story of the nineties. *The Eleven Commandments of Wildly Successful Women* gets that story out in all its richness. It helps ensure that the breadth of women's economic power and profit-producing ability will remain secret no longer.

But there's more. For every woman achieving wild success, there's another who wants to . . . but feels stuck, stymied, unsure what path to take. A glass ceiling limits women to just 3 to 5 percent of senior-level positions in major companies while the total U.S. work-force is 48 percent female. There are few visible female role models in nontraditional fields, meaning that finding mentors is harder for women than for men. Self-doubt keeps many women from getting the credit and success they deserve. In the *Working Women Count!* survey of a quarter-million American women, women of all ages and occupations told of their distress at being taken less seriously on the job than men.

Furthermore, employees and employers are redefining goals. Our economy is increasingly based on small business. And in today's service-based, technology- and knowledge-intensive organizations, nearly every worker has responsibilities for customer service and job innovation. Entrepreneurial spirit is vital to all.

Meanwhile, many women—and men!—feel trapped in a workplace world they didn't make. They seek new visions of success encompassing more than a fat paycheck or a title with clout. How to experience career success without foregoing relationships or suffering burnout . . . how to gain the skills and confidence to create a wholly new kind of business . . . how to make money while making a positive difference in the world. . . . Working women ask these questions and lots more.

Eleven Commandments offers life lessons in the form of stories shared by dozens of successful women who have struggled with these issues. The stories are honest, acknowledging the obstacles and failures that come before, during, and after success. They're inspiring *and* hardheadedly practical, making clear that in the same lifetime we need to assess our spiritual progress and learn the rules of the money game. Perhaps most important, they come from women of all ages, backgrounds, and circumstances—with or without college educations or children to support, young and starting out or older and searching for the significant challenge that will utilize a lifetime's worth of hard-won skills.

Pam Gilberd introduces us to so many different women who have created success on their own terms, there's no way to read the book without feeling you can do it, too.

Ultimately, though, real success is more than an individual woman making it on her own. By sharing hard-earned truths, affirmation and support, women help other women realize their goals. A good society—where individuals and families prosper and a million creative ideas flourish—can be built on that. As executive director of BPW/USA—the nation's oldest and largest organization dedicated to the workplace advancement of business and professional women—this is an old truth to me. But in acknowledging the value of sharing one's success, Gilberd has set her business book apart.

Gilberd's eleventh commandment may matter most: Share your knowledge, give back—and you'll create a success greater than you dream. Think of this book as a group of mentors in a paper cover—role models in black and white. Read it. Learn. But don't stop there. You too have a story to share. You can help someone else on her climb. Keep the cycle going. Doing that, you'll achieve wild success—not only for yourself, but for all of us.

Now onward—to wild success!

Audrey Tayse Haynes
Executive Director
Business and Professional Women/USA

Acknowledgments

Great thanks to the "cast of thousands" (or so it seems) who have made this book possible. Thanks to:

- My encouraging family—to my patient and supportive husband, thanks for all the great dinners; to my son at home, thanks for rubbing my tense shoulders; to my daughter in Boston, thanks for being my greatest promoter; to my mother, thanks for being there for me and earnestly listening to the daily update; to our other sons in points around the globe, thanks for cheering me on; to my dad and his wife, thanks for your enthusiasm; and to my brother, thanks for believing.

- All of the wildly successful women I interviewed for generously sharing your time, insights, and knowledge—the wellspring of this book. And a special thanks to Sally Edwards for suggesting I call her literary agent, Mike Snell.

- Mike Snell for your wildly clever input and assistance, your undying belief in me, and for your wonderful laugh. And for finding a great publisher for this book.

- Dick Staron, Editor-in-Chief of Macmillan Spectrum, for being the champion of this book for your new imprint, Macmillan Spectrum.

- Sheryl Fullerton, my "fairy god-editor," for coming in at the eleventh hour and guiding me with your experience, intelligence, and wit.

- The many other advisors of this project for your words of wisdom.

- My friends for reading the work-in-progress and offering your candid advice: Amy Rothberg, Joyce Routson, and Bev Olivier. A special thanks to Shirley Dennis and Myrna Nickelsen.

- Julie Payne, who supported my efforts and helped me with my urgent computer questions.

- The Business and Professional Women/USA for writing the foreword. And special thanks to Audrey Tayse Haynes, Executive Director, and Marcia Clemmitt, Editor of *National Business Woman.*

Introduction

I n 1982 I started a division within an Oakland, California, company to manufacture large, wood-framed, canvas-topped patio umbrellas, called market umbrellas. I became the "Umbrella Lady" and enjoyed the success my division achieved over the next ten years. In that same time frame, I also divorced and supported my own two children, then married a bachelor father who was raising his four sons. In 1992 the tough economic times proved too much for the company as it was. As a result of the company's reorganization, and despite the umbrella division's success, I found myself among the ranks of ex-employees searching for a new job and a new identity.

When I lost my job, I wondered how other people—especially women—were handling their (often unwanted) career transitions. I was curious about how they made it through such changes and still found ways to be successful. I wondered, in fact, how they defined success. Since I knew that massive change was now a fact of business and career life, I believed that their stories would be interesting to others, too. So I decided to find and interview successful, entrepreneurially inclined women—not the success icons who are featured in business or celebrity magazines but women who have overcome difficult challenges and achieved excellence in their work and lives. After 125 interviews, I have found the courage and character of these women inspiring and their advice practical and helpful. Whether they had their own businesses, were part of corporations, or ran nonprofit organizations, they were generous in sharing their stories with the hopes that what they had to say would help others. They candidly let me in on their philosophies, strategies, experiences, foibles, reflections, and wisdom so that I could in turn put them in this book and show other women how they can create their own definitions of success.

Where the Eleven Commandments Come From

As I conducted interviews with this highly diverse group of women, their differences were apparent. Some had prestigious MBAs, while others had barely finished high school. Some had extensive experience in and knowledge of business, and others had very little when they found their routes to success. They were in all kinds of businesses and industries, from public relations consulting to fashion retailing to publishing to construction to high tech, to name just a few. While the facts of their lives and business situations differed dramatically, I noticed that they shared several common attitudes and issues, and that those attitudes and issues were fundamental to their distinctive approach to achieving high levels of personal and professional success. As I listened to and sorted through our sometimes lengthy conversations, I didn't try to find hard and fast rules. Instead I looked for common threads of ideas that motivated these women and made them successful. Each spoke about her personal perspectives as well as her outlook on her business. To confirm the principles and trends I noticed, I discussed them with career counselors, entrepreneurial coaches, outplacement advisors, psychologists, and educators in the field of business. From these recurring themes I created the eleven commandments.

You might be asking yourself how these women came to be defined as wildly successful. They aren't, after all, Mary Kay Ash, Danielle Steele, or Oprah Winfrey. I wanted to find women who were closer to my—and most other women's—experiences, who have discovered their own paths, fought daunting odds, learned hard-won lessons, pursued ambitious goals, achieved significant business results, and from all of that created satisfying personal definitions of success. Those definitions include impressive material gains but also extend beyond wealth, fame, and power to include other less tangible rewards such as a passion for work, integration of career and personal values and goals, and contributions to making the world a better place.

When you look at the commandments, you'll see an emphasis on positive attitude, self-reliance and responsibility, persistence, risk-taking, preparation, and planning. These women have found that the combination of these crucial elements is the key to their success.

The Eleven Commandments of Wildly Successful Women

Commandment One: *One size does not fit all—create YOUR definition of success.*

Commandment Two: *Take responsibility for your career.*

Commandment Three: *Change your thinking, change your life.*

Commandment Four: *When the odds are against you, defy the odds.*

Commandment Five: *Fantasize your future but create your game plan.*

Commandment Six: *Get ready, get set, RISK!*

Commandment Seven: *When someone says "you can't," say "Watch me!"*

Commandment Eight: *Become financially savvy.*

Commandment Nine: *See mistakes as road signs, not road blocks.*

Commandment Ten: *Enjoy your work and your life.*

Commandment Eleven: *Give back to keep the cycle of success going.*

Who Should Read this Book

Whether you're looking for your first job, reentering the workplace after a hiatus, changing your career because of corporate restructuring, feeling bored in your current job and wanting a change, or wishing to start your own business, you're faced with transitional stress that can be overwhelming. *The Eleven Commandments of Wildly Successful Women* creates a framework to help you solve the problems of career transitions and to find your own entrepreneurial spirit. The many stories of women in this book will give you information and help in easing your job search, successfully developing your own business, or assisting you in getting "unstuck."

If you are among the many women who are thinking about starting a business of your own, this book should be of particular interest. Women who start their own businesses cover the spectrum of life—from those starting out in the workplace to those leaving their highly paid positions as corporate executives. Since job security is quickly becoming a thing of the past, more and more women see self-employment and business ownership as viable opportunities.

If you work in a corporation, you may find the strategies of successful corporate women helpful. Or you may just be curious about how other women run their divisions. The stories of corporate women in this book will give you insight into a variety of industries.

What this Book Will Do for You

By defining and explaining the eleven commandments with real-life examples of entrepreneurial women, this book will:

- Expose you to the philosophies and attitudes of successful women to help you develop the confidence to direct your own career.

- Equip you with practical tools and workable strategies to discover and use your entrepreneurial spirit in career management, workplace transitions, job searches, and starting your own business.

- Encourage you to ask yourself new questions about your goals, values, and your definition of success.

- Provide you with examples of how others have defined success and inspiring stories of how they have achieved it.

I believe you will find as much enjoyment "meeting" the remarkable women in *The Eleven Commandments of Wildly Successful Women* as I did in talking with them. Their encouragement and sound advice are meant to be part of a never-ending story—one that's continued and shared from one woman to another.

Commandment One

One Size Does Not Fit All— Create YOUR Definition of Success

If someone were to ask you whether you consider yourself successful, what would you say? With whom would you compare yourself? What standards would you use? Is success a matter of achievement? Satisfaction? Position? Money? Or what? Many of us have adopted definitions of success that come from outside ourselves, from family or the media or the companies we've joined or any other number of others who provide the yardsticks that tell us whether we're measuring up.

> **"Success is measured not necessarily by what others see but by what they don't see—personal self-worth. Success is accomplishing what you most wish for yourself."**
> —Lillian Vernon,
> Founder & President,
> Lillian Vernon, Inc.

When you talk to wildly successful women, you quickly see that they have expanded the traditional definition of success. Through hard-won business experience and personal insight, they have discovered that success is a process, not a destination. It includes not just the well-known tangibles of wealth, power, and fame, but intangibles like finding a way to make a difference in the world, integrating passion with their work, giving back to others and to their communities, and making sure that their work reflects their priorities and their values. These intangibles have in no way meant that these wildly successful women have had to give up wealth, fame, and

1

power, but recognizing them has led them to new and more satisfying ways to work and live.

Women are finding that no one else can truly determine what complete success should mean for them. Although some aspects of success may reach across all of our definitions, many wildly successful women are finding that it is individual, a matter of personal perception. Wildly successful women also know that their definition of success will probably change over time as they grow in experience and maturity. As some have reached high levels of traditional success, they have found they want to seek a balance between internal feelings of satisfaction and external manifestations of success. This more complete kind of success combines striving for clearly defined work and career goals with setting priorities and affirming values. These priorities and values in turn lead to personal success in the other domains of their lives. Wildly successful women in corporate settings—women like Micki Napp, whom we'll meet in this chapter—found that to find balance they wanted more say in what they were doing and how they were doing it. These women were willing to adjust their definitions as they developed personally—even if it meant opposing conventional wisdom or even their own earlier beliefs. In some cases it meant going for wealth and power in ways they had not imagined before. Other women decided that success meant climbing *down* the ladder of outward success to bring more balance to their lives. When they did, many found that the new balance actually led to more income and a heightened sense of themselves and their work. Finding a balance between outer and inner success was not as difficult as some of them feared.

This integration of goals, values, and priorities is important. With corporate downsizing and general job insecurity, we are all finding our old belief systems challenged and our traditional definitions of success questioned. Some people who lose their jobs or face other life-changing events free-fall for a while before realizing that they have the ingredients at hand to create their own definition of success and identify the sources of greatest satisfaction. Success becomes clearer when you see it encompassing many aspects of who you are—what your expectations and experiences have been and what your needs and wants are.

Although it's true that definitions of success aren't based solely on financial criteria, most women don't aspire to work eighty hours a week to make $15,000 a year. Money is a more-than-valid indicator of success, and all of us should be abundantly rewarded for our efforts. The trick that wildly successful women know is how to combine inner satisfaction with financial security. They see success as an amalgam of well-being, personal satisfaction, and making enough money to support themselves, their families, and their interests handsomely.

The challenge we face is not just to create a personal definition of success that suits our needs at a particular stage. It is to identify from among the many definitions the one that will be right for the long run. As life progresses, we reach cherished goals and set new ones. We accumulate a series of successes, of milestones. Becoming wildly successful means measuring success in more ways than checking off goals; it includes meeting the "test of time"—being able to step back and view success backward from the end of your life. Have you ever asked yourself:

- What would you want written as your epitaph?
- Who would come to your funeral?
- What would your dearest friend say about you in your eulogy?

Asking these questions has a way of simplifying and clarifying our lives and what we're doing with them. Wildly successful women know that what works in the short term will not necessarily suit them in the long run.

The wildly successful women we'll meet in this chapter have much to tell us about their definitions of success. All of them have found their own individual paths, emphasizing their own personal goals, needs, and values. They have found ways to integrate their personal and career goals to gain recognition for great achievement in the outside world *and* to create personal satisfaction on their own terms.

Micki Napp: Moving Up Fast and Loving It

"I think you need to get to the point where the self-confidence that got you as far as you are becomes conscious and you sit back and think, 'I really can do anything. I thought I could, but I really *can*.'"

—Micki Napp, National Manager, Women in Business, IBM

Micki Napp would be the first to say that attitude and passion for her work have been central to her success. And yet it's clear that her ambition, preparation, and determination have also been major ingredients in her many accomplishments. In 1972 she became the first woman hired directly into sales at IBM Denver. (When she started, women were usually placed in technical support.) She says, "I had one set of goals at that time, but they did go through an interesting evolution."

Micki had been planning to go to work for IBM to sell computers since she worked with her father in his office supply business in high school. "I was used to having typewriters and calculators, and I liked my dad's business associates. I thought we had to move on beyond typewriters and calculators, so I thought I'd sell computers. Throughout high school and college I took courses in computer science, programming, engineering, and marketing."

As Micki began working in sales and marketing, she quickly figured what it would take. "I had a goal of how far I wanted to get by what age, so I was pacing myself. I knew I could do what they wanted me to do, but my real goal was to *exceed* IBM goals and expectations considerably, from two perspectives. First, so my management team would realize that I could take on more responsibility and could move up through the ranks. And second, so I could make the customer really happy. I learned very quickly that if I did a great job of satisfying my customer, he or she would not only buy from me then but buy more from me over time, and would refer me to other business associates. That was my very planned, very rational definition of success, and that was probably it for about ten years of my career—to keep moving up, up, up. In the 1970s and early 1980s at IBM, that meant moving. So I physically moved back and forth across the country multiple times to get the very best position that was open and that let me move up."

Over time, as her career developed, Micki has excelled in many positions at IBM, and her definition of success has come to include some new elements. "I always knew I could do [whatever was needed], and I had proven it to myself over and over, and to other people over and over. Then somewhere in there came a breakthrough. My goals changed. Although I still wanted the responsibility and I still wanted to move up, I wanted more. I wanted more balance. I knew no matter what job I took within IBM, I wanted an intellectual challenge beyond what selling could provide.

"I also thought that I wanted to be more connected to my community. You can't do that if you move every two years. I was about thirty or thirty-two. I wanted to pay more attention to people. I was still driven, but the intellectual challenge to me meant working with people who were on the leading edge. That suggested to me I wanted to stay in Silicon Valley and work my way into a position where I could get my satisfaction out of relationships with people on the cutting edge of business/technology."

For the past five years Micki has been creating alliances with outside companies that have a solution IBM doesn't have, putting together marketing agreements, and bringing these new complementary products to market. Her area of expertise is the high-growth market. Now she's about to launch a national campaign to go after the women's marketplace—a market that is clearly identified as high-growth. She says, "I'm building up alliances with other companies, most of them with women at the top who are going to help IBM provide the solutions. It's the same kind of alliance work that I did for five years that gave me the background to be able to go after this new market."

Micki says that although attitude has not necessarily been the secret to her success, it has probably helped get her through tough times. "People say to me, 'You're always so upbeat and positive.' It is natural for me and probably comes out of childhood, but I do think a positive attitude is right at the foundation of my success. My parents encouraged me to try anything and everything, even if I said after I tried it that it didn't fit. It was okay to change my mind and even fail." That adventurous spirit has been what has made a difference for Micki. She says that the more things you try, the more you may fail from time to time, but each success is what makes you want to keep trying.

What's Micki's current view of herself and her success? "If something happened to my position at IBM tomorrow, I know I could find a challenging executive position in another company or just go on my own. You get to the point where the real confidence takes over, then I think you have the energy to focus on the people with whom you do business. That's when it really becomes rewarding, that's when you get the rewarding relationships with peers, with customers, family, and friends."

Mimi Fariña: Bringing Bread & Roses to the Community

"I don't know what else I would do that would satisfy me as much as knowing I'm doing right."

—Mimi Fariña, Executive Director, Bread & Roses

The youngest of three daughters, Mimi Fariña grew up "all over the world," because her physicist father taught internationally as an employee of UNESCO. In her mid-teens, while living with her parents in Paris, Mimi joined a dance troupe and toured Germany. She loved performing but felt in the shadow of her older sister, Joan Baez, whose star as a singer was rising. At that point Mimi believed that she wanted what Joan had: fame. That was her definition of success.

At sixteen Mimi met Richard Fariña, a singer friend of Joan's, at a picnic. She married him the following year. When the pair moved to California, they recorded two successful albums and performed at the Big Sur Folk Festival, but their stardom was cut short in 1966 when Richard died in a motorcycle accident. On her own at twenty-one, Mimi found the road to fame long and lonely.

"I was pretty disenchanted by the entertainment industry," she says. "It treated people like bottom-line items to be bought and sold. I was an exception for a while with my husband Richard—we were an overnight success. Then it was suddenly over. But I'd had a taste of the whirlwind and began to see how show business was different from art (music)." Mimi continued in show business with The Committee, a San Francisco satirical comedy group that was popular in the 1960s, and later sang on her own. During that time her cousin invited her to sing at a halfway house near San Francisco. She found the experience of bringing music to people who were confined very moving and began to see that there could be new meaning to her life and a different way to use her talent.

In 1974 Mimi founded the San Francisco Bay Area nonprofit organization Bread & Roses. Her mission was, she says, "To alleviate some of the sense of isolation felt by people who are confined in institutions by bringing them quality entertainment free of charge." The institutions have included hospitals, convalescent homes, drug and alcohol rehabilitation centers, homeless shelters, and prisons. Mimi's sister Joan Baez suggested the name Bread & Roses, which came from the lyrics of a song by poet James Oppenheim, inspired by the 1912 textile mill strike in Lawrence, Massachusetts:

Our lives shall not be sweated
From birth until life closes,
Hearts starve as well as bodies
Give us bread, but give us roses.

Today, Bread & Roses provides forty performances every month using local professional, amateur, and retired performers. It also gives performers an opportunity to donate their time and entertain on a grass roots level for their community. A partial list of the famous entertainers who have donated their talents to raise funds includes Hoyt Axton, Jackson Brown, Judy Collins, the late Jerry Garcia, Arlo Guthrie, Chris Isaak, Lily Tomlin, Robin Williams, and Peter, Paul, and Mary. "In the beginning I saw Bread & Roses as a stepping stone toward social change. I thought that we could perform in institutions, get on the news, spread the word about society's marginalized populations, and then revolutionize life in institutions. But about ten years into it I realized that Bread & Roses was never going to go beyond simply bringing entertainers to institutions, and that I had to be satisfied. Once I accepted that it was okay."

Released from the expectations of others, Mimi fully realized her passion for Bread & Roses. "Bread & Roses is a church to me, in a way. It hits a spiritual place when we're doing the shows, especially in a situation like a prison. The inmates are supposed to be 'bad people,' and the guards are assumed to be hostile. The expectation is that everyone must be on their worst behavior all the time. I consider it a highly successful prison show when the guards are listening to the music and tapping their feet, and muscle-bound, tattooed inmates are singing 'Silent Night' like sweet children. When that happens, a nonjudgmental human connection has been made through music. That's all I need. My batteries are recharged."

Mimi has realized that her focused vision of her work has led to the enduring success of Bread & Roses. "I find that if the world is judging you by a bottom line standard, then you try to live up to that and you begin to forget the love you had for your vision. The success of Bread & Roses, and why it's lasted this long, is that it has never had to deviate from its mission."

Mimi has found great satisfaction working with the "Hidden Society"—a phrase coined by a member of her board of directors.

She knows that what she does makes a difference in the lives of the entertainers as well as the audience. "I know that inside the institutions, occasionally, there's a miracle. One time, a woman who had been catatonic for three weeks began to talk after our performance. That's the kind of feedback, the 'ah-ha' experience that says, 'Yes, I did the right thing.'"

Creating *Your* Definition of Success

Micki Napp and Mimi Fariña have very different versions of what success means. Whether they work in a corporation, a not-for-profit organization, or on their own, women have expanded the definition of success beyond the traditional goals of money, fame, and power to include "inner" values: relationships (with customers, coworkers, clients, and other organizations), personal satisfaction, and meaning at work. By this time, however, you may be saying to yourself: Sounds good for Micki and Mimi, but how do I do it? How do I go about developing a definition of success that will work in my company, my work, my life? The answers are not necessarily that complicated, but they all require reflection. Interviews with wildly successful women reveal that developing a powerful personal definition of success means that you:

- Find your passion so you can love your work

- Believe that you deserve success

- Ask yourself the right questions

- Expand your view of the world

- Know your priorities and values

- Integrate your career goals and your personal goals

- Learn how to get back on track

- Give your definition of success the "test of time"

Let's see how some wildly successful women used these guidelines to develop their own definition of success.

Find Your Passion So You Can Love Your Work

"If you're working—doing something that feels good to you—that's your spirit that runs your immune system, your health, and your life."
—Jean Hollands, President and CEO, Growth & Leadership Center

You can tell from the way Mimi Fariña talks about Bread & Roses that her passionate belief in her work gives her avenues for self-expression, creativity, pride, and meaning—all part of personal satisfaction. Similarly, throughout her long career at IBM, Micki Napp's devotion to a level of personal excellence in her own performance, in her customers' satisfaction, and in the new challenges she asked to take on all reflect her passion for her work. Pride of ownership of a role, a job, a company, or a mission lays the foundation for success on all levels.

Jean Hollands, a psychologist and owner of the Growth and Leadership Center in Mountain View, California, believes being passionate about work creates the setting for success. Jean wrote a book about engineer/scientist personalities and what happened when they were with people who were not like them, at home or at work. *Silicon Valley Syndrome: How to Survive a High-Tech Relationship* (Bantam Books, 1985) was a hit. "Wives would send their engineer husbands to me and say, 'Fix him.' I would. The husbands, in turn, would ask me to fix their executive team. I did. Eventually, I turned my marriage and family counseling practice into a corporate psychology practice."

Jean believes that "finding your passion means that first of all you have to believe you deserve it. I know a lot of people who want their passion, but they can't find it because, basically, they don't feel they really deserve it. You have to do a sales pitch on yourself that you deserve to have the good life, such as, 'I work really hard and I love it, and, therefore, I deserve to have a passion in my life that feels good.' Passion can be everywhere, but some people feel that it's mysterious and hard to find. If you believe finding your passion is a process, you can take it in small pieces and not be disappointed."

Believe That You Deserve Success

"You can find that you've been shooting yourself in the foot on purpose at some level, because you were afraid of what would happen if you moved toward success."

—C.J. Hayden, President, Wings Business Coaching

Accompanying the belief that a wildly successful woman deserves to have passion in her work is the notion that she should also deserve the success that follows. While we all say we want to be successful, some women seem to fear it or at least seem ambivalent about taking steps to achieve it. C.J. Hayden, president of Wings Business Coaching in San Francisco, finds that some of her clients avoid success without realizing it. They want to be successful, but without a personal definition of success, they fear it. When they can name that fear, they start to understand the unconscious messages that sabotage their efforts. C.J. gives these examples of such messages:

1. If I become successful, then a long list of horrible things will happen:
   - I won't have time for my family
   - I won't have time for my friends
   - My friends won't like me anymore
   - I'll make more money than my husband

2. If I'm successful at this, then I'll have to do it all of the time. I'll be trapped. I won't be able to get out again.

3. If I try this and I fail, then that door is closed forever. If I don't try, it will always be my dream.

C.J. adds, "The last one is very insidious. If you try for your dream and you don't make it, then your dream is broken—as though there was only one chance. Wildly successful women take risks, which means they have the willingness to break their dream to make it come true. Simply being willing to take risks is part of the price you pay for filling your dreams. If you can't agree to take risks, then the chances of ever getting what you want are pretty slim."

When your definition incorporates your passion, personal values and priorities, and a clear sense of the rewards you seek, you are more likely to experience the sense of balance that drives out fear. If your definition of success is fuzzy, it's more likely that forfeiting relationships and personal time will worry you. Once you have a clear picture of success in your mind, you can repaint it to match your individual needs and stage of life.

Ask Yourself the Right Questions

"In order to find balance we have to be still. I thought I was looking for the answers, but I realized I was just beginning to know what to ask."
—Jeannine Barnard, President, Centerpoint Communications

One of the first things career counselors ask their clients to do is to prioritize their values. Some clients may feel that status and achievement are primary. Others may believe that financial security is the most important factor. Others value a need for adventure, beautiful surroundings, recognition, self-respect, and family. The list differs as people age and their needs and desires change.

Often, however, we don't see a career counselor, don't stop to assess our values unless forced to take stock after a life-altering event, when our needs and focus must change. If we constantly ask the right questions, we won't need rude awakenings to force us to stop and think. Stepping back to ask those questions does not necessarily mean stopping or moving backward. A pause in our routine existence can provide time to examine our direction and our values.

Jeannine Barnard, for example, left her successful fifteen-year high-tech publishing career as editor of *NeXTWORLD* magazine with International Data Group (IDG) in the Silicon Valley to ask where she really wanted to go. "I was losing touch with who I was, what I believed in, and why I believed in it. My internal strength was missing. As I lost touch with who I was internally, I felt more abstract— thinking purely intellectually rather than emotionally." After a prolonged period of reflection on a camping trip by herself, Jeannine said, "I thought I was looking for the answers, but I realized I was just beginning to know what to ask." Today she runs her own consulting company, Centerpoint Communications, in San Francisco.

One of the most important questions we can ask is "why do I want to do it?"—whatever "it" is. Faced with a situation we don't like or a need to reevaluate what we're doing, we tend to worry about *what* to do and *how* to do it, rather than taking the time to figure out *why*. In her role as a business counselor, Sheila Murray Bethel of the Bethel Institute in Burlingame, California, emphasizes the importance of knowing *why*. "As a counselor, I ask questions. I try to get people to think outside of their boxes. I sit with executives and ask them why they do what they're doing. Why, why, why. Ask why first, every step, every day along the way when you're trying something new. *How* is easy in this country. *Why* is hard."

Why is an important question, Sheila says, because we need to be focused on what we want and where we're going. "Anyone who wants to do anything in this age of technology and communication must be focused and clear. To be focused and clear, you first must ask *why*. If you answer the question 'Why am I doing this?' with 'Gee, I don't know,' you better find out. People don't do that. Instead, they say, 'Oh, I want to do that' and someone else says, 'Great idea. How will we do it?' Then they jump in, and before they know it, they have a loser on their hands. They didn't ask *why*."

People who can answer *why* tend to keep their priorities straight. They base their decisions on personal values as well as business necessities, which means they also tend to avoid conflicts between personal ethics and business decisions.

However, just asking yourself *why* is not enough. You also need to ask yourself *Why not*. Why not try to integrate your personal values with your career goals? Why not believe that you don't have to sacrifice one area of your life for another? The first step to getting a powerful personal definition of success is seeing yourself in whatever fulfills your passion and represents all of you.

Expand Your View of the World

"One day my cousin Skipper, who was running a halfway house in Marin [County, California], suggested I come and sing there, because it would be a chance to use my talent without any of the commercial strings attached that I was complaining about."

—Mimi Fariña, Executive Director, Bread & Roses

It's not unusual for people who ask themselves "why" to find that their careers no longer satisfy them. How can you become wildly successful if you're in a job that you've outgrown or that for some reason no longer suits you? Or if you're doing something because that's what you think you should do rather than what you want to do? Many wildly successful women have found that it helps, as Sheila Bethel says, "to get out of their box" and expand their view of the world and what they can do in it. Besides exciting challenges in a new or different job—the route that Micki Napp took—or a novel use of your existing talents—Mimi Fariña's tack—continuing education, hobbies, or volunteering can provide a route to this expansion of self. Gail Redman is an inspiring case in point.

When Gail Redman developed an ulcer working as a school teacher in the ghettos of East Oakland and Richmond, California, she took wood-turning classes at night to release her stress. She found that she loved wood turning so much, she wished she could do it all of the time. On her vacations Gail traveled to different countries and studied wood carving. In Auckland, New Zealand, she learned the rare art of spindle turning used in furniture and architecture from a craftsman who taught her his family wood-turning secrets.

After her traveling Gail decided that teaching would no longer be part of her life. Returning to California, she studied under an Italian master who taught her how to fashion architectural columns, newel posts, and balusters. She planned to work for two years with him, then start her own business. But that was not to be. When his business slowed down, Gail had to start her own shop six months ahead of schedule. "I approached more than 150 people with two photos of my work and a business card. I was such a novelty that people couldn't believe it." By hustling and combing the Victorian-lined streets of San Francisco, she met and got work from contractors. She has won her reputation as a master wood turner. Her view of what she could do and would do expanded to include work that is now her passion—and has been for nearly twenty years. What would have happened if she had not expanded her vision of who she was and what she could do?

Know Your Priorities and Values

"My motives got warped along the way. I didn't want to let down my investors. I put that first and foremost above my own emotional, physical, and mental health."

—Joan Barnes, Founder, Gymboree

Often it seems that we discover our priorities and values for our work and lives only when we are confronted with what we don't like about them or when we find ourselves in transition. Wildly successful women have learned—sometimes the hard way—that priorities constantly change, that even values evolve. As Mimi Fariña found in her own odyssey as a performer, because both affect your definition of success, it makes sense to address priorities and values directly and to make sure they are right for you.

When wildly successful women regularly assess their values, they find that some issues surrounding personal success have little to do with money and power and more to do with issues such as liking what you do, enjoying the environment in which you work, finding time for a personal life, living your own priorities (not someone else's), and knowing that what you do has meaning to others. An even more serious reason for determining your priorities and values is to understand what you think success will *do for you.* Success is not true success if you don't feel satisfied with what you have and how you got it.

Take Joan Barnes, the founder of Gymboree. "My definition of success has changed to feeling good about who I am. Back then [when she started her business], it was looking good. I don't mean physically looking good. I felt that if I had what other people told me was important, then I could feel good on the inside, that my insides would match my outsides. I didn't realize it, but I see now that it happens the other way around. No amount of outside success is going to make you feel okay about who you are on the inside."

When Joan founded Gymboree in the late 1970s she embarked on an exciting ride building a multi-million-dollar national business. She got off the ride in 1990 exhausted and depleted. "The only thing I did really well was run the business. I would have killed myself to succeed in my business. My kids came second. Everything came second. I wouldn't do that anymore. Nothing is that important."

Joan's original idea was to create a safe recreational area where parents could play with their babies using large, colorful balls, tunnels, and blocks—baby exercise gyms. "At the time, I was coming out of the consciousness-raising groups of the late 1960s, and, as a new mother, I really felt a need to be with other like-minded parents. [Other mothers she met] felt like 'closet mommies,' because it was not popular to have kids then—1973 had the lowest birth rate in forty years."

Soon after Joan had opened two Kindergyms, she was approached by a member of the board of the Jewish Community Center who had sponsored her to suggest they go into business together. With the $3,000 he invested, Joan opened two more Kindergyms, and within a year bought out her partner for $6,000. When Joan had six units of her own up and running, she started to franchise them under the name Gymboree.

"I was framing a business for women. It was thrilling to offer that option to women who wanted to combine a career with their parenting focus—maybe not at the level I was going for, but at a level that was comfortable for them. Women could have one Gymboree franchise or they could have eight. I understood what women were up against." Joan's business initially suited her values and priorities, but that began to change as the company grew.

Despite Gymboree's rapid growth and popularity, by 1986 Joan knew that although the franchisees were making money, the company was in trouble. "Once we went into national franchising, it was not profitable. The franchises were profitable, but the corporation was not—for six years." Joan and her management team had a major brainstorming session and decided they had to take a big step to get outside capital. Joan went to a U.S. Venture Capital board meeting and gave an impressive presentation that got her funding to design and manufacture a retail line of Gymboree clothes. She succeeded. The only problem, Joan says, was that "I already knew I was beyond what I should be doing, but they kept telling me I could do it. I started believing my own press. The gap between what I knew I could do in my gut and what they thought I could do kept growing. It grew until I couldn't do it anymore."

Not only did the gap continue to grow, but so did the distance from her personal values. "My motives got warped along the way. I didn't want to let down my investors. I put that first and foremost above my own emotional, physical, and mental health. I was in far over my head. We rolled out so many stores in 1987 and 1988 that I felt like I was going to lose my mind. In 1988 I took a leave of absence for the summer. In 1989, I said we needed to have someone else run the business. My husband and I separated. My life was falling apart."

Joan realized later that she had lost sight of her own priorities. She also learned, in retrospect, that traditional success alone couldn't fill the inner needs she sought to satisfy. "No matter how many successes I accumulated—*CBS Morning News, Today Show,* or *Wall Street Journal* articles written about me—they didn't change how I felt on the inside."

Joan stepped out of the whirlwind of growing her business to reevaluate her priorities and values. Today, Joan balances running her own marketing business with a new life complete with new husband. Her joy is using the financial proceeds from her tenure at Gymboree to give back to the community. She volunteers in the Jewish community, reconnecting with her roots, and in the greater community, where she has started programs around food, weight, and body image. She feels she is living her complete definition of success.

Joan lost sight of the personal and work priorities and values that had once given her great satisfaction. When she realized what had happened, this wildly successful woman stepped back, reassessed what she was doing, and gained new and more fulfilling ways to work and live.

Integrate Your Career and Your Personal Goals

"I think 'balance' is a fallacy . . . it sounds too box-like and linear. It's more a function of the integration of work and life in a manner that makes sense."

—Betsy Collard, Director, Career Action Center

We often hear about "balance" in the way we manage our personal and business lives. For many of us, though, it seems illusive. That's because the meaning isn't clear. The word "balance" implies that everything has to be perfectly weighted and arranged so that it won't move and get out of balance again. To maintain balance, things must remain rigid and static. Yet you don't hear many women wishing for "static" lives. That sounds incredibly boring. So what about this issue of balance—is it possible for wildly successful women?

When women say they want to know how they can balance their lives, what they're really asking is how they can set their priorities and stop feeling guilty that some aspect is getting short shrift no matter what they do. Balance is an individual matter and one of control—control through integrating, prioritizing, and staying flexible. Wildly successful women see prioritizing as an ongoing process. They understand that there will be days when their business takes precedence over family, and other days when family will come first. And they know that those days can't be predetermined.

Yet many women tend to think of "balance" as compartmentalizing. They try to determine in advance what they will do with every minute of their time. Betsy Collard, director of the Career Action Center in Palo Alto, California, says, "I think 'balance' is a fallacy. I don't like the word because, like 'career,' it sounds too box-like and linear. It's more a function of the integration of work and life in a manner that makes sense. If that's 'balance,' I'll buy it. But I tend to think when people talk about 'balance' they mean, 'I'm only going to work this many hours'—setting very strict boundaries. Each of us has our own definition of 'balance.' It involves deciding what we want out of our career. No one is going to balance our lives for us."

Betsy continues, "We used to have actual barriers before we had today's technology. Now, we can work at home. We can even work in our cars. We can work twenty-four hours a day, if we like, and some people will. We've entered an era when each one of us has to define when enough is enough in terms of work, and what role we want our career to play in our lives. But I think we were rather naive as women, particularly, in understanding the kind of knowledge-based global economy we live in today. It's not going to slow down. We have to think differently about careers and make choices. Nobody is going to make them for us."

We all know there's a time and a place for everything—even balance. As Betsy Bernard, president of the new long-distance communications subsidiary at Pacific Bell, says, "Maturity tells you that you can't run a sprint for eighty years of your life. I'm starting a transition around that. I can't convince myself that if I hadn't sprinted for the last twenty years I'd be where I am today. But I know it's fun to have some balance in my life."

Susan Corey, an attorney in the Public Defender's office in Phoenix, Arizona, feels that part of feeling successful is finding a satisfactory "balance" among the demands for time with her child, her work, and herself. "I think you have to keep trying each day. You can't let yourself get down when you don't manage to accomplish everything that day. You have to pick it up the next day and start again."

Wildly successful women simply do the best they can, when they can. "Balance" to them is prioritizing and reprioritizing. Micki Napp admits that she didn't have a personal life in her early years at IBM. But she's found more now in a marriage that has helped her to "lighten up" at no expense to her still-booming career. Wildly successful women realize that if they make a mistake with their prioritizing, they can correct it. They accept that there's no perfect solution, and they don't berate themselves for not being able to do what isn't humanly possible—be in two places at the same time and do everything perfectly.

Through setting priorities we can integrate our personal and professional goals without having to choose one over the other. It is not an either/or decision but one of varying shades of gray. Integration makes us more productive and can help us avoid worrying about home life at work and work life at home. With clearer priorities and more conscious focus, we can even find we do better at everything, from earning more money to raising our children.

Learn How to Get Back on Track

"My growth is as a teacher sharing what the secret of our success has been, because our secret runs counter to so much of the prevailing thought."

—Carol Orsborn, Founder, The Orsborn Group

Despite our best efforts to understand our priorities and values and to pay attention to them, we can sometimes find ourselves off-track, living lives and doing work that have somehow lost their savor. The obvious thing to do is get back on track, but that's easier said than done. To make the necessary corrections takes intent and courage and a sound understanding of what our personal values are and how they affect our lives. Carol Orsborn is one wildly successful woman who made major life and business changes that—despite her expectations—actually led to greater freedom and increased material success.

Starting in 1971, Carol Orsborn and her husband Dan operated Orsborn Group Public Relations, Inc., a communications company in the San Francisco Bay Area. As they built their business, they modeled it on the traditional goal of constant growth, high energy, and hard work that required long hours away from home. The results were impressive. Carol and Dan amassed their dream home (complete with hefty mortgage) in a wealthy suburb, fancy cars, all the creature comforts they had ever wanted, and two children who spent much of their time in daycare. Their focus was getting new clients and doing more. They believed they had it all.

In 1986 Carol realized she was not having it all. She saw that she'd been struggling for perfection in every area of her life and losing her sense of self among all her achievements. As she said in a *People* magazine article at the time about the "Superwoman Syndrome," she—and many women like her—had unrealistic ideas about how to be a successful woman. She believed that even the most accomplished women may come to feel like underachievers when they read magazine articles "that tell you that by good management you can cram thirty hours of stuff into a twenty-four-hour day." When she realized that she no longer wanted to continue the race to pay the bills, she and her husband decided to reclaim their time and take more control of their lives. They cut back and moved to a more modest home closer to work, reduced their work hours from fifty to thirty a week, and told their staff to quit coming in on weekends. They readied themselves for what they thought would be the inevitable financial decline in their business. Surprisingly, their refocused business began making *more* money.

As Carol says, "I think that a PR business is very reflective of the people who run it, maybe more than other companies. When a client hires an agency, they're almost getting involved in a marriage situation. I think that the people who were attracted to our agency really liked that we tried to run the company driven by inspiration rather than fear. Our people tended to be excited and alive about what they were doing."

Eventually Carol and her husband moved to Tennessee, where they opened an additional branch of the Orsborn Public Relations Group while Dan set out to follow his dream of getting involved in the music industry. Today, they've closed the San Francisco office, Dan runs the one in Nashville, and Carol spends much of her time writing books on the subject of success and spirituality, the latest two being *How Would Confucius Ask for a Raise?* (Avon, 1995) and *Solved by Sunset* (Harmony, 1995). She is also a graduate student in theology at Vanderbilt University School of Divinity.

Carol and Dan decided to go against the conventional wisdom of our times, that "have it all now" attitude. Theirs was a conscious decision to change their course and find a personal definition of success. Carol's definition is "the experience of having enough. I like to see people fill their potential whether they are my employees, clients, or myself. That's what gives me joy."

Give Your Definition of Success the "Test of Time"

"We all want to be successful, but it's been given only one definition— money. When people come close to death, they don't talk about wishing they had made more money. Yet there's very little to help people be successful in other ways besides accumulating material wealth."
—Laurie Clark, Director, Grace Family Vineyards Foundation

Today, more business, career, and entrepreneurial opportunities are available to women than ever before. With those opportunities come harder, more complex decisions—what to do, how to do it, and what is personally satisfying. Every decision has trade-offs that depend on your stage in life. Laurie Clark made the decision to cut back on her higher-paying counseling practice to head a foundation that helps children. She wanted to do it for herself, because she wanted to make a difference. Was this a bad career move? Did it make her less successful? Not at all, as Laurie explains.

"I'm a family counselor who specializes in working with adolescent children and women. Sometimes I get disillusioned with what I'm doing because I often deal with the dark side of life. It can be depressing. In the winter of 1995, I heard about a student enrichment program being funded by the Grace Family Vineyards Foundation that was looking for a counselor/director. Initially, I thought, 'I can't afford to consider the position. It would require a major reduction in my practice—and earnings. My income is the main support of our the family.' But then I realized I couldn't afford not to do it. The foundation offered a program that I knew would feed my soul and provide a needed balance in my work. The more I learned about it, the more I knew I needed it."

The Grace Family program is directed to "kids in the middle," as opposed to programs for super achievers or poor achievers. The program reaches children who have a good attitude and the potential to be successful. "There are a wealth of students like that out there who go untapped. They can too easily become part of the mass of people who settle into mediocrity rather than trying to rise above it." In this case, Laurie's definition of success is meeting the "test of time." She knows she will be able to look back at her life and feel that she has made a difference.

For wildly successful women, a personal definition of success starts with determining the kinds of monetary and material goals that are right for them. How much money do you want to make? How much independence do you want and need? How much influence and authority will satisfy you? What kind of setting for work and life appeals to you? What kinds of sacrifices are you willing to make? There is no one-size-fits-all answer to these questions, just as there is no magic amount of financial wealth that needs to be attained. Nor does the answer have to be the same for your entire life. Part of success is knowing when "enough is enough" and how to focus your energy on attaining the ingredients that will add up to *your* complete success.

Lillian Vernon's Ten Tips for Success

In 1951 Lillian Vernon started her mail-order business when she placed a $500 ad in *Seventeen Magazine* to sell monogrammed leather purses and matching belts. She spent $2,000 of the money she'd gotten as a wedding gift to purchase a supply of purses and belts and painstakingly monogrammed them herself to meet the $32,000 worth of orders the ad drew. From her kitchen table she built a business that grew into today's $235 million-dollar, publicly traded mail-order business with a catalog circulation of more than 141 million. She was ranked thirteenth in *Working Woman's* February 1996 article, "The 20 Top Paid Women in Corporate America."

Lillian offers these ten tips for business success:

1. Make time for yourself and your family.

2. Surround yourself with the best people possible.

3. Be open to new ideas and better ways to do things. Keep all lines of communication open with your staff.

4. Be prepared to take risks.

5. Like what you do and like what you sell.

6. Don't dwell on your mistakes or setbacks—learn and grow from them and then move on. Never let your mistakes defeat or discourage you. Never take criticism personally.

7. Don't try to do it all—delegate!

8. Don't grow too fast without the proper systems and people in place to handle the growth in your business.

9. Don't be afraid of new technology that can help make your business more efficient.

10. Don't spend more money than you have—set realistic budgets and stick to them. Keep your debts manageable.

Although these sensible tips are important for achieving financial and business success—and we'll see how many of them show up in our other commandments—it's clear that Lillian's definition of success also includes intangible ingredients of inner satisfaction. Her number-one tip, for example, has to do with making time for yourself and for family. And the idea of liking what you do and what you sell is not something we have necessarily believed important—or possible. Nevertheless, for Lillian Vernon, success without these key ingredients would not be success.

Questions to Help You Create *Your* Definition of Success

1. With whom do you compare yourself?

2. Who is your role model for success? What qualities does that person have?

3. By whose standard do you define success?

4. What three rewards are most important to you? How have they changed in the last five years? How would you like them to change in the next five years?

5. What do you most like about your current successes? What do you like least?

6. What would make you feel completely satisfied?

7. Are you passionate about what you do and who you do it for?

8. Is there something you wish you would do if you'd "just go for it"? Why do you wish to do it?

9. Do you have the balance and integration you want in your personal life and career?

10. What would you want written as your epitaph?

11. Who would come to your funeral and what would they say about you?

12. What's the one thing you would change to make yourself wildly successful on your own terms?

Commandment Two

Take Responsibility for Your Career

T he headlines blare the bad news: "AT&T Reorganization Planned: 40,000 People to Be Laid Off." "ConAgra to Trim About 6,500 Jobs, Close 29 Plants." "Local Naval Air Base Closes: Hundreds Out of Work." It's no wonder that anxiety is running high in the work force. Even if your job seems relatively stable, you may find yourself wondering what happened to the job security that used to be exchanged for loyalty and good performance. Do you ask yourself how you can find a safe spot in the midst of the massive and ongoing change in today's business environment? Or have you concluded, like Betsy Bernard, President and CEO of Pacific Bell Communications, that the only security we can now expect in our work lives comes from within?

> **"Career self-reliance means approaching your career as if you are self-employed, regardless of who you work for."**
>
> —Betsy Collard, Director, Career Action Center

Career self-reliance is what Betsy Bernard is talking about. It means that you take full responsibility for your career, that you approach it as if you were self-employed, regardless of who you work for. In place of the old focus on moving up a hierarchy, career self-reliance emphasizes an entrepreneurial attitude and continuous acquisition of new skills and knowledge. If you're not learning, and if you're not in charge of managing your career, you're very vulnerable in a job market and a work environment that's characterized by rapid change. Betsy Collard of the Career Action Center in Palo Alto, California, and other human resource professionals and career counselors encourage their clients to push themselves all the time to master new skills. After all, out-of-date or stagnant skill sets and knowledge bases may make employees less valuable to an organization looking to streamline, reengineer, or downsize.

Jane Seeley, a human resources director at Schlage Locks, agrees. She believes that self-reliance is not a burden but the key to expanded opportunities. "I keep pushing people to realize they have a responsibility to keep themselves employable. They can't sit back and expect the company to tell them where to go and what to do." Many companies, she says, will pay for education that will benefit the company if the employees stay, and the individuals if they move. But not enough people take advantage of it because they are complacent or perhaps afraid of change. Yet the fact is, to advance in an organization you must develop your own skills. If you don't, the company is likely to move on around you.

An essential ingredient of the career self-reliance mindset is an entrepreneurial attitude. That means looking at any job or any endeavor with the questions: What can I do to get the most out of this? Where can I add value? How can I create a win/win for me and this organization? How can I achieve my (or our) vision and goals when there aren't any rules? This kind of an orientation helps with all kinds of workplace transitions. As Betsy Collard points out, "You have to know who you are and how to articulate your value in business terms. You need to translate your skills for the workplace in the language that a buyer will understand. You need to answer, 'What relevance do I have for the workplace?' Then you can research the marketplace and find where you might fit." Taking the initiative in this process is part of the entrepreneurial attitude.

We often think of job changes as forced transitions or job loss. Moving up within a corporation, however, is a change that can present its own challenges. In today's corporate environment, anyone who wants to move up understands that it's a very different game from the one being played even just a few years ago. With the flattening of corporate structures, "rising in the ranks" in a hierarchy is no longer the way to get ahead. Instead, people win by taking personal responsibility for creating opportunities, outperforming expectations, and expanding their areas of responsibility. Career self-reliance is an invaluable attitude if you're an ambitious person who wants to move up.

In the stories of the successful women in this chapter, we'll see the ingenious ways they have managed themselves, their careers, and a variety of workplace and personal transitions. Their entrepreneurial attitude and willingness to be flexible are important parts of their success. Honesty in assessing their situations and the commitment to create their own solutions are other ingredients. Betsy Bernard has chosen to rise to the top of one of America's largest corporations, while Gale Ricketts found her success where she least expected (or, at one point, wanted) it—on the streets of New York.

Betsy Bernard: The Wisdom of Self-Reliance

"Whether you are in a corporation or not, you absolutely have to depend on yourself."

—Betsy Bernard, President and CEO, Pacific Bell Communications

Betsy Bernard, President and CEO of Pacific Bell Communications, has been charged with the mission of making her new subsidiary a successful competitor in the long-distance market now dominated by AT&T, MCI, and Sprint, the giants who currently hold 90 percent of that $70 billion market. Her goal is to make Pacific Bell Communications a one-billion-dollar business in just four years—by the year 2000. She says that one secret of her past and current success is the "confidence factor." "If I believe that something can be done, I'll get it done." But there's much more to the story of how Betsy has excelled in her corporate career, largely through practicing an especially savvy brand of career self-reliance.

Betsy was recruited by AT&T during her junior year of college at St. Lawrence University in Canton, New York, to work for the summer in Albany in a sales position. "Actually, I was on my way to work for my father that summer when AT&T called. I was at a turning point. Did I want to go to graduate school, probably in law, with a notion of taking over my father's business? Believing it would be better for him and myself if I worked for someone else first, I accepted AT&T's offer." She also believed that her summer experience with a Fortune 100 company would be helpful no matter what she decided to do. She liked working with AT&T and enjoyed the relationships she had developed there so much that during her senior year, when she looked around at other jobs (and got offers from PG&E, IBM, Xerox, and GE), she chose to work at AT&T after graduation. Betsy was also impressed by their policy of paying for additional education and with their management development program. "It was up or out; you weren't going to languish in a first-line entry job. I started moving up the ladder."

Over the next few years, Betsy obtained her MBA, attended an executive training program one summer at Williams College, and in 1988 was one of two employees from AT&T selected to go to the Stanford Sloan Program for a full year with her salary and all expenses paid. These experiences were, Betsy says, crucial in helping her grow, expand her skills and knowledge, and develop a broadened sense of her potential. As a member of a corporation that has done more than its share of downsizing, she observes, "There are people who have been thirty years in a place and they haven't learned anything new in the last twenty-nine years, and there are people who have spent thirty years in a place and yesterday learned something new that made them more valuable and updated their skills. If you're not continually investing in yourself, in the many ways there are to do that, why should others? I don't have a lot of patience with people who complain that their job is being eliminated when for thirty years they worked in a place that offered opportunity and they didn't take advantage of it. Whether you are in a corporation or not you absolutely have to depend on yourself."

When she reflects on other elements of her career success, Betsy says, "You have to be the best of the best, and you have to have a little luck. How much does luck have to do with it? I've worked six to seven days a week, twelve to fifteen hours a day. I've moved where it was necessary to get a great job. I've lived outside of my comfort zone so much that it seems natural to me. Is there really an element of luck? Sure, but I've made 90 percent of it."

Betsy defines living outside her "comfort zone" as taking on ever bigger and greater responsibilities. "My favorite example of that was when I was twenty-four years old. I ran a central switching office at AT&T that operated seven days a week, twenty-four hours a day. I had sixty people reporting to me, from union workers to first-line supervisors. I look back at that now as an adult and I wonder why I wasn't overwhelmed by it. I was too young to know, but I've always been given and accepted opportunities that expanded me tremendously. Today, I'm still outside my comfort zone—I've never run a billion-dollar business as a president and CEO—but I'm as confident as I was at twenty-four, and I'm a lot more willing to ask for help and counsel."

Betsy advises women to "believe you can do anything you want, be accountable for your decisions, and understand that every day we make decisions that have significant consequences for ourselves. I was having a conversation the other day with someone who was bemoaning that he had not been served a great hand. I told him, 'You're forty years old, you've been working for a company that provided tuition aid, but you've never gotten an MBA. You've never done all these things that were available to you.' I'm not saying that everyone has to get an MBA or that everybody has to continue to invest in their skill set. But at the end of the day, if you're not getting opportunities, it's because you haven't owned up to that. Be accountable for your decisions and make them consciously. Don't wait to see what happens or wait for someone else to take care of them."

Betsy also very much believes in having an entrepreneurial attitude, being able to work in what she describes as "an unstructured, chaotic world." She says she was never one to "stay within the lines." That's especially useful in the new venture she's heading. "In this kind of environment, you have to say, 'Let's start with a clean sheet of paper.' There is no tradition here. I think in an organization you need to be aligned around your vision, your mission, the key values of the corporation. My leadership team and I are jointly developing those and we're in a better position to deploy them throughout the organization. They create our touchstone and our frame of reference, but they are still pretty wide. Everybody needs to be clear: What's the vision? What's the mission? What are the key business strategies and values we aspire to?"

When Betsy describes what she's set out to do, it's easy to see the importance of vision and mission and values in the work she's doing now. "Building the infrastructure to support a billion dollar revenue stream is not your normal start-up where you grow to $100,000 then maybe triple that every year. It would be very easy to say, 'Gee, are we really going to bring in a billion dollars in revenues by the year 2000? What if we don't? What if we build this big infrastructure and we're not successful in acquiring customers and revenue? Maybe we ought to scale it back a little bit, don't go for a big end but operate on an incremental basis.' But we don't. We're staying the course, saying we have one shot at being successful. We *are* going to be successful."

Betsy says that in the new flatter organization, scope of responsibility, not how employees fit in a hierarchy, is what counts. "You look at the size of their sandbox [responsibilities] and their ability to expand it. You need to help people have a career path, but it looks different than it did in my day where it was based on a series of steps. We work in processes, not in hierarchies and functional expertise.

We start by defining success from a customer perspective and then work our way back into the business. That's how we're organizing ourselves, and it's the real reason hierarchies don't need to exist anymore. But I think you can give people a sense of direction and progression based on skills that they're acquiring. You make sure it is a continuous process and that they understand that they can do self-inventory today and set targets for themselves for tomorrow. Then you see that they have help in continuing to invest in themselves and develop their skills."

Betsy believes that people need to ask themselves, "How do I continue to improve my own worth in this company? The answer lies not in moving up but in developing a set of skills and seeking out experiences that help develop those skills. Then it's a matter of influence and authority. Ask yourself, 'How can I make my sandbox bigger? How can I take on more responsibilities? What do I need to know or learn to expand them?' You don't need promotions anymore to increase your opportunity to have greater influence in this kind of structure."

Gale Ricketts: Ready to Roll in New York

"I was trying to get work as an actor and running this limousine company, but I really didn't want the limousine company because I wanted to work as an actor. I would bang my head and struggle, but full-time acting wasn't going to happen. I'm more aware now of the importance of staying flexible."

—Gale Ricketts, President, Ready to Roll Limousine Service, Inc.

Gale Ricketts grew up in southern California, studied at the American Academy of Dramatic Arts in Pasadena as a member of the founding class, and graduated from the University of Southern California. Like many young people who want to be actors, she moved to New York to seek more opportunity. And like many young actors she found that it was challenging to keep going to acting classes, auditioning, and just plain surviving, even with occasional work. But Gale had plenty of ingenuity. She and a friend started a Greenwich Village roller skating rental service called Ready to Roll with a hundred pairs of skates and a leased van. With her roller skating business on the side and roles in plays, a few in films, and a soap opera, she says, "We starved, but we made enough money not to starve too badly." As it turned out, however, roller skating was a trend that abruptly came to an end. "One day everybody in New York decided not to roller skate anymore. We went out of business. I realized that I still had no skills. I didn't even know how to wait tables like my other actor friends."

Not one to give up easily, Gale had another brainstorm. "I realized that since I grew up in southern California, I did know how to drive. I took a job as a chauffeur for a limousine company, which afforded me the time off to go on auditions and do summer stock." For Gale, driving a limo continued to be just a way to make some money, nothing more. She still saw herself as an actor, but another opportunity kept knocking at her door. When Liza Minnelli started requesting her as her driver on a consistent basis, Gale began to think about what she was doing in a different way. "One day," Gale explains, "Liza said to me, 'Why don't you get your own limousine and I'll be your client.' I said, 'Why don't you buy a limousine and I'll be your driver.'" Gale eventually decided to take the chance. She says, "I didn't have any money, but I had Liza as a client. I knew another chauffeur who had started his own business, and I subcontracted a car from him every day on an hourly basis."

Liza kept Gale busy. "I didn't have any time to spend my money, so everything I made I put toward a down payment on a used limo with some very high financing—worse than credit cards. My first limousine was a 1982 Lincoln stretch, burgundy and black, with a burgundy interior. Liza named it Angel, after the character she was playing on Broadway."

Even after Gale incorporated Ready to Roll, her limousine service, in 1985, she still considered herself an actor who drove limousines. "I didn't get it that I had a business until about 1992. It clicked that the bigger the limo business got, the more it was a serious thing. I could hire someone to answer the phone twenty-four hours a day, instead of me. I could hire drivers, instead of me. Since the business was taking off, it became something that I really had to pay attention to and manage, or not do it at all."

With that realization, Gale finally understood that the opportunity she had seen as a sideline was actually more satisfying than the acting career she had been pursuing with little success for years. "The combination of interests has made Ready to Roll more than a business to me, because many of my clients are in the entertainment business," Gale says. "I feel like I'm still in the entertainment business, and my clients know that I understand them." Gale acknowledged that owning a limousine company gave her a better return for her time, energy, and emotions than being a struggling actor.

"My advice for women in transition is to go to the door that's opening. If what you want is full of disappointment and not working out, and something else seems more effortless, I say, go for what presents itself." Gale adds, "I was trying to get work as an actor and running this limousine company, but I really didn't want the limousine company because I wanted to work as an actor. I would bang my head and struggle, but full-time acting wasn't going to happen. I'm more aware now of the importance of staying flexible." In the new world of those who are self-reliant about their careers, flexibility and opportunity go hand in hand.

The Six Principles of Career Self-Reliance

Career self-reliance and flexibility have played a big part in Betsy Bernard's and Gale Ricketts' stories. Both women understand transitions and the need to seize opportunity with passion and an entrepreneurial spirit. Career self-reliance can be expressed in six simple but powerful principles:

- Adopt an entrepreneurial attitude

- Describe what you want

- Keep the big picture in mind

- Use transitions to evaluate your work choices

- Be willing to change gears

- Create your own solutions

Adopt an Entrepreneurial Attitude

"Be accountable for your decisions and make them consciously. Don't wait to see what happens or wait for someone else to take care of them."
—Betsy Bernard, President and CEO, Pacific Bell Communications

An entrepreneurial attitude means taking responsibility for change—seizing the initiative. Whether you're moving up the ladder, surviving corporate reengineering, or starting your own enterprise, such an attitude will make the difference between failure and success. The same goes for the job search process. By focusing on the steps you can take to make progress in your life, by facing the fact that you may need to retool or change careers, you can lessen the negative impact of forced transitions. Self-reliance means knowing what you want in any job and in your overall career. Take responsibility for exploring what kind of business you want to be in, what kind of corporate culture and work environment suits you, what skill sets you need to acquire. In today's volatile business environment, entrepreneurially minded people are the kind most companies—especially those that have shifted away from the old command-and-control hierarchies—are looking to hire. They want employees who can plan and implement strategies, who can organize themselves around key processes.

Taking an entrepreneurial attitude toward finding a new job means taking the time to research what that company does and how it's managed. Get a clear picture of the job description. Meet as many people as you can. Pay attention to surroundings, the way people are allowed to individualize their work areas and schedules. Some human resource managers say they can tell the enthusiasm level of an applicant by the amount of company knowledge she has acquired before her interview. By the same token, if you're thinking of leaving a position you currently hold, know why you're doing it. Is it the management style that dissatisfies you? The people? The project? The pay? Or the lack of opportunity?

Cheri Comstock and Jackie Larson, co-owners of The Focus Group, a Chapel Hill, North Carolina, technology recruiting firm, write about the entrepreneurial attitude in *The New Rules of the Job Search Game: Why Today's Managers Hire and Why They Don't* (Bob Adams, Inc., 1994). "When we give seminars, no one picks attitude as the number-one reason someone gets hired, but it is," Cheri says. "People who have an entrepreneurial attitude, who have the ability to learn new skills and bring in fresh ideas to a business, seem more appealing."

The self-reliant individual who can show that she takes the initiative gets the job more often than someone who waits for "friends" to call her back. She has a clear mission and is less likely to take the first job that comes along. "Another thing about job seeking," says Cheri, "is that many people can't focus or articulate what they want. They can't say what their skills are, or they have no idea of what they can do or have a passion to do. If they can't say it, it's a disaster. They have to have a vision, or they come off as desperate." Starting with an entrepreneurial attitude puts you in the positive frame of mind that will be essential in navigating any kind of change.

Describe What You Want

"I decided I had to be able to stay in Manhattan and I had to be able to afford it. I was going to give my son the best education I could. Those were the goals I set for myself. Then I focused my entire life on making them happen. Raising him was very important to me. Equally important was my career."

—Harriet Mosson, President, Liz Claiborne Dresses and Suits

As Cheri Comstock points out, the most successful career changers and job applicants can articulate what skills they have to offer *and* what they want to do with them. Being able to describe what you want—whether it's your own business, a position you seek, or the qualities you desire for your personal life—is the first step in being able to make it happen. It begins with inspiration and moves to the more concrete steps of specifying exactly what your vision is, how it fits you and your goals, what value you can offer or provide, and why the vision is so important to you. There's no reason your vision cannot balance work and home and family. The key is to be purposeful, to create and articulate what you want—not let situations dictate what you can do. Harriet Mosson is one example of a wildly successful woman who had to clarify her vision for herself and her life in a time of crisis. In the process she learned that describing what she wanted made it all the more satisfying.

When Harriet Mosson, currently president of Liz Claiborne Dresses and Suits, found herself in a profound transition—widowed and three months pregnant at age thirty-two—she had to plan for her future and that of her unborn child in ways she had never done before. "I was earning $13,000 a year as an assistant buyer at Macy's. I decided I was going to have the child no matter what. After the delivery, I had $1,800 in the bank. I started to really focus my life with this child. I set very strong goals at the time, probably for the first time in my life."

"I was almost paralyzed with fear with all the responsibility. My mother and father were moving to Florida and offered me their house in Queens, but I decided I had to be able to stay in Manhattan. I had to be able to afford it, and I was going to give my son the best education I could. Those were the goals I set for myself. Then I focused my entire life on making them happen. Raising him was very important to me. Equally important was my career."

Over the next several years, Harriet worked herself up the ladder at Macy's until in 1980 she was running all of Better Sportswear and making good money, almost $80,000 a year. "I was saving money and struggling through those times. But I was able to afford a two-bedroom apartment and quality child-care that I could depend on."

Since Harriet knew what she wanted to accomplish, she worked to better herself and was constantly promoted. She believes strongly in setting goals as a way of describing what you want. "I read about a Yale study that said the students who entered school with expressed written goals became more successful than the ones who didn't," she says. "I understand that very well. If you have a vision and a goal you can work toward achieving it. That gives you a better chance of success than if you have no goals."

In 1980 Harriet left Macy's to become founder and president of Liz Claiborne Dresses, a division she ran until 1986. Then, after years of climbing the ladder, she took a hiatus to reassess her values and her goals, spend time with her son, and study art history. For several years she worked as a freelance retail consultant. In 1991, Harriet was asked to rejoin Liz Claiborne to evaluate the company's potential for entering the women's suit business. The ability to see what she wants and describe what she sees has been as valuable in Harriet's professional work as in her personal life. She says, "I try to bring the world in and discover the reality of why people buy things. What they're looking for. How their life is going to be impacted by it. How the world is changing today. The environment is changing, lifestyles are changing, and so is the need for clothes or the lack of need for them. What is going to motivate my customers to buy our clothes?

Why would they buy them at all? If we don't think about things in an intellectual way, we cannot be successful in today's economy."

Harriet believes we all have the ability to create our own success—if we accept responsibility for doing so. "Once you can say, 'This is my life and I'm going to make it happen,' then you can. Life is a constant challenge and you can't be defeated by it. You always have to take the upward road." You too must to be able to describe what you want. Remember, like Harriet, you may someday be faced with a life very different from the one you thought you would have.

Keep the Big Picture in Mind
"I realized I had to be true to who I am as an individual."
—Linda Kral, Human Resources & Operations Manager,
SyberVision Systems, Inc.

When you take responsibility for your career, it's not unusual to feel overwhelmed at times. This may be a sign that you have lost the "big picture," that overall sense of the passion, goals, values, and desires that add up to a meaningful life. The big picture is what tells us that our definition of success comes from within, not from those around us. Keeping the big picture in mind can save us from getting lost in the day-to-day stresses of work, even when we feel pressured to do something that doesn't feel right. That pressure may represent a conflict in ethics, or it might just be a tradeoff that we know will not produce the desired results. Linda Kral, an executive with responsibilities in sales operations, administration, and human resources at SyberVision, a language education telemarketing company, found that keeping the big picture in mind gave her the fortitude to weather a difficult management situation.

"I had a particular incident last year," Linda says, "where the president of the company wanted me to manage differently. We were going through a challenging time. We weren't getting the results we wanted, and I was being asked to 'kick butt' in the sales staff to get better results. I wasn't 100 percent convinced it was all the fault of the sales department. So I decided to do a test. I decided to trust my own instincts, the way I work with people, and the way I thought I could get results."

Instead of "kicking butt," Linda spent time trying to get the sales group to understand the predicament. She believed that if she told them the true seriousness of the situation and its consequences in a way that motivated them instead of making them fearful, it would work much better. These conversations let the sales group know that her job—and their jobs—were at stake. Calling on the rapport she had already built, Linda asked them to work with her in order to get the results that her boss had asked for.

Linda's faith in the sales staff and her vision of what she wanted to achieve were part of the big picture she had to keep in mind. SyberVision got the results they wanted—in fact they exceeded them. There was another benefit, too. When she talked to the president, Linda says, "I explained that I decided to do what I did because I didn't feel right about [her boss's approach]. If you ask someone to do something they fundamentally do not believe in, then you can't expect to get a favorable result. The president said he was glad I had followed my instincts and appreciated the way I communicated with him."

Linda calls this experience a turning point in her career. "I had worked very hard to prove that I was good at what I do and to produce results. Still, I suffered from the 'Good Girl Syndrome'—doing what you're told to do and being cooperative and flexible. I'm always flexible and I'm always cooperative, but I also have to be true to myself. It was either that or quit. It was gratifying that the consequences were such that I didn't quit my job and I came to a new level of understanding with the president of the company. I think he has a new respect for me because I stood my ground, and maybe he has a better understanding of what my parameters are."

Linda adds, "I saw that situation as a door shutting. But I also know that no door shuts without another opening. I looked at the situation as a business challenge and also a personal challenge. I never really doubted myself. I just tried to think about why it was occurring. I remember thinking that I have had all this success so far, so why can't I be successful again? I didn't see that I had any other choice. I didn't want to be where I couldn't be myself."

Use Transitions to Evaluate Your Work Choices

"It's an interesting thing in our society that we think a career drives who were really are, yet somehow we minimize it [a career] by assuming it can happen without really investing in it."

—Eunice Azzani, Vice President and Partner, Korn/Ferry

When faced with a career challenge like a layoff, our first inclination is usually to fill the void immediately. Instead of really taking the time to evaluate our work choices, we focus on short-term needs, such as the need for income, and fail to address long-term needs for greater job satisfaction and ultimate success. The transition period can be the time when you expand your horizons. You might consider taking a stop-gap job while you redefine and home in on the work that will bring you the most satisfaction and fulfillment. Even if you are currently satisfied with your job or your work, periodic evaluation keeps your mind open to opportunities.

Eunice Azzani, a partner in the San Francisco corporate recruiting office of Korn/Ferry, observes, "We do complicate our lives by not trusting ourselves. We'll invest in the stock market, we'll invest in real estate, but the last thing we ever invest in is ourselves and our careers. I say that because I have people coming to me and saying they need a job in thirty days. I laugh and say, 'You know what, if you came in here and told me you needed a partner to share your life with in thirty days, I would say you were crazy. So why are you approaching your career life the same way?'"

This urge to stay busy, to replace an old job the minute it goes away, may not be based solely on financial needs. It may come from the fear that something else, something better, won't materialize. Not surprisingly, the successful women I've interviewed have learned that rushing to fill a job void may significantly reduce their chances for career satisfaction and success. This is why Mary Donnelly, formerly co-owner of Metrosoft, decided to use the time when her business ended to evaluate what *she* wanted from a career.

Mary Donnelly left her MBA program early and started her career in the financial department of a Honda dealership in San Diego. She was eager to achieve the items on her mental checklist—money, power, possessions, status—and didn't particularly notice that the list was lacking some of the personal goals of a more balanced life. She thought she knew what she wanted. She carried that same list with her when she left the car dealership and became a partner in Metrosoft, a start-up software company that made proprietary software for Steve Jobs' NeXt computer. Everything was fine—she was getting what she was striving for—until the software her company was developing became obsolete overnight when Jobs withdrew the NeXt computer from the market. Faced with a major transition, Mary began questioning her old values and realized it was time to reevaluate her choices. She needed to write a new checklist of what she wanted from her work. She's learned three important lessons of career self-reliance: Don't put your life on hold until your career hits a certain plateau; don't assume that success in business guarantees success in life; and don't assume that the goals you were trained to reach fit you.

"Here's where I find myself: I'm thirty-five. I'm financially set because of building my company for five years, but I don't have a personal life. I'm not married. I'm not even in a personal relationship." Mary adds, "The natural urge is to jump right back into another career, and I'm getting job offers all the time. Yet if I jump back into the computer industry, when would I ever develop my other side?"

Mary is also reflecting on how she had been playing the game. She says, "I had all this stuff, but I was not enjoying it—I didn't have the time. I didn't even have time to spend the money. My job was my life. Nevertheless, I felt that I had accomplished something. With my own company I was willing to work hard as long as I knew the end results would be a balanced life with flexible hours. My idea was that I would work hard for five years and develop my company. I would make enough money to hire people to do the grunt work, then oversee the business and get the satisfaction of owning it."

"Now," Mary says, "my plan is to take this time to learn to relax, learn to enjoy being by myself, and learn that who I am isn't based on my career." You may reach a different conclusion from the one Mary did when she faced her transition, but even the decision to step back is a form of career self-reliance. Mary's lessons are good ones, because without that kind of reflection, it's unlikely she would have the clarity to take complete charge of this next phase of managing her life and career.

Be Willing to Change Gears

"If I were projecting, or hanging onto the past, or trying to recreate something that was no longer appropriate for me, I would have missed this opportunity. If you have a rigid image of yourself, you reduce your options. And to me, life is only options."

—Judy Meegan, Vice President of Operations,
Advanced Bioresearch Associates

Gale Ricketts, the founder of Ready to Roll, is a prime example of someone who had to make a big shift in how she saw herself and what she was doing. All transitions involve change, and most change is unpredictable—not to mention uncontrollable. That's why staying flexible is so crucial. Flexibility allows us to recognize opportunity and reorient toward it. When one opportunity did not yield the results Gale wanted and she realized an acting career was going to keep her struggling forever, she used the modest foundation of business knowledge she had gained to build a successful limo business.

Judy Meegan, currently Vice President of Operations for Advanced Bioresearch Associates in San Ramon, California, was someone who made an unusual shift mainly because she stayed flexible enough to recognize another opportunity. There are many stories about women who have left the corporate world to start an enterprise on their own. There are fewer about someone like Judy, who left her own successful consulting business, Meegan Management, to join Advanced Bioresearch Associates, a consulting firm that helps other companies get their pharmaceutical products through the FDA approval process. Judy explains: "I was totally immersed in my business and enjoying it. One day I was working with a client of four years doing strategic planning for their organization. They needed a very key person. When we talked, one of the owners said jokingly, 'That sounds like a Judy Meegan job.' We laughed, but then we began thinking about the possibility of my taking the position.

"I thought, 'I'm doing what I love, but the opportunities that have come into my life have often come when they were not expected, and from a direction not anticipated.' I try to be aware of what's going right now, instead of projecting far into the future or hanging onto something in the past. Yet many people said to me, 'Oh, how can you give up your business?' I didn't feel like I gave up anything at all. In fact, I felt that I had just added something new and rich. Everything that I've been doing in business for twenty-five years has come into play. If I had hung onto the past, or tried to recreate something that was no longer appropriate for me, I would have missed this opportunity. If you have a rigid image of yourself, you reduce your options. And to me, life is only options. If you cut yourself off or paint yourself into a corner, you miss the experience.

"Someone asked me, 'Gee, do you think you can retire from there?' I answered, 'I don't know. Why do I have to decide today?' Why is that relevant? I feel like this is an unfolding."

Create Your Own Solutions

"If you're not pushing yourself out of the box all of the time, your skill sets are going dead."

—Betsy Collard, Director, Career Action Center

Faced with all the challenges of workplace transitions, the best place to look for solutions is within yourself. That's a major part of career self-reliance. You can expand your responsibilities, as Betsy Bernard would advise, change gears, as Gale Ricketts did, or create solutions that use a completely new angle on the problem. All of these approaches involve not only an entrepreneurial attitude but also knowledge of yourself and what you want.

Betsy Collard of the Career Action Center agrees. Creating solutions begins, she says, "with knowing who you are, then moves beyond that to research—scanning the environment to set a realistic target about what you want to do. One principle is: Leverage your strength. Look at your background and your strengths and build on what is transferable. Follow up research with contacts and networking. Learn from that and try not to jump too early."

Part of creating your own solutions means reviewing and creating your own checklist of what you want in a career. Mary Donnelly found that the career checklist she took from business school ultimately didn't suit her. Individual solutions must meet your own needs, not those that others think you need.

When Harriet Mosson was a pregnant widow, she realized that she had to create her own solutions if she were going to balance caring for her son and moving up in her career. She found solutions to each problem as they arose—a place to live, child-care, career, money. Successful women know what "career self-reliance" means to their futures. It means continuously learning so you don't get run over by the rapid changes in the workplace, in technology, and in the business environment. It means staying challenged, sharp, and flexible. As Betsy Bernard says, "If you're not continually investing in yourself, why should others?" Successful women have often found that they are surprisingly resourceful when put to the test. That test, whatever it involves, sharpens their senses and their ability to take complete charge of their lives and work. They don't anticipate that the world will ever return to the days when they could count on a company, the government, or any other person to take care of them throughout their lives. Self-reliance, career and otherwise, is not a trend—it's a reality, and an opportunity.

Dr. Jennifer Starr's Eleven Tips for Courting Opportunity

Dr. Jennifer Starr, one of the leading researchers on entrepreneurship in the United States, is a Visiting Research Scholar at Wellesley College's Center for Research on Women. She is developing a training program for owner-managers of growing firms using cases of successful women entrepreneurs as a project of the National Foundation for Women Business Owners and the Kauffman Foundation's Center for Entrepreneurial Leadership. By invitation, she participates in an initiative of the National Women's Business Council, a federally funded think tank, to develop policy and research recommendations relating to women-owned businesses. She regularly makes presentations to industry and trade groups, both in the United States and abroad.

Jennifer is also president of UptoData Partners, a firm specializing in solving the operating problems associated with business growth. She has been the founding member of two start-up ventures and currently serves as an advisor to rapidly growing small and mid-sized owner-managed firms, including several in the Inc. 500. She teaches courses in Entrepreneurship and Managing Growing Businesses in the Executive MBA

continues

---

program at Suffolk University Graduate School of Management in Boston and has taught at the Wharton School, Babson College, Boston University, and the Ohio University School of Medicine. Here are her eleven tips for courting opportunity:

1. Be an Information Junkie. Everything you read, hear, or learn is raw material for uncovering opportunities. Develop a mindset that continuously asks, "How can I use this information?"

2. If you want to hear opportunity knocking, forget what your parents told you. Always talk to strangers. Curiosity will not kill the cat. The early bird is not the only one who catches the worm.

3. Look for chaos, confusion, and contradictions. There is an inverse relationship between the availability of data and the potential for opportunity. You may be on to something if you see possibilities and connections that others do not see or cannot understand.

4. Cultivate an ethic of change. Enjoy the process of discovery. Don't accept the status quo. Wherever there is change, there is a chance to make a difference.

5. Ideas are a dime a dozen, but novel and appropriate solutions are one in a million. Shape your idea to fit a specific situation and take action. If you think you have a good idea, ask someone to pay for it!

6. Three powerful questions are guaranteed to open up possibilities: "How can I help?", "It's not done this way now, but what if . . . ?", and "What would it take to . . . ?"

7. Remember that opportunities come in all shapes and sizes. An introduction may simply be a way to get your foot in the door or lead to the chance of a lifetime.

8. When the stakes are high, critically evaluate the dimensions of the opportunity. Is the window opening or closing? What is your distinctive advantage? Is there room for mistakes and experimentation? What are the economic and non-economic benefits? What is the worst and the best that can happen? Can you live with the consequences?

9. Travel down the Corridor of Opportunity. One thing leads to another, but if you do not open the first door, the subsequent opening will never appear. To get started, take on small projects that move you forward. Have patience; be adaptable and flexible. The impossible just takes a little longer.

10. Learn to substitute information for capital. Spend time and imagination rather than cash. You may be surprised to find that people are willing to trade in a variety of currencies that may be just as good as, or even better than, money.

11. Don't be afraid to turn down opportunities. Knowing how and when to de-commit is just as important as knowing how and when to commit. Ask yourself, "Is this an opportunity for me at this time?" You know you have a strategy when you start saying "no."

Reflections for Managing Workplace Transitions

1. Can you articulate the skills you have to offer and what value you add in compelling business terms?

2. Can you describe what you want? Write down your goals and aspirations. Ask yourself how well your current work situation is meeting them. Describing what you want begins with inspiration, with discovering your passion, and moves to a concrete plan. Being able to describe what you want, whether it's your own business or a position you seek, is the first step in being able to make it happen.

3. What changes in the job market are affecting your line of work? Do you know what the companies in your field of interest look for in an employee? What corporate structure do you think would be most appealing to you? What kind of company culture?

4. Have you thought out what you will need financially in your life in the next six months? In one year? Write out a time line, starting with the present, and include all the factors—marriage, children, housing, education—that have an impact on your life. If you have children, include their requirements on your time, as well as financial needs like daycare, hobbies, and college tuition. Note job requirements such as travel, overtime, and take-home projects; include personal elements like vacation, recreation, and entertainment. Do the same exercise in five- and ten-year increments. This helps you assess where you are now and what issues you need to consider in the future.

5. Have you set up an action plan to spend a realistic amount of time each week researching companies, making phone calls to companies, and networking? Keep track of every contact and conversation. Make this part of your "job transition."

6. Do you know how to find jobs on the Internet? Have you kept up with technology? If not, take time to learn all you can so that you are comfortable and current.

7. Are you taking things too personally? As Betsy Collard says, "Taking things personally is both a power and a curse. It gives you some insights and helps you in many ways, but it can paralyze you."

8. Are you focused on your efforts? Do you know where to get support and advice to keep you focused and keep your spirits up?

9. Have you communicated clearly what your goals are and how you plan to reach them? Keep your family informed of your action plan and your goals. Let them understand your situation so that they can assist you with their support rather than worry about you.

10. Have you kept a flexible outlook? Are you willing to change gears?

Commandment Three

Change Your Thinking, Change Your Life

uccessful women know the "magic of believing"—believing in themselves, believing in possibilities. They succeed by creating a vision for themselves and by being willing to take responsibility for their own future. When faced with a challenge they ask themselves, "Why not?" Their lives are changed, not so much by what they do or how much they know but by how they think. They know the secret of linking constructive thinking with flexibility, clear goals, and forceful action.

"You have to put yourself in the frame of mind that you're going to be a success no matter what."
—Audrey Rice Oliver, President and CEO, Integrated Business Solutions

Many of the successful women in this book changed their lives by changing their attitude. They learned to avoid or remove negative beliefs that could hold them back, beliefs such as:

- I can't get ahead because of . . . (divorce, downsizing, whatever). Things keep happening to me.
- I will never succeed because I'm too old/too young.
- I don't have enough education or money.
- Nothing else has ever worked out before, so it won't now.
- I'd change my life if I could, but I'm stuck where I am.

Such beliefs can turn into walls that separate us from our own success. When we change this kind of thinking, we can change our lives. It's *how* we look at things that makes the difference in moving ahead to a more successful life. That's why it's always appropriate to ask: *How* do I want to spend the rest of my life? *How* can I do what I want to do? Such questions get to the heart of our basic attitudes about ourselves and our work. Wildly successful women, when confronted with challenging situations, believe they can do whatever it takes. They refuse to feel like victims or to waste time blaming others. They focus on what they can learn from any situation and on how they can deal with it productively.

Have you ever met someone who has survived a life-threatening experience? Have you noticed that person's appreciation for life and its lessons? People who have come close to death have a *joie de vivre* that most of us find fascinating and enviable. They have often taken their "second chance" to change their attitudes and set new priorities. We can all do that, if we choose to. Since attitude determines outlook, we can choose how we set our priorities, how we spend our time, and what we think. Amy Garrett and Audrey Oliver, two wildly successful women, are cases in point.

Amy Garrett: The Law of Expectation and the Law of Belief

"People told me it would take me a year to get another job, that I would have to take a cut in pay, a step down—they were advising me with the best of intentions, but I didn't like the picture they were painting. I believed I could do something to change that."

—Amy Garrett, President, The Garrett Marketing Group

When Amy Garrett left the University of Arizona in 1969 with a degree in interior design, the owner of the top design company in Phoenix advised her to go to Sears or Montgomery Ward to learn the basics. She got her basic training at Montgomery Ward and moved to Sears a few years later to work in the design department for the next ten years. When an opportunity to train other designers at Sears fell through, Amy took the job of an assistant manager of the design department of Rich's, Inc., part of Federated Department Stores. "The man who hired me was in the antiques department, and he wanted me eventually to run the design department." When her boss left shortly thereafter, Amy says she had to figure out what to do. She believed she could run the department until someone else was hired, then came to believe she deserved the job. So she set to work. "I got us involved in decorator showcases. I started in-store design seminars. In six months I turned the numbers around." Nine months after she was hired as assistant manager, Amy became design director for Rich's design departments in eight locations. She made them the most productive design studios at Federated. But then, she says, "I lost my job when Robert Campo did the hostile takeover of Federated."

After her nine successful years at Rich's, Amy had to put together a résumé and look for work. People advised her that she would have to take a cut in pay and move, and that finding a new position would take months, even a year. "I started going to seminars, reading books, and listening to tapes. I started training myself. It helped me have inner strength. I approached things from the positive, even when my job was cut. I saw a lot of people who had a lot going for them professionally get stuck in anger, anxiety, resistance."

Amy chose a different approach. "I decided to see this [job loss] as an opportunity. I wrote down what my next job would have in it: a lot of autonomy, a lot of variety, in a large metropolitan area, for more money, a step up with a large corporation that was the Cadillac of its industry. I wrote all of that out and more, and in three weeks I had my next job. Of course, I networked like crazy, and the opportunity came from someone four times removed."

Her opportunity came from a sector she had never dreamed of entering: the kitchen and bath industry. "When people told me plumbing, I thought 'Plumbing? I don't know.' But when someone that I respect says go talk to this person, I talk to them. I got the job, and it included everything that I had written down on my list. I was just learning how to create something from visualizing what I thought it would be. Before that I just gutted things out—full steam ahead, because that's all I knew."

What was the key to her successful approach? "I changed my thinking from what I should do to what would I like [to do]. What would I like to draw to me? How do I make that happen? That came about like a miracle, but when you're working with these kinds of visualizations, it does work."

Amy says her core belief is the law of expectation and the law of belief. "We all draw to us what we expect. We are doing that anyway, but some of us are more aware of it than others. It's not about personally faking yourself out. I don't believe in just hyping myself up. But it is believing something could happen. Stephen Covey would call that 'Begin with the end in mind.'"

But Amy would be the first to say that belief must be coupled with action. "This is not about thinking your way to a greater life. It starts with thought, then you have to act. What I was doing from the Friday that I got my pink slip until the following Monday was calling everyone I knew." And all those people helped Amy, both with referrals and with moral support.

While she was at the plumbing company, Amy expanded the market from new construction to remodeling projects through networking with interior designers who were dealing with high-end consumers. Before she arrived, the company had no marketing strategies; their idea of marketing was, as she says, to "turn on the lights and open the doors." Using many of the techniques she'd learned at Rich's, she developed their markets. She rose in the company and was eventually nominated to be a member of the National Design Counsel sponsored by Masco. After only two years in the industry, Amy sat on the board of that counsel.

Looking for new challenges, Amy took her skills in marketing and started her own consulting company, The Garrett Marketing Group, in August 1995. She is now getting into the corporate training and public speaking arena, particularly on the topic of motivation, and is represented by one of the largest and oldest training companies in the United States. As Amy says, "To me success is the everyday progress toward my goals. I'm satisfied that I am on that path. I'm at the beginning of another cycle in my life."

Audrey Rice Oliver: Creating a Vision and Living It

"I believe that you are in charge of your own destiny. If you're thinking clear and positive thoughts, you'll generally be optimistic. That's the kind of energy you want to create and generate for your life."

—Audrey Rice Oliver, President and CEO, Integrated Business Solutions

Audrey Rice Oliver, a woman who has succeeded time and time again in her diverse career paths, readily admits to being an optimist. She found out early in her life that a positive attitude is the only alternative for someone who wants to achieve her goals and live a happy and satisfying life. As she says, "If we are able to change our negative thought patterns about our circumstances, then we can create something very significant in our lives."

Audrey has always had dreams for herself, but it wasn't until she learned the hard lessons of an abusive marriage, the birth of her children when she was barely out of her teens, and a business failure that she began to see the role that optimism plays in realizing those dreams. She began her career in 1971 with the opening of a men's shoe store in Denver called the Boot Broker. Using a $25,000 loan she had received from the Small Business Administration (with her house as collateral), she became the first African-American to own a retail store in downtown Denver. After a year in which the street in front of the store was torn up, followed by an energy crisis that crippled the economy, Audrey had to close her store. She says her own inexperience played a role, too. She felt she was naive about running a business, particularly forecasting, and believes she could have paid more attention to fashion trends. Audrey had managed to pay off the SBA loan, but the store didn't survive.

With three growing children to support, Audrey took a job as a secretary with the Denver Regional Transportation Agency. That was a difficult time for her. "I saw myself as taking a step back. In that circumstance, most people would feel that they had hit rock bottom and would wonder if there was any hope or any thought of something good happening. It would have been easy to take the negative side and get depressed." But Audrey didn't, although an incident with her children was the key to a breakthrough in her attitude. "When I got the secretary job, it was awful. One evening when I went home, I was so upset over it. At the dinner table, my six-year-old twins asked me what I did at work that was making me so tired. They kept asking me questions: What did the bus do? Why were we riding the bus? Where did it go? I was tired, but I answered their questions. Afterwards I went upstairs, feeling very discouraged by my circumstances. As I started to reflect, I began to realize that I wanted to change my thinking. I knew the best way to do that is to try to see the good in any circumstance. I dozed off to sleep for awhile. When I woke up, I stayed up until 3:00 A.M. writing down exactly what my children and I had talked about that evening." When she went to work, she typed it up and showed it to the general manager. Audrey turned it into a coloring book for children to tell them about Denver's transit system. It eventually became the pilot program on transportation in the Denver public schools. Audrey won an award from the school district and the agency for her work and put it on her wall as a daily reminder of her progress.

Audrey stayed at the transit agency for ten more years. After she created the coloring book, she was asked to move up to customer service and eventually became head of the thirty-eight-member customer information center. Audrey's energy, positive attitude, and optimism were noticed. Her next position was in the emerging minority business department. "The management said I get such good momentum going that it would be a good place for me. I developed a program for them that helps women and minorities to get contracts at the agency to provide goods and services. I designed and ran a program that went from $300,000 to $6 million in minority contracts in one year." Audrey's success in Denver was beginning to be noticed nationally. She was asked to go to Washington to help write the Department of Transportation's regulations for minority business.

In an odd way, her growing national prominence did not serve her well in the agency in Denver. After a difference of opinion with management there, she pursued and got a job as a supervisor in customer information at AC Transit in Oakland, California. Before long, she found another job even closer to her interests as a manager of a program for minority business for a Bay Area water district. Once again she dramatically increased the amounts being spent with minority and women-owned businesses. At the same time, she had started Audrey Oliver and Associates, a consulting organization specializing in minority procurement. Like many successful women, that move was part of her positive sense of career self-reliance. She says, "No matter who you're working for you are self-employed. You are the product, you get paid for that product, and you market it. In marketing that product, if it's good, you get rewarded, and if it's not— that's when attitude becomes very important. You put yourself in an optimistic frame of mind and you believe that you can accomplish whatever you put your mind to. You have to be able to see where you want to go. Successful people can see. The unsuccessful stagnate because they are constantly dwelling on the 'poor me' syndrome. 'Woe is me' doesn't make it. You have to ask, 'How can I make the best out of the circumstance that I'm in?' The first way to do that is to change your outlook on your circumstance."

In her case, Audrey says, even her job as a secretary had positive aspects. It was where she learned to express her thoughts in writing, which led to the coloring book, her job in customer service, her work in Washington, and her current consulting firm, Integrated Business Solutions (IBS). Today, IBS specializes in software development, analysis, consulting services, and systems integration. Her multimillion dollar business contracts include clients such as AT&T, Pacific Bell, Pacific Gas & Electric, Bank of America, and Bechtel, and has offices in San Francisco, Sacramento, and San Ramon, California, as well as Chicago, Illinois.

Audrey is a living example of how a positive attitude combined with action can create impressive levels of success. She was recognized as running one of California's Best Women Owned Businesses by Governor Pete Wilson in 1992 and in the same year was given the "Best Supplier" award from the State of California. She attended the Clinton administration economic summit in 1992 and has testified several times before Congress on minority issues. In 1995 Audrey was a delegate and chair of the California delegation to the White House Conference on Small Business.

The Art of Changing Your Thinking

Amy Garrett and Audrey Oliver are powerful examples of the difference a positive outlook can make in women's lives. Amy wasted no time thinking of herself as a victim in her unexpected job transition. Her combination of positive attitude and forceful action led her to new challenges and eventually to a whole new line of work. In the same way, Audrey's entrepreneurial attitude and ability to deal forthrightly with problems and mistakes were what led to her success. Such women combine belief in themselves and their visions with actions that often take them outside their comfort zones.

Success is not purely mental, but the art of changing our thinking begins in our minds. A few key principles can make a tremendous difference in the way successful women view the world and handle the challenges that come their way:

- Use the power of belief to create success

- Adopt a "Why not?" approach

- Choose to deal with your circumstances

- Remember the importance of flexibility

- Stretch your comfort zone

- Practice optimism

Use the Power of Belief to Create Success

"You can learn to change the way you think, feel, and behave in the here-and-now. That simple but revolutionary principle can help you change your life."

—Dr. David D. Burns, Clinical Associate Professor of Psychiatry, University of Pennsylvania School of Medicine, in *The Feeling Good Handbook*

We all have heard over and over how essential it is to foster a constructive outlook and to believe we can create our own success. Some versions of this message can seem vapid and unrealistic, but they're based on an important truth: What we tell ourselves about who we are and what we can do has a dramatic effect on what we actually feel and accomplish. Positive thinking is not about telling yourself that bad things in your life don't exist or haven't happened to you, or that life will be easy if you just think the right thoughts. It is about understanding that thoughts affect outcomes. That's why wildly successful women know that paying attention to what they think is basic.

Sheila Murray Bethel, acclaimed lecturer, business counselor to a host of Fortune 500 companies, and author of a best-selling book, learned this lesson early in her life. She says, "I remember coming home from my first-grade class and asking my mother, 'Are we poor, Mommy?' My mother asked, 'Who said that?' I told her, 'The kids at school said we're poor.' 'We aren't poor, Sweetheart,' my mother said to me. 'We just don't have any money.'"

At that time Sheila and her family lived in a tenement in Oakland, California. Her mother, who worked twelve hours a day cutting pears in a cannery during the summertime, also made their clothes. Her father made the furniture. They hooked their rugs by hand, and they had an ice box when everybody else had a refrigerator. But they never let their current circumstances become their future. In her professional life, Sheila has seen how that attitude affects individuals and, in turn, entire companies.

"When I started work in the late 1960s I trained brain-damaged children. I was the coordinator for an institute. In the three years I was there I got on-the-job training in behavioral sciences, but I never went to college, even though I had a personal study plan to learn about the arts, ancient civilizations, and other subjects. I've always believed we have to be very broad in our knowledge and very specific in our expertise."

Sheila next took a job in sales in the mortgage banking industry. She was quickly recognized as a top salesperson and asked to teach her techniques to others in her business. She jumped at the chance for advancement, because she had recently gotten divorced and needed to support herself and her two teen-age sons. Sheila found that the secret to her sales success was her habit of listening carefully and understanding what her customers needed, then responding promptly and thoughtfully. She also recognized the power of a positive perspective in a sales situation. Her customers sensed her sincere desire to make a difference in their business and responded enthusiastically.

In 1977 Sheila attended a seminar and realized that she wanted to do what the speaker did. So she set out to do that by creating Sheila Murray Associates and giving sales seminars. But, she says ruefully, "I learned all the lessons the hard way." When Sheila first started, people didn't want to hire her because she was unknown and a woman. She now finds those qualities can be a benefit. "When I went into this business and saw that there were no women, I got my banker to loan me $7,000 on my 'good will.' He knew I would break my neck to pay him back. Unfortunately, I blew through that money in the first year because I didn't know how to run a business. So then I had to start all over again owing $7,000—worse than when I first started." But Sheila's persistence in developing her speaking career paid off— and also allowed her to pay off her loan. Today she is in the top one-half of one percent of female lecturers in the country.

What carried her through? Sheila says it's her philosophy about being successful. "If you make a difference in people's businesses or their lives that helps them become successful, and you do it enough times, you won't be able to carry the money to the bank. My whole philosophy and passion is about making a difference." That philosophy manifested itself in her books, *How to Organize and Manage a Seminar* (Prentice Hall, 1981) and *Making a Difference: 12 Qualities That Make You a Leader* (Putnam-Berkley, 1990). She still believes that defining your own success is important. "From day one I defined success. From day one I planned where I wanted to be in five years. From day one I planned all of my (promotional and sales) materials as a writer and a speaker—they were all more professional and advanced than I was at the time. I let my fantasy become my reality."

Seeing the good in difficult situations is a perspective successful people consciously choose. Indeed, research has shown that the link between positive attitude and life events is extraordinary. As David D. Burns writes in *The Feeling Good Handbook* (Plume, 1990), negative thinking patterns can actually *cause* people to feel depressed and anxious. When people think about problems in a more positive and realistic way, they experience greater productivity. "You can learn to change the way you think, feel, and behave in the here-and-now," writes Dr. Burns. "That simple but revolutionary principle can help you change your life." Dr. Burns refers to self-defeating attitudes and fears as "silent assumptions." Among them:

- Other people are to blame for my problems.

- The world should always be the way I want it.

- It's not really safe to feel happy and optimistic.

- I'm hopeless and bound to feel depressed forever because the problems in my life are impossible to solve.

Successful women avoid these silent assumptions. Amy Garrett, for example, would never have been able to land on her feet so gracefully if she had spent her time blaming the villains in the hostile takeover that put her out on the street. And Audrey Oliver would not have been able to achieve her impressive levels of success if she had believed it wasn't safe to find the good in her difficult circumstances or that she was doomed to remain forever at the bottom of the heap. Successful women know that they can go further and find greater success—however they define it—if they begin by believing in themselves and in their ability to handle whatever comes their way.

Adopt a "Why Not?" Attitude

"When I was writing the history of perfumes, I discovered computers. I needed more and more fields in the database, but I couldn't find a program on the market for what I needed. My interest in history, in science, and in techniques gave me the confidence to create one myself."

—Marylène Delbourg-Delphis, Founder and President, ACI US, Inc.

There are lots of reasons *not* to do something: money, time, other obligations, doubts, physical constraints. But successful women tend not to focus on why something can't be done. Instead, they ask, "Why not do it?"

They may, as Marylène Delbourg-Delphis did, turn frustration into opportunity. Even though she wasn't a software designer, Marylène thought, "Why not me?" Marylène's background as a philosophy teacher at the Sorbonne in Paris and a writer of research books on the history of perfumes was an unlikely beginning for her successful career in the computer industry.

Since most computer software is made in America, no one expected a French person, let alone a French woman, to produce innovative computer software. But Marylène did. Out of her frustration with the existing database software came Marylène's motivation to do the extensive research and networking necessary to get the technological support to develop "4th Dimension," a best-selling relational database program for Macintosh that received a four-star rating in the March 1996 issue of *Macworld*. As the article said, "The program has survived and beaten back a half-dozen serious competitors over the years—so successfully that ACI US's only hope of market expansion is on the other side of the fence, in the Windows domain...."

ACI stands for "Analyses Conseils Information," or "the analysis and control of information." US stands for the United States branch. Today, just ten years after she started it, ACI has six international branches and sales of more than $40 million.

Marylène has a philosophical approach to success. "I never perceive what I do as success. Success is the way people qualify what you've done—not what you felt. My purpose was to accomplish something which made sense." This kind of "why not?" attitude made it possible for Marylène to create a valuable product that solved her research problem and created a thriving cross-national organization.

Choose to Deal with Your Circumstances

"When you're too busy thinking of the negative, you can't get past that to be creative or have the obvious come through that there are possibilities. It is a mental attitude that creates the positive results."
—Audrey Rice Oliver, President and CEO, Integrated Business Solutions

There are plenty of circumstances that are simply out of our control, but wildly successful women concentrate less on what happens than what they can do about it. They don't ignore the problem, wishing it would go away. Instead, they focus on the next step, on the future, not the past. When things seem out of control, they choose how they will react and deal with the issues head-on. In doing so, they often discover abilities they never knew they possessed and opportunities they never before considered. New York advertising copywriter Joy Golden is a woman who did that, who used adversity as a spring-board to a new—and even more interesting—career.

"In 1979, when I was almost fifty, I was fired from a big advertis-ing agency. I was one of the associate creative directors, but there was a political problem at the agency, so they dumped me. But if that hadn't happened, I never would have gone into this business. I would have stayed at that agency forever." Still, figuring out how to deal with this turn of events took time.

"I wasn't sure what I was going to do, so I decided I would freelance while I figured out what I would do with my life. At fifty I knew I wasn't going to work for anyone else. It's age discrimination, but I wanted to figure a way around it. When you freelance, it's the differ-ence between being engaged and married. I was making money freelancing but was not married to the agency. I freelanced for several agencies, including Tragos, Bonnange, Wiesendanger, and Ajroldi (TBWA)—people refer to it by its acronym because the names are too long. I fell in love with that agency." When they asked Joy to write a radio commercial, she wasn't excited about it. "I thought, 'Oh no, radio. It's so boring.' But as it turned out, it was the one thing that I did best. I had to stretch my comfort zone, but it must have been in the cards."

The client did not, however, like the first radio commercial she wrote. "The client said, 'Oh God, Joy, that's so boring. Why don't you write a schtick.' I asked, 'You mean funny?' If my client hadn't suggested writing funny, I never would have thought of doing funny." But as it turned out, her funny commercials were tremendous hits.

Joy is probably best known for her humorous radio commercials for Laughing Cow cheese. The campaign ran for more than five years, delivered record-breaking sales, and the commercials became clas-sics. The ultimate recognition (which Joy says was "the happiest

moment since my second divorce") came when her work was chosen
to be part of the permanent collection of the Museum of Television
and Radio. In case you don't remember any of the Laughing Cow
commercials, here's one:

> Enid: "Last night my husband woke me and said he had a
> little craving. I said, 'I'll go to the all-night supermarket
> and get you a little round laughing cow in a red net bag.'
>
> He said, 'I don't care if she's in lace with high heels, it isn't
> what I had in mind.'
>
> I said, 'So what do you want, Stuart?'
>
> He said, 'Something sort of soft and a little nippy.'
>
> I said, 'So you want Mini Babybel from the Laughing Cow.'
>
> He said, 'No.'
>
> I said, 'So what do you want, Stuart?'
>
> He said, 'Cheese.'
>
> I said, 'What do you think I was talking about?'
>
> So I went to the dairy case and I bought two red net bags
> with five mini cheeses in each. Mini Bonbel and Mini
> Babybel. Delicious, natural, bite-size. Then I went home
> and I said, 'Look, Stuart—a little laughing cow in a red
> net bag freshly wrapped in wax with an easy-open French
> zipper.'
>
> He said, 'Enid, don't talk naughty to me.'
>
> Then he ate all ten mini cheeses and said it was the best
> treat he ever had in bed . . . so I smacked him."

Joy continues, "Those Laughing Cow commercials changed my
life. It had never dawned on me to write radio commercials. It was
not the chic medium in my day. Television was very hot in the sixties,
seventies, eighties. Radio was not considered the 'class' medium. TV

was really the art form at the time because it was newer." Joy had never considered starting her own business, much less at age fifty-five. But the success of her Laughing Cow commercials changed her thinking. "That success gave me the self-confidence to start my own business."

Joy asked everyone she knew how to run a business. "I picked a lot of brains until I could figure out how to do this. I had enough money from freelancing, and I had thirty-three years of advertising experience." When she announced in the trade papers that she had opened her own comedy radio business, she immediately got clients. "I took all of the shoes out of my closet and put in a shelf (as my office) and I was in business." Eleven years later, Joy Radio continues to grow. And she's moved it out of her closet.

She looks at her transformation philosophically. "You have to believe in yourself. You have to keep a positive mental attitude. You can't be depressed by failure. Failure is the greatest road to success. Nobody succeeds without failure. Nobody should be set back because they got fired or whatever. A lot of people get fired in middle age, but that should not set them back, that should light a fire under them to show the world."

"I always say it's never too late to change your life," she continues. "I mean, really never, as long as you're committed to what you really love. If you love what you do, you can make a business out of anything. If you have enough enthusiasm for it, it's bound to be a success."

Life can bring all sorts of challenges. It's what you choose to do with those challenges—your attitude, your outlook—that transforms them from hardships to intriguing possibilities.

Remember the Importance of Flexibility

"It's easy to blame it on something else . . . but I think there has to be flexibility in handling every situation—and not a rigid preconceived idea."
—Dr. Marilyn Rosenwein, Obstetrician/Gynecologist

Successful women are optimists. Instead of seeing walls and hurdles, they see windows of opportunity and avenues to success. These women are not ignoring reality. They hope for and plan for the best outcome, but they know they also have to be flexible. Narrow expectations can limit options, stunt reactions, and lead to unnecessary disappointment.

Dr. Marilyn Rosenwein, a gynecologist and obstetrician in private practice in San Mateo, California, says she sees the effects of attitude in women all day long. "It's great to see someone who's upbeat. Some patients come in who have such severe problems—their husbands may be dying of cancer or their kids are in trouble—and when I ask, 'How are you?' they say, 'Great.' They feel healthy. Then I see a woman who shouldn't have a care in the world, but she comes in depressed, with a bleak attitude. She's created her own illness. We all have ups and downs, but some people have a great attitude about dealing with life."

Marilyn believes that one of the biggest problems for women in any transition is their rigid and narrowly defined expectations. "For example, a woman thinks she'll have a perfect baby and it has colic. I see her six weeks later and she's in severe post-partum depression. She can't believe this is happening to her because she envisioned a fairy tale situation with her baby. It was all going to be wonderful."

Women who stay flexible have an advantage in dealing with transitions. Marilyn's advice is, "Don't have your mind fixed on what you think the outcome *has to be.* You can have a general idea of what you'd like it to be, but if you're rigid, you set yourself up for disappointment. There are emotional problems from disappointment that can lead to depression. It's easy to blame it on something else, but I think there has to be flexibility in handling every situation. It's great to have goals, because you're working toward something, but you can't think that your goal is the only possible outcome. It may not be."

In some cases, women contribute to their own problems by forecasting a negative outcome for normal life events. As Marilyn explains, "Some patients come in whose mother had problems going through menopause, and they're already prepared to go crazy and have problems. They've set themselves up, as opposed to some women who say, 'This is going to be easy.' Very often situations are what you anticipate. If you're totally rigid about it, you have a much harder time dealing with it."

Marilyn sets a good example. She didn't plan to specialize in her particular branch of medicine, but she seized an opportunity when it presented itself. "I was lucky enough to go down the right path, but I'm sure if I had gone down another direction it would have been okay, too. I can't say that anything has been a disappointment. Some things have been difficult to deal with, but they all worked out. I think (success) is very much based on attitude."

Stretch Your Comfort Zone

"There was a mystique about owning a business, and, for a long time, I didn't think I could do it."

—Diane Jacobs, Owner, The Cakeworks

Throughout the book you'll notice that successful women don't try to hide the fact that they didn't know everything when they changed course in their careers or started their new endeavors. More often than not they started with an entrepreneurial leap of faith that landed them well outside their typical comfort zone.

Amy Garrett and Audrey Oliver certainly did. They took the attitude that they would learn as they went, that they would take action to find out what they didn't know. Successful women aren't afraid to stretch; in fact, it's a strategy for taking risks. And when they stretch they feel most proud of their successes, when they knew they truly had to challenge themselves to attain their goals. Diane Jacobs is just one of many, many success stories of women who were willing to let their reach exceed their grasp.

Diane Jacobs had thought about owning her own bakery since she was fifteen, but her education didn't include business training. Her dream was so important to her, however, that she was able to look at her fears philosophically. "The worst part of failure is thinking how everyone will look at me. I can't stand that thought. The question is, 'What is it that I'm trying to learn here—what would I be learning if I failed?'" She was willing to be outside her comfort zone and to learn as she went.

Diane had studied at the Art Institute of Chicago and earned her degree in architecture from the University of Cincinnati, but she loved baking—and especially decorating cakes. It had been her passion since she was twelve years old growing up in Ohio. Unfortunately, there was no market for art cakes in Ohio. "I saw a bakery in California that made beautiful cakes featured on a television show, and I wrote to the owner to ask about job opportunities. I sent pictures of my cakes and got a job." At twenty-one, Diane moved to California to start her new career, but the thrill of working for even that talented baker faded. "I found working for other people difficult. There was no flexibility. Someone was always trying to dictate what I could or couldn't do with my art. I didn't like the constraints."

Besides the artistic constraints, her job was never secure. The bakery often changed ownership, and her pay was disappointing. "At first I earned $5 an hour, and after six years I was only earning $8 an hour. I got tired of hearing people say that I should make more money, and I felt that I could run a shop better than any of my previous employers at the bakery."

"There was a mystique about owning a business, and for a long time I didn't think I could do it. After all, I had majored in architecture. Yet everything I studied came into play later in my business. Photography classes helped, because I ended up shooting the photographs for the brochure for my bakery, and I produced the layout work. With my architectural background, I designed the shop to suit my needs."

What Diane didn't know she learned from books. "I went to the library and got books on how to write a business plan. I came home with seven of them. I wanted to learn all the different perspectives." After Diane wrote her business proposal, she took it to investors to get start-up capital. Her family helped her with one-third of the start-up money needed to secure a Small Business Administration (SBA) loan. "The federal SBA office and Service Corps of Retired Executives (SCORE) advise people that the SBA doesn't *lend* money [they guarantee it]. They referred me to Pacific Coast regional, a development corporation, that guarantees state SBA loans." When Diane talked with an officer at Pacific Coast, that's where she says her business plan proved to be a valuable tool. "I talked to him about my business and he was sold. He took it to committee. It didn't take as long as I thought to get the loan—about eight weeks. Before that I went to a lot of banks, but I had no collateral and no business background, so they couldn't grant me a loan."

Today, Diane owns The Cakeworks, a bakery that pleases customers from movie stars to passers-by, who see her imaginative cakes in her store window in the fashionable La Brea area of Los Angeles. Her "signature" cake is one that looks like a basket filled with real wild flowers. Some of her other unique cakes include one shaped like a couch to commemorate the one-hundredth episode of Roseanne's television show, a life-size computer cake, and one that looks like an autographed publicity photo of Orson Welles.

Diane feels her success comes from within. "The only meaning of success for me is the feeling I get when I've done something myself, and I've done a great job. Analysts say people can tie their self-worth into something material. If my business burned down, would that mean I have no value? No. My value lies in making my own decisions and providing for myself." One of Diane's best decisions was to stretch her comfort zone.

Practice Optimism

"People can learn to be optimistic by accentuating the positive."
—Jean Hollands, President and CEO, Growth & Leadership Center

Can you actually practice optimism? Is it a temperament, or is it something that can be learned? The answers to those questions are yes, no, yes. Jean Hollands, corporate psychologist and owner of the Growth & Leadership Center (GLC) in Mountain View, California, says, "My pervading philosophy is that if you can't be optimistic, you may as well be dead." That may be overstating the case a bit, but Jean holds strongly to her convictions. One of her activities at GLC is to teach people to become optimistic. "People can learn to be optimistic by accentuating the positive. We help our clients figure out when they generalize—such as thinking that if they're not good at some things then they're not going to be good at other things. We help people to stop deducing that 'if I made one mistake today, then I'm going to make mistakes the rest of the day.' Instead, we encourage them not to generalize and to think more positively; 'I'm not lucky in love, but I can still be lucky in business.'"

Jean wrote *Optimistic Organizations: How to Get, Grow and Keep Positive Power in Your Company* (Select Books, 1992). "The prevailing hypothesis of the book was that you can be powerful if you're optimistic. If you have parents who didn't believe that they were the lucky ones—even if they say you're the lucky one because you got a better education—you're still hassled by parents who weren't lucky. So you grow up with a handicap. You need to overcome parental messages, teacher messages, and cultural messages. Plus, people are always being measured. To off-load and compensate for this over-measuring, we have to give ourselves extra care, love, and nurturing."

Jean finds that people in transition need to be optimistic. "My advice is to be practical. If you have to do a job that will feed you for a while, do that job. But on the side, spend the other twenty hours a week—the ones you would spend in depression—preparing for your next vocation or avocation. Never give up. Always believe. Do a lot of imagining, dreaming, and fantasizing about your next event."

Successful women master the art of changing their minds. It's not only a prerogative, it's often necessary for success. By changing your thinking, you change your life. Try it and see!

Joy Golden's Nine Tips For Changing Your Thinking

1. Stop thinking so much and act on what you've been thinking about.

2. Don't give up your dreams because you're too old, too tired, too fat, too single, still single, or single again. Be glad you're alone and don't have to listen to snoring all night.

3. What would you tell your best friend if he or she came to you with your exact same problems? Whatever you would say you should do yourself.

4. Give up the word "Can't." This is a dirty four-letter word.

5. Get a computer and learn how to use it. Your whole life will change.

6. Did you know the lobster sheds its shell in order to grow? Take the risk. Shed yours.

7. Try something you have always wanted to do. Yes, tap dancing will free your spirit. Tap dancing? Right.

8. All the lessons your mother taught you weren't necessarily the word of God. Let your own internal engine drive you from here on. Be free.

9. Don't live your life the way you're living it right now just because that's the way you've always done it. One tiny experiment a day will help you change your thinking and give you courage to do two the next day. Did you ever think of throwing out your furniture? Great catharsis.

The Wildly Successful Woman's Guide to Getting "Unstuck"

People who want to change their thinking and their lives but don't, often feel stuck. Women in careers often feel stuck because of to the "glass ceiling" or the "mommy track." Others are bored and feel they're only working for a paycheck. They realize they aren't having any fun, but they don't know what to do about it. They just feel stuck.

Most successful women will tell you that to get *un*stuck, you have to work at it. Quick insight and inspiration don't usually solve the problem. It takes time to explore different avenues. Amy Garrett and Audrey Oliver set goals and worked in different organizations before they decided to start their own businesses. But it took action to get them to the levels of success they enjoy today. Here are six tips to consider if you ever feel stuck:

1. **Take little steps.** You often hear entrepreneurs say that if they had known all the steps they had to take to become successful, they would have been too frightened to start. Take little steps to keep from feeling overwhelmed. Every morning when you wake up, think about what you can do that day to advance yourself toward your new goal. Do something each day, whether it's making one phone call or writing a letter. But keep moving!

2. **Get out.** Successful people know they need to connect with people who can help them. Get out and mingle with other people. Attend club meetings and lectures. Gather new ideas from people in an industry that interests you. Talk to them about what you may like to do. Ask them questions and listen carefully. Brainstorm. See and hear what else is going on in the world around you.

3. **Post a "have done" list.** Many successful people keep a tally of their accomplishments, great and small. Appreciating how far you've come helps remind you that you can achieve your goals,

one step at a time. List all the information you gather and from whom, the seminars you've attended, the calls you've made, the letters you've written. Post the list where you can see it.

4. **Acknowledge the things you *do* have control over.** When faced with situations that seem out of their control, successful people analyze the situation and look for areas they can control. Perhaps you don't control your job situation or the economy. Fine. Find the things you do control: how much you exercise or when you work on a special project or when you can say "no" to extra assignments or when you meet with people you manage. Start with the basics, then elaborate. When you identify the many different things you can control, you regain your sense of having the power to choose.

5. **Don't say "yes" to people just because they ask you to do something.** Successful people stay focused. They try not to overcommit or accept responsibilities that throw them off course. Practice saying "yes" to yourself first. If what you're requested to do fits with what you want to accomplish with your time, fine. If not, politely decline. Pick and choose your yeses to keep you on track.

6. **Call for support.** Call on family and friends when you need help or encouragement. Successful people don't try to go it alone when they are down. When you feel stuck, go for a walk with friends. Tell people what you need. Attend a meeting of a professional group you belong to and get involved. Many wildly successful women have found that helping others truly helps themselves.

Commandment
Four

When the Odds Are Against You, Defy the Odds

If you think of life as a card game, we are all dealt a variety of hands. Sometimes the odds are against us, sometimes with us. When all is said and done, though, the skill of playing—and the tenacity to stay in the game—determine success. Successful women who beat the odds opt to get in the game even if they have to learn the rules along the way or write their own. They simply turn a deaf ear to naysayers and keep playing.

Regardless of the hand you have been dealt, the belief that you *can* beat the odds is essential in playing the game to win. Whether you face a corporate reorganization, dizzying levels of change in your markets, a forced layoff, or any other life-altering event, a first response may be a temptation to fold. What differentiates successful women is that, by playing their hands well, they remake the odds in their favor. Their entrepreneurial spirit, positive attitude, and pure perseverance are their "aces in the hole."

If you ask successful women how they defied the odds, their answers most likely will be a variation of something like this: Play

> **"When you come from a different field, in a way that is an advantage. You're not jaded. You have to work harder. But it's good because it's your point of differentiation. I believe if there's a will, there's a way."**
> —Josie Natori, Founder and CEO, Natori Company

the hand you've been dealt the best you can—but get in the game. Determination makes the difference. Nancy Battista and Josie Natori both defied the odds and have become master players in the game.

Nancy Battista: The Fresh Tomato

"When I started this everyone told me I was doing something that was impossible—including the authorities."

—Nancy Battista, Founder, Pomodoro Fresca Foods

Everything should have been wonderful in Nancy Battista's life in 1988, but her marriage of four years was in trouble. "I asked my husband, 'Do you love me? Do you want to be here?' He said, 'No.' I said, 'All right, pack your bags, I'll drive you down to the station.' It was just like that. The entire way down to the station I expected him to say, 'No, I want to stay.' When he got on the train, I realized he was really going."

At twenty-six Nancy was left with her two-year-old son, a mortgage on her condominium, car payments, and a drastically reduced family income. But she had no time to feel sorry for herself. "I didn't come from money," she says. "I couldn't count on getting money from family. I had to find another source of income, but I couldn't afford full-time child care."

Nancy looked around and assessed her circumstances. To add to her income as a textile designer, she began catering her company's New York showroom events when they presented their new lines of fabric to interior designers. Nancy prepared Italian "peasant food" using her family's recipe for homemade fresh pomodoro (tomato) sauce, which eventually became the trademark of her catering business.

Word of her catering spread. "Within four months I had a great business, catering to the galleries and studios in Soho. I was working my design job during the day and catering five nights a week. This gave me a chance to save some money, but I was completely worn out. I thought I would have more time with my son, but I hardly saw him."

"Although my parents helped me with baby-sitting and catering, I realized I had to let go of something." Nancy's distinctive fresh tomato sauce had become such a hit that people asked to buy it—cases of it—and were willing to pay any price. Nancy decided to quit her textile job and her catering to make and sell her tomato sauce full time. Although she knew nothing of the food industry, Nancy rolled up her sleeves and got started.

Armed only with a strong belief in her product, Nancy took her first step by bringing her sauce to the Food Emporium, an upscale supermarket chain on the East Coast. "I waited around for hours. It was a Friday and all of the managers were there. When I finally got in, I started rattling off my whole spiel about Pomodoro Fresca, but they were talking another language, supermarket language: one in ten, slotting fees, etc. The deli manager looked at me and asked, 'What are you going to do for me?' I looked at him and asked him exactly what he meant. I didn't have a clue that he wanted me to pay him for shelf space. I said, 'What are you talking about? I'm here to make money and you're trying to get money from me!' I broke down and cried."

The buyers at the Food Emporium were impressed with Nancy's sauce—and they felt a little sorry for her—so they gave her an order. They also told her what she needed to know about liability insurance and what she had to put on the label. She left with an order for five stores and a promise for an order for the entire chain of twenty-five stores if the sauce sold. With a lead time of two months to get it together, Nancy thought, "What more could I ask for?" She soon found out she needed much, much more.

Finding a way to produce her sauce commercially was Nancy's next problem. Nancy had heard about co-packers—companies that process food products in quantity—but she was not prepared for the response from the first one she called. "He told me he couldn't make the sauce using fresh tomatoes." Every other co-packer she called said the same thing. "I thought I was having a communication problem. I couldn't believe that what I wanted was unique."

Nancy called the U.S. Department of Agriculture and Markets for their advice. They asked her what her food background was. "I told them, 'I don't have a food background, I do designs for the textile industry.'" When they told her to go back to her design studio and draw tomatoes, not cook them, she said, "Listen, I'm not going to forget it. I'm doing this. I'm on a mission. You don't understand. I'm going to make it, but you have to tell me how. That's your job!"

Her persistence paid off. They advised her to go to the Cornell University Cooperative Extension campus. "I put everything I needed for the sauce into my Volkswagen and drove six hours to Cornell's testing lab. It was like going to see the Wizard of Oz." At first the director was not optimistic, but Nancy cajoled him into helping her develop a recipe and the exact legal requirements for commercially manufacturing her sauce. Still she had no commercial kitchen willing to make it her way. She would have to figure out a way to produce it herself, but she didn't know where she was going to get the money or the people to do it.

Nancy had used half of her savings to incorporate her business and had barely enough money to buy tomatoes, jars, and labels. Nancy asked family and friends for help. "My brother had an ice cream parlor which had gone out of business, and he offered to let me use it. My father revamped the space into a manufacturing facility." Friends sent her a used stainless steel sink and a sub-zero refrigerator. Her mother and sisters cut the fresh tomatoes and packaged the jars. "We shipped the Food Emporium their first order on time, and it sold out within a week. They put my sauce in the entire chain of twenty-five stores."

Now the challenge was keeping up with the demand. Within six months Pomodoro Fresca was in every major specialty food store in New Jersey and parts of New York and Connecticut. Nancy had to do everything herself to get her company up and running. Her biggest problem, besides not having enough hours in the day, was ensuring a steady supply of good, fresh tomatoes. She not only had to survive harrowing midnight sorties to New York's produce market to buy fresh tomatoes, she had to contend with their fluctuating prices. With restricted cash flow, Nancy was finding she couldn't afford to make excess inventory when the price was low and couldn't produce at all when the price was high. Worse, the erratic production schedule meant she couldn't hire outside help or create a steady supply of her product. Her family, already weary, would not be able to keep up with the increasing demand. Nancy was savvy enough to know that now that she had established the market, if she didn't fill it someone else would.

To overcome her production problems, Nancy made two of her biggest decisions. She became partners with one of the co-packers she originally had contacted, a man who had been intrigued with what she wanted to do. When he purchased a large building for his own business, he offered Nancy a partnership in exchange for creating special equipment to produce her sauce. That solved her production problem, except for the problem of tomato prices, which have continued to be troublesome. Her second decision—to hire a distribution company to deliver the product—allowed her to stop the hectic running around that she had been doing during the early years.

In the last two years Nancy has moved her business to a larger, state-of-the-art facility. She has expanded her line with medium-priced sauces. With greater success, Nancy has found more time for her personal life, has remarried, and is expecting another child. Nancy loves to tell her story about all the obstacles she encountered, the odds she overcame, and the importance of persistence. Was it all worth it? Unequivocally, yes. "I get a real feeling of fulfillment every day. Every day I come home and I feel I've accomplished something." Nancy Battista is a wildly successful woman.

Josie Natori: Out of Wall Street and into the World

"You have to have belief in yourself and belief in where you're going. That's the long-term vision."

—Josie Natori, Founder and CEO, Natori Company

Josie Cruz Natori came to the United States from the Philippines to study economics at Manhattanville College in New York City. After graduation in 1968, she worked in the securities industry, first at Bache Securities and later at Merrill Lynch, where she became a vice president. But she was bored. "I left Wall Street because I wasn't learning anymore and I wasn't challenged." She and her husband looked at all kinds of businesses, and Josie realized that whatever she chose, it had to interest her and it had to be connected with the Philippines. So she tried furniture, then baskets. She says, "It was a process. First, start my own business; second, do something with the Philippines; and third, try different products. It evolved into apparel."

Josie thought of importing Filipino embroidered blouses called "barongs." When a buyer at Bloomingdale's suggested she make the blouses longer and turn them into nightshirts, her empire was launched. "I had zero background in apparel. Some people assumed that I was educated in fashion, my family was in the industry, or that somebody helped me and I had connections. I had none of these. On top of that, I had no mentor telling me what to do. I learned it the hard way." That approach may have cost her money and led to some mistakes, but Josie says, "When you don't have any preconceived idea of how you're supposed to go, you do it by instinct. Some of it was not practical from a business point of view, but I think it brought us to where we are today. People who've been in an industry feel that they have a formula for it. When you come from a different field, in a way that is an advantage. You're not jaded. It's part of the thrill. You have to work harder. But it's good because it's your point of differentiation. I believe if there's a will, there's a way." Her will and her way have created an apparel company with sales of $40 million that is world-famous for its lingerie, inner-outerwear, and "24-hour dressing."

Josie attributes much of her success to the support of family and friends. "I could not have done this on my own. You need moral support, whether from your friends or your family. Certainly I could not have done it without family help." She also counted on her customers to help her develop her business. "You hear your customer wants it this way, and then you go after that. You listen, you pick everyone's brains. At the beginning, if they told me to do it in green and red, I did it. Obviously, I feel a little differently nineteen years later. But I still listen. That's how you learn."

Her tenacity, business instincts, and creativity continue to serve Josie well in today's business environment. "In the 1980s you couldn't do anything wrong. In the 1990s you have to reengineer, restructure, and rethink, because it's a different mindset. In the 1980s we didn't worry so much about costs; we had to keep evolving our collections and following what our consumer wanted. We now have to be cost efficient. Now I have to be more responsible in a business sense, I have to look at everything. I look at margins; it now costs more to do less. The retailers demand more. We have fewer retailers because of bankruptcies. It's been good, though. I don't think there is any company that hasn't had to reevaluate things."

Today, Josie is preparing for a piano concert she plans to give at Carnegie Hall in celebration of her fiftieth birthday in 1997. To accomplish this she is following the same principles of defying the odds that she did with her business: she sees herself as a player (in this case, a concert piano player), she's taken the first step (set a date), she refuses to believe conventional wisdom (that having not played piano for years should hold her back), she's doing what she knows (she had played solo at age nine), she has gotten support (encouragement from her family), she knows when to get help (she's hired a piano instructor), and she's willing to learn the hard way, if necessary. At age forty-nine she continues to do what she has done in her business: Make her own odds and play the game to win.

Perseverance: Defying the Odds to Win the Game

Nancy Battista and Josie Natori, two very different women from two very different worlds, would not let any obstacles stop them. Driven by their personal goals, by their own definitions of success, and by their desire to succeed, they overcame odds most others would have found daunting. Were they blessed with some innate character strength? Yes, probably. Did they believe they had to stay in the game? Certainly. Can the rest of us learn what they know so that we, too, can master the secrets of tenacity? Absolutely!

Perseverance is no mystery. You can learn it, just as you can learn to play a card game to win. The key ingredients for any wildly successful woman are to:

- See yourself as a player

- Take the first step

- Refuse to believe conventional wisdom

- Do what you know best

- Get support when you need it

- Know when you need help and ask for it

- Be willing to learn the hard way—or any way

See Yourself as a Player

"When people asked me what I would do if this didn't work out in six months, I was shocked. I never doubted it. I was playing the game for real."

—Sharon Leone, President, Sweet Favors

To become successful at anything, you must see yourself as a legitimate player who is more than entitled to sit at the table—or to start your own table. When you begin, you may not know all the rules of the game or all the other players or even what all the cards mean, but you can learn it all with practice and perseverance. That's exactly what Sharon Leone did.

When Sharon was attending the University of California at Berkeley, her friends called her the "candy girl" because of her enthusiasm for her work in a local candy store near campus. After graduation Sharon worked for a while in commercial real estate, but she missed the happy atmosphere of the candy store. Besides, her appetite had been whetted for owning a business.

Sharon tried to buy the candy store where she had worked—three times. On her third and final attempt, Sharon tried a new approach. "I wanted to open up candy stores like theirs all over the state near college campuses. The owners liked the idea but wanted to maintain ownership of the new stores themselves. Even though they had forty other businesses, they wouldn't sell me the candy store. They said they would rather kill the business than sell it." After three tries, Sharon realized that particular game was closed.

When she couldn't create a way to buy into the candy business, Sharon decided to sell candy from her home to corporations instead of to individuals. She had never heard of the terms "premiums" or "ad specialties" and didn't realize she was entering a new game in the field of promotions. She began by approaching a chocolate company to make candy for her with corporate logos on it. She started out small, spending $500 for six chocolate molds. "I had hand-written labels. I took terrible pictures and sent them to people, but I didn't know they were terrible then. Even if I'd had the money, I wouldn't have known how to use it wisely. I wouldn't have known what I wanted from the brochure or what identity I wanted to present."

Sharon started talking to people at large corporations about buying candy with their company logo on it. She approached realtors, the University of California, all kinds of companies that seemed good candidates to her. Many of them bought her candy. She did her marketing homework by reading the local business and community newspapers. If she read about a company that she hadn't heard of, she researched it. "I felt I had no right to call on a company unless I knew what their logo looked like and what they did."

Her big break came when Visa gave her an order for $16,000— 62,500 embossed chocolate coins. Still working out of her house, Sharon bought an embossing machine and called on her parents and her five brothers and sisters to help. It took them three weeks to emboss, wrap, and ship the coins. From there sales took off. Sharon sold 117,000 coins in her first year. In 1992 she moved to a 700-square-foot office and expanded to double the size in 1994. She quit counting coins that year when they broke the one-million mark.

Today, with the birth of their first child, Sharon and her husband have bought a new home with space for her business so she can run it from there rather than put her daughter in daycare. During the hectic holiday crunch she will rent space again. "I realized that since I own the business, I can do what works best for me. However, I put in six years of long hours and hard work to grow it to this stage. If I hadn't been so focused, I could have easily quit in the second year. But then I would never have known how easy it was going to be as I learned more about this business and how to deal with peak seasons."

Take the First Step

"I talk to women all the time who want to do something but can't decide what to do. I tell them to come up with something, anything, and start. It may not be exactly what they'll doing in six months, but it is a mental commitment."

—Caroline Hull, Founder, *ConneXions*

Every successful woman started with a first step in the direction she wanted to go. Nancy Battista had to make her sauce and present it to the Food Emporium. Josie Natori had to start out by importing baskets and furniture. They managed to overcome any fear that the odds were stacked against them. Taking that first step breaks down fear and inertia and substitutes anticipation and excitement—and accomplishment. But how do women take that first step?

To assist clients who want to get over the fear of taking the first step, C.J. Hayden, a business and career coach in San Francisco, suggests beginning by "feeling their way" along. "They do have to have a vision of where they're headed," says C.J. "I don't want to disregard that, but they don't plan it out step by step for five years. They take their vision and take only one step. Then they think, 'Is this going toward my vision or away from it? Oh, toward it. Okay. I'm going to take another step in that direction. Is that toward it?' That's feeling your way."

C.J. has also found that by setting up all of the conditions for something to occur, her clients can get ready for what they want to happen. That's a step, but as Caroline Hull reminds us, it's not yet action. In 1990 Caroline created *ConneXions,* a newsletter that for five years provided local resource information for women who were at home with their children and who wanted a way to make professional connections. Caroline comments, "I talk to women all the time who want to do something but can't decide what to do. I tell them to come up with something, anything, and start. It may not be exactly what they'll be doing in six months, but it is a mental commitment. I tell them to say to themselves, 'I'm going to do this [business]. I'm going to get my business license. I am going to get zoning for my house. I'm going to get inexpensive business cards. I'm going to go for it.' I encourage them to take action."

If you find that you have a long list of things that you "must" accomplish before you start something new, whether you're looking for a new job or starting a business or beginning that big new team-building project, look at your list again to see whether the items on it will actually help you get where you want to go. Are you practicing "productive procrastination"? Productive procrastination can clear away things that take your mind off your mission, and to that degree, it may be useful. If you have to get your taxes done before you can concentrate on your business, that's helpful. If you need to finish your year-end report before you start a new initiative, that makes sense. However, if you have to reorganize your files, put the photographs from the last nine years into albums, or reconfigure your database, beware. It helps to give yourself a time line. "Some day" isn't specific enough to call you to action. When you have a specific time frame in mind, you can set the conditions for what you want to occur.

Refuse to Believe Conventional Wisdom
"I have always felt there was a voice there saying, 'Do it.'"

—Hung Liu, Art Professor and Artist, Mills College

Conventional wisdom can be helpful, giving us the benefit of others' experience. It can also be a restraint, a chorus of naysayers who believe they know better than we do. It may imply that your situation can never change, or that what you want is impossible. It may assume that you're too young, too old, undereducated, overeducated, or simply clueless about what it takes. Conventional wisdom may be absolutely right, but that doesn't mean it's right for you. You know your strengths. You know your ability to hold on to an idea and make it work despite the odds.

Conventional wisdom doesn't apply to women on a mission like Nancy Battista or to a hard-working, intuitive businesswoman like Josie Natori. Nor did it stop a courageous woman like Hung Liu, who crossed continents in her efforts to defy the odds. Hung Liu grew up in newly formed communist China, worked in corn and wheat fields as a forced laborer, painted Chairman Mao propaganda murals, and emigrated to the United States in 1984. Twelve years later she became an American citizen, an associate professor at Mills College, and an award-winning artist. The odds she faced were daunting. Conventional wisdom said she could not get into graduate school, would never receive permission to divorce, and certainly could not obtain a passport to leave China. Yet she did all of that—and much more. "I have always felt," says Hung Liu, "there was a voice there saying, 'Do it.'"

Hung was born in Manchuria in 1948, the year before the People's Republic of China was established. Her parents named her Hung, meaning "rainbow." Six months later her parents were forced to separate after the Civil War. Her father, a captain in the Nationalist Party of Chiang Kai-shek, was considered an enemy of the people and imprisoned. He spent the next forty-six years in prison labor camps.

At age eighteen, Hung was sent along with other students to become "re-educated" by working in the fields of southern China when the colleges and universities were closed during Mao's Cultural Revolution. Despite the stigma of being the daughter of an "enemy of the people," and despite the fierce competition among students, Hung trained, and eventually taught, at the Central Academy of Fine Art in Beijing. "I competed with a lot of people throughout the country, and it's a big country. I was not scared. I knew there were people who made decisions beyond my control, but what could I do? Do my best. I didn't care if I competed against a man, or someone with more experience. I always felt that I was going to do it."

While Hung was in graduate school she married, but realized immediately it was a mistake. She also realized that in China she would never have the artistic freedom she wanted. So she set out to change her circumstances, despite the constraints of tradition and even law. "It's hard to get a divorce in China. Whether you're getting married or divorced, you have to go through your employer and get a formal letter." Her professor at graduate school in China gave her permission to divorce, as well as custody of her baby son. In 1984, after waiting four years for a passport, Hung emigrated to the United States to attend graduate school at the University of California, San Diego, where she received her Master of Fine Arts degree.

Hung believes that expectations are actually explorations. "If you expect something, it may not happen that way." Yet Hung refused to believe that what she wanted couldn't be done. An art professor at

Mills College since 1990, she has traveled the country sharing her insights as a lecturer. She refused to believe conventional wisdom, and today bridges American and Chinese cultures through her attitudes and through her art. What would her life have been like if she had followed the conventional rules?

"I have other Chinese friends who came to America, some have Ph.D.s and others work in big corporations. They are still very Chinese. They are humble and demure. There's one old friend of thirty-plus years that I took shopping for bright-colored clothes. She later told me that she never had a chance to wear them. I said, 'What do you mean you didn't have a chance? You give yourself the chance.' I have sent her other things, and she has said there was no way she could wear them. The kinds of limitations, boundaries, and programs that we all learned from an early age we carry around with us for a lifetime. Even if we don't consciously try to."

Do What You Know Best

"I had rolled the problem [of ferrying customs officials to and from ships] around in my head for years. It may have looked to others like I was leaping into this, but I had clearly thought out the idea."

—Mary Shaver, President, Anchorage Launch Service Co.

When the odds were against her, Nancy Battista decided to do what she knew. She realized her strength lay in something very close at hand—her family recipe for pomodoro fresca sauce. Josie Natori didn't know fashion, but she always knew she wanted to be an entrepreneur. And she knew she wanted a business that had to do with the Philippines, her homeland. Both relied on a product that was part of her heritage—something familiar, something they knew.

Doing what you know may mean more than just doing the same kind of business. Some women faced with transitions want or need to make complete career changes, as Josie and Nancy did. But the fact that there was a thread of familiarity in their choices helped ease their way.

Doing what you know is an excellent way to face intimidating odds. Mary Shaver, for example, survived by doing what she knew best after one of the most stressful years of her life: a year in which her mother died, her daughter was born, her husband divorced her, and she lost her job working in the family business.

For many years Mary and her husband worked in her father's tugboat business on the Columbia River in Portland, Oregon. Part of their work was ferrying the customs agents, crew, and, depending on cargo, any other people who needed to get to and from the 1,500 ships that anchor on the river every year. Often, however, if they were busy passengers had to wait for the tugs to come and get them.

Mary had suggested using smaller, faster boats instead of the tugs to ferry the river passengers, but her father replied, "We have done it with tugboats for a hundred years and we will for the next hundred." She didn't forget her idea, though, and it eventually became the business that supported her.

Mary started her own business after her divorce when it became apparent that she couldn't get a job with the competition. Tugboat companies feared she would eventually return to her family business. "I was backed into a corner, and I didn't have time to think about it. I didn't have a clue about forms or anything to do with business. I was only concerned with putting food on the table."

Although Mary had long seen the need for a fast ferrying service, she conducted her own survey of the marine community in Portland before she started. People encouraged her. "I had rolled the problem [of ferrying customs officials to and from ships] around in my head for years. It may have looked to others like I was leaping into this, but I had clearly thought out the idea." She took her half-interest in the almost defunct fishing boat ("the only thing I got out of the divorce") and her version of a business plan—"it was more like a résumé that explained what I had done in the marine industry and why my idea was needed"—and went to banks for a loan to buy out the partner.

"I got laughed out of almost every bank in town. One banker thought the idea was so ridiculous he laughed like a hyena. It was a humiliating experience." In 1982 there were very few women in the industry and only one bank in Portland that handled marine accounts. Mary defied the odds. Eventually she persuaded a friend to help her set up a meeting with a vice president of another bank. Mary took the loan officer to lunch and told her all about the industry and her need to make her idea work. She got the loan and used it to buy out the other partner's interest, clean up the boat, and start her business.

Today, Mary's twelve full-time employees and four boats service between 400 and 500 ships a year. She has weathered a variety of obstacles as a woman in a male-dominated industry, even competition with her skeptical and unsupportive father and price cutting from other tugboat operators. But, Mary says, "The business is even better than ever. The challenges always change, but they are always there." Mary's definition of success is "knowing I can be bottom-lined [when things are as bad as they could possibly be] and continually rise above it." Mary believes that she has been successful because when she was in a pinch, she called on what she already knew—then built a company to serve her customers in new ways.

Get Support When You Need It

"I've found that most women don't think in terms of 'I can't share with you.'"

—Maridel Moulton, Independent Business Training Consultant

Even the toughest and most tenacious among us needs to feel supported in what we're doing. We all need that occasional verbal pat on the back: "You can do it"; "You're on the right track"; "Here, let me help you." To begin and persist in any adventure—career, business, life—we need support. Although we may hesitate to ask for it, there is nothing wrong with seeking and finding support. In fact, we often learn so much in the process that we end up succeeding even better.

Of course, getting constructive advice from friends and associates depends both on their intentions and on your ability to receive it in the right frame of mind. Asking for advice or support from people who are reluctant to give it or who do not genuinely have an investment in your success can sometimes make you feel defensive or belittled. Yet, even then, if you can lower your defenses, listen carefully, and ignore what isn't useful, you can get helpful information.

Judy Meegan, now Vice President of Operations for Advanced Bioresearch Associates in San Ramon, California, relies on support from a women's networking group that she presided over as president for a while. "It is imperative that you build up your network of support. See that you have a place where people love you and believe in you and will be honest with you. You can use them as a sounding board."

Joining professional groups can be helpful whether you work in a corporation, a nonprofit organization, or your own business. There are professional organizations for almost every industry that offer support and education. Organizations such as the National Association for Female Executives, Inc. (NAFE) has 200 local chapters around the country and 200,000 members. It offers contacts, opportunities, information, and support for female executives and entrepreneurs. The National Association of Women Business Owners (NAWBO) has 60 chapters across the country and provides a network of support, management and technical assistance, leadership skills, and business contacts and referrals. The National Federation of Business and Professional Women's Clubs, Inc. of the United States of America (BPW/USA) is 70,000 members strong, with chapters in every state, Puerto Rico, and the U.S. Virgin Islands. It offers meetings, scholarships for women, seminars, and the BPW/USA bimonthly magazine, *National Business Woman.* (An annotated listing of more organizations and how to reach them may be found at the end of this book.)

If you can't find a support group for your specific field, be like Maridel Moulton and form your own. Maridel Moulton, now a business training consultant, remembers when she took a job as the

Executive Director of the Contra Costa Center in charge of Transportation Systems Management (T.S.M.). "I didn't know what T.S.M. meant, but I learned from other counties' models. I called other transportation systems managers in the nearby counties. I've found that most women don't think in terms of 'I can't share with you.' And this was true of these transportation systems managers. They were happy to show me their manuals and explain what they did. We didn't see each other as competitors. I had a luncheon roundtable meeting every six weeks with five women from different T.S.M. organizations."

By joining support groups, you'll find other women willing to share experiences and to encourage you. If you belong to a group where you feel comfortable, and you respect the knowledge of the others, you have a safe place to discuss what you don't know in an atmosphere of understanding and camaraderie. If you haven't been part of a professional group or women's club, you may not fully appreciate the value of having like-minded women surrounding you.

Know When You Need Help and Ask for It

"I didn't realize how many bows they would want [referring to her first order from Wal-Mart]. I was scared to death. That was when I began to call for help."

—Amelia McCoy, Founder and CEO, Rainbows and Halos by Amelia

The wildly successful women in this book not only understand the value of asking for help; they also know *when* to ask. Feeling that you have to struggle heroically on your own will not lead to the kind of success that the women in this book have achieved. Remember, asking for help at a crucial point is not just about responding to crisis. Successful women plan ahead and think strategically, asking themselves, 'What kind of help will I need? When will it be most effective?' Nancy Battista kept ahead of what was going on in her business, getting help from family and friends to fill her first order, forming a partnership with a manufacturer when she needed it, finding a distributor who could take some of the burden off her. Help comes in many forms, from family, friends, and colleagues to temporary agencies, consultants, and professional associations. Once you know the sources and resources that can be helpful, the next step is to determine when you can use them to best advantage. Amelia McCoy learned this secret early on.

The day Amelia McCoy was interviewed for this book, she was preparing to fly from her home in Oklahoma to the CBS Studios in Hollywood to tape a segment of the television show "How Did You Do That?" Recognizing that Amelia had grown a multimillion dollar business from her talent for making pretty bows for her granddaughters' hair, the producers of the show were curious: How did this woman become the Small Business Person of the Year in 1992? Part of the answer is that she knew when to ask for help.

It all started with a compliment. Amelia had made her granddaughters beautiful bows for their hair to match the outfits they wore in dance recitals and beauty pageants. "Mothers came up to me to ask where the bows were purchased. I was thrilled to tell them that I made them myself. This made me realize, 'Hey, I could do this.'"

Amelia didn't need a business background to recognize the potential in her product. Her first break came when she was commissioned to make all of the seventy-seven bows for the Miss Diamond Pageant in Oklahoma. Amelia ventured further into the community to craft shows and beauty shops; then, buoyed by her successes, she walked into the local Wal-Mart store. It was December 1978. "I asked the store manager if he wanted to buy my bows. He said, 'Of course I would, but I can't do that.'"

When Amelia asked, "Why not?" her business education began. Until then, Amelia wasn't aware that large corporations had their own purchasing departments, or that a store manager alone could not make a decision to buy an item. "Understand, I didn't finish high school. I was married when I was sixteen. I had never worked a day away from home."

The store manager brought Amelia in to present her bows at a district meeting that happened to be held at the store that day. When they asked how she packaged them, she had no idea what they were talking about, so she asked them. At the end of her presentation, the purchasing manager agreed to let her stand in the front of the local store and make bows as a Christmas promotion. "I started the second day of December. I turned fifty-two on the sixth of December. Everybody loved my bows, and mine became some of the first bows Wal-Mart carried."

Amelia was thrilled to win Wal-Mart as a customer, but she was shocked how many bows they wanted. "It scared me to death. I called for help. I called my daughter, daughters-in-law, and all of my neighbors. We managed to assemble sixty bows in two days." Amelia netted $1,700 during that Christmas promotion. She was officially in business.

Within a year Amelia was selling her bows in five states. Today her hair accessory products are carried by more than ten national chains. How did she do that? She learned her business one step at a time. She learned how to sell and she got help from her board of directors. But most effective of all, she called on people in her community to make the bows. "I have many older people making bows. Others are young mothers with children. They all make the bows in their homes—they're cottage industry workers. I'm providing a better way of life for 600 to 800 employees."

Be Willing to Learn the Hard Way—Or Any Way

"Some people assumed that I was educated in fashion, my family was in the industry, or somebody helped me and I had connections. I had none of these. On top of that, I had no mentor telling me what to do. I learned it the hard way."

—Josie Natori, Founder and CEO, Natori Company

The truth is that there is probably no easy way to achieve high levels of success. It takes dedication and energy and many other qualities.

Nevertheless, many wildly successful women learn much of what they know the hard way, through concerted, hands-on experience, with a few failures here and there along the way. Regardless of how much education, success in another field, or previous earning power they have, they are willing to do any and every job they can to master what they need to know in their new endeavors. Sometimes, as happened to Susan Bauman, that willingness to do anything and learn the hard way inadvertently leads to the discovery of a new career interest.

At twenty-four Susan Bauman was the senior traffic coordinator at the J. Walter Thompson Advertising Agency for worldwide broadcast advertising for RCA Victor and Pan American World Airways. It was the late 1960s. "I handled between $40 and $60 million in advertising for those clients, yet the agency couldn't even give me a raise to $125 dollars a week. Now, years later, I find that amusing. I wanted to go into account work, but they didn't *allow* women to handle accounts in those years."

When Susan entered the work force, the term "glass ceiling" didn't exist, but it was very much in place. But Susan was willing to learn anything she could about the advertising business, barriers or not. "In the 1960s J. Walter Thompson had what they called 'General Staff.' Those on the General Staff could fill in for anyone on vacation. That was the only time they *allowed* women to work as secretaries in all of the different departments. That sounds so archaic, and would be considered sexist today. However, years ago, it was a fabulous opportunity to find out how an advertising agency worked."

As a member of the General Staff, Susan learned what many of the 1,800 employees at J. Walter Thompson did. "The one department that I really liked—which happened to be the low-man-on-the-totem-pole position—was the traffic department. We scheduled the commercials, got the films or video tapes to the television stations, and made sure the commercials ran in the right time slots."

After a few years bumping the glass ceiling at J. Walter Thompson, Susan left and worked for a few other smaller agencies. She liked what she was doing, but she didn't care for the way most of the companies were run. "My dissatisfaction prompted me to say to myself, 'Just try it.'" She admits, "I was a little scared but confident that I could do it and thought, 'If it doesn't work, I can always get a job.' Those were the years when it wasn't hard to find work."

With moral and financial support from her mother and her future husband, Susan began her business. "I left my job on a Friday at one o'clock, because those used to be the summer hours in the advertising business, and got on a plane to Boston to go after a very large client. I opened a business bank account and spoke to an attorney, an accountant, and a payroll company. My first office was in one of my future husband's cutting rooms. He was a film editor in those days." In July 1973 Susan started her own business, Broadcast Traffic and Residuals, Inc., in New York City.

Twenty-three years later she says, "We're redesigning our computer systems so the business will be functioning differently. Our markets have expanded internationally and we are responding to the new media." Susan continues, "I'm from a different generation from the women in their twenties and thirties who are fighting their battles today. I didn't have opportunities. I just made them out of sheer stick-to-itiveness." She was willing to learn the hard way—and it made her a successful player in business. Today her company is the second-largest of its kind in the industry.

Wildly successful women like the ones we've met in this chapter found their success in all kinds of places, doing an impressive variety of things. They took the bad hands they were dealt—from lack of business knowledge to bias against women to divorce to seemingly overwhelming barriers of every description—and they remade the odds. They played their hands skillfully, stayed in the game, and would not let the noes they were hearing discourage them. Their stories are inspiring, but tenacity and persistence do not belong to them alone. Those qualities can belong to all of us if we're willing to play the game—and make our own odds.

Josie Natori's Tips for Tenacity

"My father always taught me that life is like a tire. Some times you're up and sometimes you're down. When you're up, you know you'll go down, and when you're down you know you'll go up. I have enough confidence that when I'm down I think, 'Okay this is bad, but it is a question of time before it goes up.' But I work at it. You have to believe in yourself and believe in where you're going. That's long-term vision."

Her advice for sticking with it in business:

- You have to want to be in the game. Just to say you're going to be in it isn't enough.

- You'd better love what you're doing and be good at it. If you stop loving it and just want to survive, then it will fall apart.

- When times are tough, love the work, then look for the challenge.

- Never lose the vision of where you want to go.

- If you truly want your vision, all of the problems are just little hiccups. You will survive.

- If something doesn't work, pull the plug right away and go on to the next thing. Don't dig in your heels.

- Stay on top of your marketplace and what's going on all the time.

- Remember that everything connects. Everything you do will connect with the next thing. If you believe in something and it's not working, but you still believe in it, you have to work it a different way. There is nothing that I've done that hasn't contributed positively to the next thing.

- Always find something positive in any situation.

- Always ask questions. Always be hungry. Always be on top of things.

How Tenacious Are You?

1. What game do you want to be in? If you're not in it, what's holding you back?

2. What is the biggest obstacle you face right now in your career or personal life? Where does it come from?

3. What is your *least* effective reaction to obstacles you encounter? What is your *most* effective response? What's the difference between them? Name one thing you can do to meet your biggest obstacle with the response that you know works.

4. What is missing right now in your career or life that would make you more successful? What can you do to create it? Will you do it?

5. You have a great idea you've been nurturing for years. What is the first step you need to take to begin to make it a reality?

6. How much are you affected by what others will think of you? Do you worry about what people will say if things don't work out as planned? Do you prefer to play things "safe"?

7. Do you scrap ideas when someone "shoots holes" in them? Name a time when you could look through the holes to find better ideas.

8. Do you know enough to know what you don't know? And when to ask for help? Or do you hate to admit ignorance?

9. Are you willing to do something over and over until you think you get it right? Once you think it's right, are you willing to do it over again until your market thinks it's right?

10. Are you willing to trust others who give you advice when you ask for it? Are you willing to accept advice when offered? If not, why not?

11. Do you know where to get support? Have you researched groups or organizations that would enhance your career and provide networking opportunities?

Commandment Five

Fantasize Your Future
But Create Your Game Plan

Y ou hear it over and over: If you can't "see" it, you can't do it. Call it fanta- sizing, visualizing or day dreaming, it's what successful people do. Daring to dream, to create your future in your own mind, and to see yourself doing what you love is the beginning of any successful venture. Luck may play a role, but most successful women know that good fortune begins with vision and comes about as a result of their own preparation and just plain hard work.

"Whatever money your company is making now without a long-term plan, you can make twice as much with one!"
—Judy Stewart, President, Creative Sense, Inc.

For women who find themselves enmeshed in the day-to-day realities of stressful jobs, balancing career and personal life, or facing a major transition, it's especially important to fantasize and visualize your future. Although it's difficult to stop and take the time, successful women know the value of focusing on the positive aspects of the changes they anticipate and envisioning what they can gain from those changes. This is an inherently optimistic approach to work and life, one that can lead to accomplishments others only dream about. Others will say you're "lucky," but you will know how it really came about.

Planning is the bridge between fantasizing and realizing your dreams. It requires a well-thought-out sense of goals and outcomes, as well as the tools, resources, and skills you'll need to acquire to make your dreams come true. As Judy Stewart explains to her corporate clients, "Planning is a thought process. The key to a good plan is the 'whys,' 'the logical reasons,' and the awareness of the external environment, not the financial numbers. Strategic planning should be a normal part of management's daily responsibilities, not a process that a company thinks about once a year. A good future-planning process helps you ascertain whether your personal goals are being realized through the business." Or, as another wildly successful woman, Sandy Gooch, puts it, "Even before the first store opened, I had goals, ideas, aspirations, themes, and the way the store would look written down on paper." Both these women, whom we'll meet shortly, knew that behind every great plan is a fantasy—a vision of the future.

Sandy Gooch: The Carefully Planned Fantasy

"I believe that all things are possible and that you make your own happiness or sadness. I was determined to make my business a success."

—Sandy Gooch, Founder, Mrs. Gooch's Natural Food Markets

After a combination of the antibiotics she was taking and the food additives in a soft drink she had ingested nearly killed her, former school teacher Sandy Gooch started going to health food stores to find alternatives to the kind of foods she believed had made her sick. What she found bothered her—and gave her a business idea. "As I went from health food store to health food store, I realized how circumscribed they were in their product mix. I was upset and angry that people didn't have access to better food to make them feel better. I thought the only way people could have good healthy food in Los Angeles was if I were to open a market."

Sandy spent a lot of time visualizing what she wanted to do in her store, what she would carry, and what kind of retail environment it would be. She founded Mrs. Gooch's Natural Foods Markets in 1977 after two years of thinking about it, looking for the right location, and talking to people who could advise her how much it would probably cost—attorneys, accountants, real estate brokers, and food wholesalers. Though her only business background was working in her father's medical supply business during summers and weekends growing up, she says she learned an important lesson from him: "I had the perception that there needed to be precision and excellence in business."

Sandy explains that she reflected on her goals every day and planned as an ongoing process. "Some were mini-goals, such as: 'By next week, we will have a cash register, an accounting procedure, whatever.' There were mid-range goals, such as: 'One year from now all of our supplements will be under Mrs. Gooch's private label.' Long-range goals included such things as: 'Within four years we will have two more Mrs. Gooch's markets and this is how we will go about doing it.' To this day, when I'm starting a new business or consulting with others, I do the same thing. I have a platform that I look at when I consider a new business."

Over sixteen years, Sandy expanded her chain of natural foods markets to annual sales of $90 million. "The timing was right, and people flocked to the market. It was an avant-garde idea in the 1970s, but it became the largest supermarket of its kind in the country." Sandy sold her business in 1993 to Whole Foods, Inc., a publicly traded company. Money, however, was not her mission. "I had the satisfaction of giving hope and opportunity to others. I received many thank-you letters saying things like, 'You saved my life and my family,' and 'My son was doing poorly in school; now he is doing well.' My definition of success is having the knowledge and evidence that the business you have chosen to develop is thriving and making a positive difference in people's lives. You could have a tire company and have the same feeling."

With this kind of vision and level of success, it is no surprise that Sandy has been recognized with many prestigious awards, including being named the 1992 Entrepreneur of the Year by *Inc.* and Ernst & Young and being included in the 1993 list of Top Fifty Women Business Owners in the United States by the National Foundation of Women Business Owners. She has also been featured in *Working Woman*. Today, Sandy travels the country sharing her knowledge by lecturing on the benefits of natural foods and the secrets of running a successful business. Since the sale of her natural foods markets, she has envisioned, planned, and started three more companies— a design company, an import-export company, and a bagel cafe that she plans to turn into a nation-wide chain.

Judy Stewart: Planning for Success

"Actually, the planning process for your business is the same thing that helps you in your personal life. It's a matter of understanding your strengths and weaknesses, who you are, where you want to go, and the external environment and your position in it."

—Judy Stewart, President, Creative Sense, Inc.

Judy Stewart began planning her life and her work at her father's knee. "I got my drive from my dad. I was his oldest daughter, one of five kids, and a chip off the old block. He groomed me, not for a specific job but for being a business executive, and it appealed to me because I thought it was exciting. To me, business is really creative problem solving. I would sit down with him and we would discuss my strengths and weaknesses, what to do about them, and where to go. It was all planning in a funny way. We did this every year, and we realized that my strengths were in the retail field where at that time a woman had a better chance of going to the top. If I were a biochemist like my dad [who later became CEO of such companies as Standard Packaging, Sheaffer Pen, and Speidel Watch Bands], I would be a disaster, because my qualities and traits don't match."

During summers and holidays in college, Judy worked at Saks Fifth Avenue in White Plains, New York. "Saks had a training program that lasted six months, but when I went to work for them full-time after graduating from Northwestern, I was on the training program only three weeks because I had already worked in the store so much. My intent was never to be on the selling end; it was to be on the buying and executive end. I got noticed. I was a buyer within one-and-a-half years in the Contemporary Sportswear department." Put on the fast track, Judy ran that department for five years.

"I went from Saks to Bloomingdale's to being president of August Max, the national women's apparel specialty chain that was a subsidiary of the United States Shoe Corporation. That gave me the experience in running specialty stores where I was every position from President to General Merchandise Manager to Chief Financial Officer to Chief Cook and Bottle Washer." Judy repositioned the floundering August Max, evolving a totally new company at every level. The result was a tripling of sales to $30 million and the turnaround of a losing regional specialty retailer into a profitable national enterprise.

Judy's success didn't go unnoticed. A head-hunter came to her to see whether she'd be interested in running a new division of Toys 'R' Us that would specialize in children's clothing. She signed on to start Kids 'R' Us. Judy reflects on the importance of planning and vision in her work in the new subsidiary. "What I really learned running Kids 'R' Us was that in order to get big, you had to think big from day one. Even before you exist, you think that way. Before we opened the doors, we really thought out what we had and what we would need to succeed. We thought out the kinks. We knew every competitor cold. I knew where the business was going and why. Although I had done planning before, this job really nailed it. It was the epitome of classic planning, although we weren't afraid to be spontaneous. It was my baby and now it's a billion-dollar company. I'm very proud of that."

With nearly seventeen years of experience in developing fast-growth companies and start-ups and in doing turn-arounds, Judy decided she wanted to have her own company. In 1984 she formed Creative Sense, a management consulting firm that specializes in positioning companies for fast and professionally managed growth. Some of her clients have included Donna Karan Company, Rockefeller Center, Mrs. Fields, Ringling Brothers-Barnum and Bailey, and Montgomery Ward, to name a few. Judy plays an unusual role that goes beyond consulting in that she is brought in to manage businesses for a few years to get them running smoothly and successfully. She enjoys it immensely and finds it an excellent use of her strategic planning and management skills. "After you've been in business for a while, you develop the skills to tell if the signals you're seeing make sense. Some of the best decisions I made when I was young, I absolutely couldn't make today because they would be deemed too risky. I was young, I was going to make it happen no matter what, and I did. But it was a risk that I couldn't do to a business today."

Judy tells a story about taking a risk on behalf of her vision of her customers and what they needed. "When I was at Saks, I was one of the youngest buyers and headed up Contemporary Sportswear, a $10 million division and one of the biggest sportswear departments in the country. Contemporary at the time looked somewhere between Missy, which looked like your mother, and Juniors, which looked like your younger sister. It was a middle world. I thought something was wrong there. You look either old or young. The truth is that the market was such that you couldn't get clothing that was right for thirtysomething customers at that time. When I was in Europe, I saw a line called Cacharel that had gorgeous flannel, quality gabardines, great looks. It didn't look old, it didn't look young; it was contemporary and you looked 'with it.' It was twice the price point of anything in the department, but I decided to put it in some of the biggest of the stores I bought for. I look back and I'm amazed that I did that. The Cacharel story is an example of how you mature and go through growth stages just as your company does. You should never ignore the spirit and gut intuition of the young, but you need to balance them with the pros and cons of the older, more experienced people: it's the combination that's so great."

In her view, planning is a natural part of life and work. "Actually the planning process for your business is the same thing that helps you in your personal life. Because it's a matter of sorting. It's a matter of understanding your strengths and weaknesses, who you are and where you want to go, and noticing the changes in the outside— looking at voids and needs and understanding the external environment. It is the same kind of process you go through when you hire a housekeeper for your kids. You have to ask yourself, 'What do I need? What are the strengths and weaknesses of this family? What do I need to fill in? What are we looking for in the person? What's the range of potential help out in the marketplace?' You fit the external to the internal to get it to work. But the key is preplanning it, prethinking it, and not overreacting. You don't hire the first person who walks in the door. You've thought about your needs and how to get them solved. It's the same process."

Planning to Make Your Dreams Come True

The stories that Sandy Gooch and Judy Stewart tell about what they've done and how they've done it demonstrate the importance of having a vision of a destination and a plan for getting there. As every successful woman knows, plans may be imprecise navigational charts, but they are musts for any voyage to a great future. The vision or the dream can come out of a need that you see, as Sandy's did, or out of a drive to succeed, as Judy's did. But both would agree that the time, thought, and research they invested in planning were key to their success. The clearer your vision and the more specific your plan, the more likely you are to succeed. The women in this book say that the lessons they've learned came from just a few essential principles:

- Create a vision from your dreams.

- Know your destination.

- Create your own "luck."

- Make preparation part of planning.

- Use action plans to make your dreams reality.

Create a Vision From Your Dreams

"I have wanted to make my own wine ever since I started in the wine business."

—Cathy Corison, Owner/Winemaker, Corison Wines

Sandy Gooch and Judy Stewart began with dreams: Sandy's, to create a grocery store providing healthy, additive-free foods; Judy's, to realize her vision of herself as a highly successful business executive. Visions and dreams can come from all kinds of sources and be sparked by all kinds of people and situations. Cathy Corison, owner of Corison Wines, wanted to make wine in her own distinctive way. She had a vision of "her" wine—a vision that led her to capitalize on her many years learning her craft and making wines for other companies and create a plan that brought her wine into existence "on a winemaker's salary."

Cathy Corison studied viticulture at one of the United States' premier enology schools, the University of California at Davis. For twenty years she made wine for other people, most notably award-winning Cabernet Sauvignons for Chappellet Vineyard. "Sometime toward the end of my tenure there," she says, "I felt that I needed to make a wine without compromise, or at least without someone else's compromises. Chappellet is a world-class vineyard with a fabulous history of great cabernets, but they are a mountain cabernet and my own favorite cabernet comes from the bench land area of the Napa Valley, which I think is the quintessential place to grow cabernet grapes, perhaps in the world."

The first step in Cathy's plan was to find another winery that could produce her wine. Etude Wines, famous for its outstanding pinot noirs, became the perfect vehicle. In 1982 she became a business partner in Etude, and in 1987 started Corison Wines as a division of the winery. Eventually, it was spun off in a reorganization. "I had enough years and experience to give me the confidence to know exactly what I wanted. Etude's success allowed me to start my own project on a more commercial level." Another part of her plan prioritized her spending. Since housing was provided when she worked for Chappellet Vineyards, Cathy says, "I bought grapes and barrels instead of cars and houses."

Using her academic degree in wine-making and her lengthy experience in the wine industry, Cathy next called on her instincts about the business and her experience. "Wine is a wonderful mix of science and art. My intuition serves me well, but I've also watched many wineries over time and have seen many things that I wouldn't want to repeat. I have a good technical foundation, but the added measure that makes a wine great, instead of just good, gets into the realm of art, intuition, and feel. That's what you can't learn in school, and that's what takes a long time to develop."

Cathy Corison has combined her knowledge of the wine industry, her vision of her perfect wine, and her focused long-term plan to find the best grapes and to create her own "luck"—the right situation to produce her wine—to make her dream reality. Cathy concludes, "There came a point when I felt really confident about my project. I never felt that confident about anything before. I tend to be a worrier and nervous about most things, but making my wine feels like the right thing to do. My definition of success is making the best wine I can, my way." Praised by the critics, Cathy's wines add their own testimony to this definition of success.

Know Your Destination

"You have to set up a road map to get you from where you are to this great future that you believe fits your needs and strengths and also fills a void and need in the marketplace."

—Judy Stewart, President, Creative Sense, Inc.

Having a dream and creating a vision are essential, but equally so is knowing where you want to end up. The destination you choose will determine how you will travel, what route you will take, what (and who) you will take with you, and many other things about the journey. You have to ask yourself:

- Where am I now?

- What is my desired destination?

- Have I researched this destination to be certain it's where I want to end up?

- Who and what will I need to make this a successful journey?

Judy Stewart agrees. "The first thing you do is look at where you are now, whether you're already in business or not. You have to set up a road map to get you from where you are to this great future that you believe fits your needs and strengths and also fills a void and need in the marketplace. To do that you have to know who you are, your strengths, your business; you have to know the marketplace and the voids and needs within that to create a unique selling proposition and the positioning that will allow your company to win."

Not everyone grows up like Judy, already knowing where they're going. It takes some of us a while to figure it out, and many people change jobs and careers repeatedly in a quest for variety and challenge. For those who don't feel they know what their destination is, who don't know what they want to do next, it helps to sit down and analyze the factors that affect them, both internal and external. Jane Seeley, a human resources executive at Schlage Locks, often sees people who have been downsized wondering what to do next. "There are so many ways of finding what you want to do. Many career centers offer assessment tools, there are people and associations to network with, and there's volunteering. With a clear personal destination, opportunities increase because you have mentally prepared yourself by taking the responsibility to broaden your basic interests and acquire the skills you need to get there. Don't wait for your direction to fall in your lap—be willing to find it yourself."

This is another kind of self-reliance, the self-reliance to name your destination. It's what you need to develop your career direction; just as importantly, it assures you that you will be able to support yourself and get where you want to go. Rita Channon, host of the nationally syndicated PBS show *Today's First Edition*, knew her destination early on, and knew that to get there meant taking charge of her career and her life. "I would say to a woman my age what I say to girls in high school and college—and I believe it with all of my heart—that the only way to have any clarity in your life is to become self-reliant," she says. "I'm talking about financially, emotionally—everything. You've got to be out there on your own. You have to go through being scared and doubting yourself, all of that, to know that you can come through to the other side. That is very powerful."

Rita has learned that a large part of becoming self-reliant is being willing to take responsibility and knowing that hard work and persistence create opportunities. From an early age Rita envisioned herself in television. She started her career at fifteen by hosting a TV dance party. Later, she entered the University of Kentucky to go into television news, only to be told that women weren't used in television news because they weren't credible and "no one would want to listen to a woman's voice." That was in the late sixties. Yet, even when a marriage and children interrupted her college career briefly, Rita never lost her vision of her destination. In 1977, after years of working toward her goal, she became the first female news anchor in Kansas City. "At first Kansas City wouldn't talk to me [about news], but they had an opening for a weekend weather reporter. I was willing to do it to get my foot in the door." Her next step was to prove she was intelligent and understood what the viewers wanted. She wrote consumer reports on her own and showed them to the management, knowing that they were always in need of that kind of news. "I showed them my reports and said, 'Let me have a shot at it.' The first time out I had a really good story and they said, 'Okay, you don't have to do weekend weather anymore.'" Rita got in the door by accepting a job that wasn't her ultimate goal, but she had a plan and took action to create something better. It was a strategy that worked for her repeatedly. She adds, "You have to be willing many times to do things you don't want to do."

Even so, she says, "My biggest disappointment was that the main thing TV management was concerned about was the way I looked. Most of my mail from viewers said, 'I hate your hair' or 'I love your hair,' or 'Don't ever wear yellow again.' To be fair, television is a visual medium. That's what's so compelling about it—identifying or having a gut reaction to that human image on the screen. I persevered and did the news until 1984. After that I moved to San Francisco and worked as a travel correspondent and co-host of a local evening show on the CBS affiliate, filling in for a host who was out on maternity leave."

Later, when Rita was trying to syndicate a series called *The Human Condition*, the then-president of San Francisco's PBS affiliate saw it and called her about his project, *Today's First Edition*, a show about writers and books. Rita says, "I thought, 'Wait a minute, could this be real? Someone is going to *pay* me to read—something that I love to do anyway?' With the show, I go all over the country and interview writers in their homes. Working on the show has been wonderful."

Today Rita is happy to have a career that combines her love of reading and her curiosity about writers in one program. She also feels it's her time. "I'm moving toward what I really want to do in the second half of my life. I had responsibility early in life; I thought I was so grown up. You have to go through all those passages. I know that now, but I didn't then. I remember being ten years old in Mayfield, Kentucky, and thinking, 'I'm in the wrong place.' I just didn't feel comfortable. Women were not encouraged. When I grew up in that small town I saw the tunnel vision those people had, and how unfair they seemed, and I wanted to help change that somehow."

Rita kept working toward her destination, relying on herself to get ahead in a career that was not that open to women at the time. She was one of the first few women who persisted and got jobs in television news. She raised her two children on her own and eventually remarried. Rita's success was not luck. It came about because she had a clear view of the road ahead.

Create Your Own "Luck"

"I'd like to know what luck is, because it's inexorably entwined with success. Are we making this luck or is it falling in our lap? I think wildly successful women make it—they just show up in the right place where it looks like it falls in their laps."
—Ursula Hermacinski, Senior Wine Auctioneer, Christie's Auction House

Remember what Betsy Bernard said about luck in her interview in chapter 2? "I've worked six to seven days a week, twelve to fifteen hours a day. I've moved where it was necessary to get a great job. There is an element of luck, but you make 90 percent of that." Judy Stewart echoed those sentiments: "You create luck by being intense, by being a real student of what you're doing so you understand the factors that change the business, and by seizing opportunities. A lot of luck is caring and having passion about the business you're in, about the marketplace you're in, about the people. After you've been in it for a while and get better at it, you see how the pieces of the puzzle fit and where the opportunities are. Then if these opportunities fit your business, your personality, all of these factors, you go right after it. It's taking your vision and your view of the opportunity and absolutely going for it."

For Ursula Hermacinski, having a vision for herself and where she wanted to go was crucial to creating the opportunities that made her one of the "lucky" ones. Ursula developed a vision of herself as an auctioneer in part because of the pleasure she got from childhood visits with her mother's family in England. "I thought an auction house would fit with how I fantasized my future. I thought it would involve international travel or, at least, travel between England and America. When I went to college, I always had it in the back of my mind that I wanted to work for Christie's Auction House. Most of the people I've talked to say the same thing, that they thought about what they wanted. It's creative visualization."

After college Ursula took all of her savings and enrolled in Christie's Fine Arts course in London. "I thought that by attending the course, I would have a shot at working for Christie's and make up for the fact that I hadn't studied art history in college. That was the best academic year of my life. I was in my element. I was in London, and I was studying at Christie's."

There was no question in Ursula's mind that the next step was to work for Christie's in New York. But to her shock, Christie's wouldn't hire her. Ursula sent resumes to art galleries, museums—she kept getting rejections. She finally landed a position at the Milwaukee Auction Gallery. It was far from New York City, but it turned out to be fortunate for her and her career. "In Wisconsin I was able to be up at the podium as an auctioneer straight away. I was terrible at the beginning, but I got encouragement from the dealers in the audience. Even though they could hear my voice shaking, they would tell me that I was getting better, or that I would be good, or that I had a strong voice."

Eager to get to Christie's, Ursula left the Milwaukee Auction Gallery within a year. "I moved to New York City without a job and basically sat on Christie's doorstep until they hired me." She waited tables for a summer and called Christie's once a month. "Then one day they hired me in an area I could have cared less about—rugs and collectibles. It didn't matter, because I was in Christie's."

Within a year Ursula advanced from being secretary in the rug department to working in the decorative arts department. "I was very encouraged. And because I had that experience on the podium at the Milwaukee Auction Gallery, they let me be an auctioneer right away.

At twenty-four I was the youngest female auctioneer they had ever had. It was just what I had fantasized—an auctioneer for Christie's at a really young age."

Even so, Ursula's enthusiasm for her work faded. "After about five stressful, hard years, it just wasn't fun any more. I quit, took some time off, rested, and regrouped. I traveled in Egypt and Mexico. When I returned to the States, I went to California. Christie's had heard I was back and contacted me. I went to work for the Beverly Hills office, where I started doing their two wine auctions a year. I fell in love with the wine world." She has stayed in the wine world at Christie's ever since, specializing in benefit wine auctions. Today, Ursula says that for her, "Success is the incredible sense of freedom and well-being, knowing that you have the opportunity to do what you want." Would you say she got where she is through "luck"?

Make Preparation Part of Planning

"I thought, 'Why not have my own business?' . . . but I really didn't know anything about starting a business. I didn't do any research. I thought I could just put out a shingle. I thought that anybody could consult. Of course, it didn't work."

—Clara Villarosa, President, Hue-Man Experience Bookstore

Wishing for goals and a vision that you haven't carefully thought through may have unintended consequences. If you think big, you'll prepare for big. If you think small, you'll stay small. But if you don't really think at all, you may just find out what Clara Villarosa did—it just doesn't work.

Clara Villarosa opened Hue-Man Experience: An African-American Bookstore and More in 1984 in Denver, Colorado, after she had had two successful corporate careers, a divorce, and one business failure. That failure taught her that if you're going to dream of a goal, you must also *prepare* for it.

Clara did not start her career in the bookstore world. At a young age she became Director of the Behavioral Sciences Department of

Children's Hospital in Denver. "It was quite an achievement, considering I'm an African-American female social worker and all the previous directors were white male psychiatrists." From that position she went on to become assistant hospital administrator. "I did very well and began to look at myself differently."

With her broadened view of herself, Clara began to long for the challenge of owning her own business. She went back to school to get a Ph.D. in social work, even though she was fifty years old at the time, had two daughters in college, and was in the middle of a divorce. While she was in school, she started a consulting business to help corporations develop their African-American administrative personnel. It didn't work, because, Clara says, she hadn't prepared. "I really didn't know anything about starting a business. I didn't do any research. I thought I could just put out a shingle. I thought anybody could consult. Of course, it didn't work."

Clara took a temporary job at the United Bank of Denver. "It became a permanent job, and I moved up the ladder very quickly. But I hit the glass ceiling. I said to myself, 'Maybe it's time to rethink owning a business; but *this* time I'm going to make a business plan, take some classes, and learn from my failure.'"

Clara, who had always been an avid reader, felt she wanted to sell a product that she already knew something about. "I felt we needed a bookstore experience that people hadn't seen, the largest group of African-American books in one place." One book wholesaler thought she was crazy when she told him that she planned to open this kind of specialized bookstore. "He said, 'You want to do what? Do you know how many bookstores are closing?' But my vendors and publishers have been my greatest allies." Although Clara had no specific background in a retail business, she called on her corporate experience in banking, human resources, and large-scale money management. Her training as a psychotherapist had taught her how to gather information, do analyses, solve problems, and implement a plan of action. All of that was very useful in her new venture. Still, it was a struggle. "Because it was undercapitalized, it was necessary to reinvest all moneys in the business. I didn't take a salary for three years, and supported myself in a significantly lower lifestyle by seeing patients in my psychotherapy practice. But by the time I started the business, I only had myself to support, and I was willing to make sacrifices."

She had found affordable space for her store in a two-story row house in a commercial area on the fringe of downtown Denver. It was much less expensive than other commercial areas, and it also gave her store the welcoming ambiance she sought. Within two years she expanded into the neighboring row house, giving her store 3,000 square feet for her more than 4,500 titles.

Clara has some words of wisdom for those who want to own their own enterprise. "Starting your own business seems so glamorous, but it's really difficult and demanding. When you start from scratch and are undercapitalized, you don't have the money to hire somebody to clean. You have to do everything. You have to understand that about business, and about yourself."

Today, in her mid-sixties, Clara feels she has achieved her dream. She says, "I do anything that promotes reading among African-American children. I've formed a Fifteen-Minute Club to encourage parents to read to their preschoolers at least fifteen minutes a day. I work with ninth graders and try to form small groups to offer reading as a form of recreation. I also work with inmates in prisons to help them learn to read." Her bookstore continues to grow and gives her more than a place to encourage literacy—it also gives her a voice. "It's given me influence in areas that I had never had before. I can speak with authority, because I've done many things."

Clara focused on her vision, then developed the tools and expertise she needed to make it happen.

Use Action Plans to Make Your Dreams Reality

"It's like planning a vacation. The fact that you don't know the airline schedule to Hawaii doesn't stop you from saying, 'I want to take a vacation in Hawaii.' You express your intention, then you figure out the logistics."

—C.J. Hayden, President, Wings Business Coaching

As Judy Stewart, Sandy Gooch, and the other successful women in this book will tell you, action plans are the way to put wheels on your dreams. Action plans are strategic maps that lay out the steps you need to take to reach your destination. They can be precise, step by step, or more loosely arranged to fit your personal style. C.J. Hayden, President of Wings Business Coaching, works extensively with women on creating action plans. "The more traditional methods of planning were very linear: 'The way to get from point A to point B is to follow these six steps.' That serves as a barrier for some women, because they aren't used to thinking in a linear way. That's what causes them to say, 'Well, I can't do it this way. Maybe I could just find somebody's blueprint I can copy, somebody who knows how to do it this way.' Sometimes women will tell me that they want to consult with someone who can tell them how to run their business. My response is, 'If I could tell you how to run your business, then I would be running your business instead of consulting with you. There is not a blueprint. You have to make it up. Yes, of course, you can gather facts and talk to a lot of people and do your homework, but in the end, *you* have to make it up.'"

Although the nonlinear approach works for some women, others prefer to have an action plan. Action plans are not business plans, although writing a business plan may be part of the process. Coming up with action plans takes time and concentration, but they can mean the difference between having a dream and actually living it, whether you're starting a business, conducting a successful job search, or moving up in a corporation.

When Sandy Gooch wants to turn a business idea into reality, she goes through a six-step action plan she calls her platform: "Let's say that I'm going to develop a new face cream. First I look at the concept and ask what would be the overall design of the product. The answer might be, 'I'm going to have a face cream that is going to miraculously remove wrinkles overnight, and it's going to be a nationwide product.'"

Second, Sandy asks what the product would look like, what the mechanics of it would be, and what people would be willing to pay for it. "The answer might be something like, 'The mechanics of selling the face cream will be through a multilevel marketing operation based in Utah, and I know people will be willing to buy it because there has never been anything like it.'"

Third, Sandy looks at marketing the product. What are its benefits? "For the face cream," she says, "I would look at the research, who would use it, what would be the profile of the users, and where they lived. I would think of how I would position this product against all other anti-wrinkle creams. I would identify the competition—who is out there selling it, and how mine is better or different. I would think about the design of the label, the brochure, the print and television advertising. I would consider what the salespeople would say about the product."

Fourth, Sandy analyzes the economics of the product and what would be required: development costs, research, projections, accounting, finance, and cash flow. Then she examines legal issues such as what will need legal protection, the structure of the corporation, the trademarks, copyrights, federal regulations, and local, state, and federal licenses. In the same category would be human resources issues, insurance, and who to pick for the board of directors.

"Finally," Sandy explains, "I look at the systems. What mechanisms are needed to bring this product to market? They include machines and tools, computers, registers, faxes, phones. I look at operations—how the product would be produced, transported, and warehoused. When you can answer those questions with clarity," she says, "Then you know you have the data and information to determine whether your business has an opportunity to be successful or not."

Action plans are the final step in a process that begins with whatever fantasies and dreams you have about your life and work. Turning fantasies into visions that can be developed into destinations involves the usual: hard work, perseverance, and, most of all, planning. Successful women know that planning is the process that grounds our dreams and makes them possible.

Judy Stewart's Guide to Dynamic Planning

"Planning is a dynamic and flexible process that is meant to be changed and revised as internal and external factors constantly evolve and affect your business strategy."

—Judy Stewart, President, Creative Sense, Inc.

Judy Stewart describes the long-range planning process as an organized, multi-step process that creates a business "road map that anticipates the future and enables one to address key issues before they become crises or missed opportunities." Long-range planning is a process of deciding:

Where are we now?	(Present)
Where do we want to go?	(Future)
How are we going to get there?	(Road map)
How soon?	(Time frame)
With whom?	(Personnel resources)
How to get organized?	(Structure)
What costs?	(Financial)
What benefits?	(Upside)
What risks?	(Downside)

Planning: The Key Steps

1. Analyze the external environment—economic, political, demographic, social, and technological.

2. Appraise the company's resources and capabilities—human, physical, and financial, plus intangible assets like good will, service, and quality.

3. Analyze the company's strengths and weaknesses compared to key competitors—financial strength, cost structure, corporate structure, pricing policy, product quality, advertising and public relations, research and development, sales and marketing, management expertise, and service.

4. Identify marketplace voids, opportunities, niches, and crucial success factors.

5. Develop and prioritize realistic strategic options; list all your options and possibilities, then balance, research, dissect, prioritize, and get consensus. Keep the creative process going. Sometimes the best option may be a combination of two options; sometimes you may need a short-term option to get you to the long-term option.

6. Define the company's future business—put in one simple, clearly stated sentence the scope and nature of future business and the company's guiding statement of purpose.

7. Establish objectives for the areas of the business that affect your company's mission—growth in sales and earnings, profitability, market standing, innovation, productivity, financial resources, employees, and social responsibility.

continues

8. Develop specific action plans to implement the strategies. Identify and rank the critical business issues, define the specific objectives, define the chosen strategy, detail the necessary steps to implement the strategy, develop priorities and responsibility and authority, establish a time schedule of events, assign resources, evaluate profitability and risk.

9. Create a system to periodically review, monitor, and revise the strategies through regular meetings, status reports, tracking of key strategic issues, updates on competitive analyses, reviews of environmental trends, and analysis of action plan results. Then revise as needed.

Creating Your Plan: An Inventory

Clara Villarosa, who learned the importance of preparation and planning from hard experience, offers the following questions to ask yourself in creating a plan to make your dreams come true.

1. Are you creative? Can you conceptualize, develop, and implement? Are you willing to sacrifice time, money, and social/family life? Do you require others to plan for you, or are you a self-starter?

2. What is the business? Retail, service, consulting? Develop and write down a compete description of the business as you conceive it.

3. Who else is selling the product or service? Who is your competition? How is yours better and/or different?

4. Who will buy your product? Who will be your customers? How much information do you have about them? What do they look like and what are their buying habits?

5. Where and how will you locate the customers and motivate them to buy from you?

6. Where will you get the money to start and run your business? If it is from others, what do you need to motivate them to loan you the money?

7. What form will your business take? Partnership, sole proprietorship, corporation? Have you researched the advantages and disadvantages of each form and matched it to your situation?

8. What will you call your business? How will you describe it to the potential customer? What is your image?

9. Where will you locate the business? Why?

10. When will you be ready to do this? What specific steps are necessary to get ready?

Commandment Six

Get Ready, Get Set, RISK!

isk is an inherent part of everyday life. Staying in what we think is a safe spot may make it seem as if risk has been eliminated, but it hasn't been. Successful women have learned to view risk as a necessary and important part of their careers and work. They enjoy the satisfaction of never having to say, "If only I had . . . . " All have risked; sometimes they've won, sometimes they've failed, sometimes they've regretted a decision. But they have discovered a couple of essential principles: that we risk by default every day, and that it is often a greater risk to do nothing at all. Through the risks they've taken, successful women have become stronger and more prepared to get the results they really want. Significantly, they realized that every risk has both an upside and a downside. Focusing on the downside leads straight to fear, while concentrating on the upside creates a mindset that tolerates risk and the tough decisions that accompany it.

What makes these women able to be risk takers? For one thing, they have the entrepreneurial attitude that we've talked about so much in this book. They know that risk is part of responsibility, part of the volatile business environment, and part of opportunity. They also

> **"The safety net we want doesn't exist—it's an illusion. Coming to see that enabled me to go for it."**
> —Mary Jane Ryan, Partner and Executive Editor, Conari Press

realize that there's no security either in corporations or in their own businesses. By seeing risk in a positive light, they avoid a "let's jump off the cliff and see where we'll land" attitude. They take the "leap of faith" with a sense of direction, armed with a network of supporters and resources and fortified with skills from their past experience. They combine information and intuition in a way that helps them succeed in all kinds of situations—especially during transitional periods in their lives and careers.

When successful women think of taking any risk, they ask themselves questions like:

- What would happen if I didn't take this risk?

- What is the alternative?

- Is this the right time to take this risk?

- To what extent is my decision based on my own gut feeling, and to what extent on others' opinions?

- Will I still like my decision in five years?

- How have others handled situations like this?

Such questions place risk in a decision-making context rather than letting it remain stuck in whatever doubts or anxieties accompany it. Answering them, formally or informally, lets you begin to see a risk more clearly. Then you can decide what information you need to make the best decision you can at a given point in time. The questions set the framework for feeling in control. Successful women know that there are no "sure things," but they are willing to take a calculated risk: to go through the soul searching and fact finding, to make decisions based on available knowledge, and to consider the long-term consequences of those decisions. Although this kind of calculated risk taking can be frustrating—because there are usually no clear, clean, obvious answers—they know that the alternative is much worse. They don't leave risk to chance. At the same time, they realize that it's impossible to know everything in advance about a decision and how it will turn out.

Although there's no way to *teach* someone to take risks, risk-taking skills may be honed by seeing how successful women have handled their own difficult decisions. Mary Jane Ryan felt compelled to start a company even when she didn't feel at all comfortable gambling her resources or being without a job. Kate Coburn, using completely different tactics, used the support of networking with her colleagues and peers as part of her risk-taking strategy.

Mary Jane Ryan: Risking for a Reason

"I remember going to a publishing seminar, and the speaker said, 'I want everyone here to raise your right hand and say, "I am a compulsive gambler."' That's what half of publishing is. It's been very hard for me to learn to be a gambler."

—Mary Jane Ryan, Partner and Executive Editor, Conari Press

Mary Jane Ryan was not a born risk taker. "I think people's feelings of terror are legitimate," she says of the overwhelming nature of some of the risks that people in business often have to face. She has never felt comfortable "gambling"—which is how risk taking seems to her—but she has learned to do it, with admirable results.

Mary Jane Ryan had edited magazines for many years, but she was really more interested in books. One in particular changed her life. "I started freelance book editing on the side, and I helped a friend create a manuscript that I thought was really wonderful. She got an agent who shopped it all over New York, but it didn't sell." Although Mary Jane wanted to publish it herself, she was afraid of leaving a salaried position as editor of a women's magazine and having her husband support her efforts. She liked her independence. Nevertheless, her strong belief that her friend's manuscript should be published led her to establish Conari Press in 1987. In the process of founding her company and making it successful, she learned to become a risk taker.

Mary Jane describes how she and her husband at the time began: "We started with no money. We borrowed on our credit cards to pay the original print bill, around $10,000. But then we had success with our very first book, and that bankrolled us into the future." The book, *Coming Apart* by Daphne Rose Kingma, has sold over 200,000 copies.

Knowing she faced tremendous risks in establishing Conari and her first book in the tough self-help/psychology market, Mary Jane took steps to acquire the knowledge she needed to succeed. "I bought a book called *1001 Ways to Market Your Book* (Kremer, Open Horizons Press, 1995) and just did everything in it. Every single thing that I did worked! It said to send the book to women's magazines and I did—*New Woman* magazine excerpted it. It said to send it to book clubs and I did—The Literary Guild took it. It said to send it to mass market houses for reprint and I did. We got Daphne on *Oprah!* and *Donahue*. There was a big auction for the paperback rights to the book, and we made a lot of money that funded the press for a couple years. And the publishing house that bought the book at auction was one of the many that rejected it initially. It was incredible."

Mary Jane continued to educate herself through reading and talking to others in the publishing field. "I remember going to publishing conferences, telling my little story, and getting told, 'It's not going to be that easy every time.' Seventy-five books later, I found that's true, although in general it's been easier than I suspected. But *Coming Apart* definitely gave me the boost to keep on publishing."

Mary Jane believes that her intuition has helped her decide which of the many manuscripts she receives to publish. "In trying to decide whether to publish a book or not, ultimately we go on instinct. We do research on what other books are on the market, how this book is different, and how promotable the author is. But ultimately the reason comes down to whether we really feel *compelled* to publish it. Experience also helps. I've gotten to the point that when I hear of an idea, I can tell whether it will work or not, and, at least in general terms, how well. Of course, there are always surprises."

Mary Jane's approach has worked well for Conari Press. They have published such successful books as *Random Acts of Kindness* (1993) and *Wonderful Ways To Love A Child* (1995). Although the majority of small publishers are essentially outlets for their own message—what they want to say to the world—Mary Jane doesn't do that. "We go up against the big New York publishers in exactly the same fields that they're publishing. It's difficult to do. It's been surprising how well we've done."

Today, Conari Press ranks in the top ten in sales volume of the 150 independent publishers that Publishers Group West, a prominent distributor, represents. *Publishers' Weekly* recently named Conari the fifth-fastest-growing small publisher in the United States, featuring it in an article about the secrets of their success. Mary Jane claims that a major factor has been her passion. "You have to be totally, passionately interested in your idea and at the same time be willing to take feedback from other people. There is a very fine line between losing your vision with too much input from others and not taking constructive advice. The world is littered with marketing ideas that failed because people didn't listen to advice. But you also hear story after story of things that worked when people said they wouldn't. Surviving between the two poles of that paradox is what entrepreneurship is all about." Learning to live with risk is another.

Kate Coburn: Creating a Network of Support

"Networking is not only important personally; it's really helpful in a corporation. Part of my value to this company is the relationships that I've built over the years."

—Kate Coburn, Vice President of Retail Leasing
and Marketing, Rockefeller Center

Kate Coburn got sidetracked from plans to go into retailing after college when she found her way into real estate through a temporary position at Rockefeller Center in New York City. "When I came to Rockefeller Center, it was Christmas time. They were putting up the Christmas tree. There were concerts every day." She loved it—and she liked what she was doing. "I was stapling press releases, pasting captions on photos, but I did all of it with 100 percent energy and enthusiasm. It was recognized." Two months later, Caroline Hood, the Vice President of Public Relations at Rockefeller Center, asked Kate to stay on as her administrative assistant. When Caroline retired eighteen months later, Kate realized that she had put her job at risk because she had not developed a relationship with the number-two person in the office who was set to take over. Kate decided to look for another job, but Caroline had spoken so highly of her that the President of Rockefeller Center asked her to wait six months, when there would be a new opportunity. Caroline was the first strong anchor in what would become Kate's extensive and well-developed network of professional colleagues and contacts. That network would become her resource for furthering her career and providing support for the risks she wanted to take.

The opportunity Kate was promised turned out to be in the new marketing department for all of Rockefeller Center. Her work in that department also led to her entry into commercial real estate. The marketing department was part of the renting department at Rockefeller Center. "I was very fortunate because the Vice President of Renting, Walter Douglas, was a strong advocate of networking for the whole department. He wanted people to achieve as much as they could on their own, to be recognized. He felt that if everyone was known as a strong person, the department and Rockefeller Center would be perceived as a much stronger entity. He suggested that I get my real estate license and my brokerage license."

Kate had some networking tendencies of her own that she had picked up from her first boss, Caroline Hood. "I decided in whatever field I was going to pursue, I was going to get involved with associated professional organizations and lead them. Caroline was the first woman member and president of the Public Relations Society of America. She also started the Women Executives in Public Relations."

When she got her licenses, Kate joined the Real Estate Board of New York and the Store Brokerage Rentals Committee; she also attended meetings of the Young Men's Real Estate Association, an organization founded after World War II by sons of real estate developers and brokers. "When I joined I was the sixth woman member. I had really made a point of knowing the members, personally and professionally. And I volunteered for all kinds of assignments. I ran for chairmanship in 1983 and became vice chairman; then in 1984 I won chairman. The year after that they changed the name to Young Men's/Women's Real Estate Association."

Even so, Kate saw the need for women in real estate to form their own organization. She is one of the founding members and a former vice president of the Association of Real Estate Women and is currently membership chair of Commercial Real Estate Women. "The lesson is really to network, but you have to network from the heart. If people perceive you as a climber and a user, that's not valuable."

Networking took Kate out of Rockefeller Center and into one of New York's top real estate brokerage firms, the Edward S. Gordon (ESG) Company. "A former chairman of the Young Men's/Women's Real Estate Association had seen how I worked. He needed someone in the downtown office to do marketing and sales and bring in new business. That job took me out of negotiating store leases into handling commercial office buildings, dealing with ad agencies and brokers, and marketing office buildings." Although she had never marketed an office building, Kate says, "I had been exposed to the language of it, I had an innate sense because I had worked in real estate. It was a risk, but I knew I could do it."

When the real estate market took a downturn in 1989, Kate mentioned to a friend who had served on her board at the Young Men's/Women's Real Estate Association that she was considering changing jobs. "Within two hours I had a phone call from her saying that she had someone who wanted to talk to me. It was all networking. I started working at Park Tower Realty, marketing their development in the U.S. and overseas. They knew my skills and they knew me."

At Park Tower, Kate volunteered to take over six office buildings around the country, which involved renegotiating leases with IBM. "At the time I had never negotiated an office lease. But I trusted my intuition and my related experience. I knew enough to know that I didn't know everything. But at least I knew the questions to ask. That's the key. There's nothing wrong with saying 'I don't know.' If you're a logical thinker and you ask the questions, you're halfway there. And it's easier to take the risk."

Kate had been with Park Tower for four years when she received a phone call from the woman who had taken her job in retail leasing at Rockefeller Center. "She was leaving and wanted to recommend me to replace her! Coincidentally, I ended up working for someone who served on my board at Young Men's/Women's Real Estate Association—Alan Stein—whom I work for today."

The value of networking is clear in Kate's career. Her contacts and colleagues helped her learn her business and take advantage of the opportunities—and risks—that she sought out and that came her way. For Kate, risk taking and networking are not just concepts but integral parts of her life that have helped her achieve her own personal definition of success: "doing something that at the end of the day makes you feel happy and proud."

Taking Risks: What's The Alternative?

Some women actually like taking risks. It makes them feel alive and invigorated. Others, however, have to learn how to take risks. Women who successfully override their fears of risk taking, as Mary Jane Ryan did, develop healthy attitudes that help them work through those fears. They see risk taking as a process rather than a cliff they're about to jump off. "If I were going to say anything to women who are thinking of starting a business," Mary Jane says, "it would be two things that were incredibly useful to me. One, never risk more than you can afford to lose. I don't know if that is good financial advice necessarily, but it certainly allowed me to sleep at night. Two, risk taking does get easier the more you do it."

What Mary Jane is saying is that risk can be mitigated through experience and self-knowledge. Understanding what you can tolerate, pushing a little past it, and seeing how risk taking pays off can help to integrate it as a normal part of life instead of a terrifying abstraction that stops you in your tracks. And, as Kate Coburn's story amply illustrates, reaching out to others in the same business or situation can put your own risks into a broader context, as well as locate resources and advisors to help you evaluate what you want to do.

Another crucial point about risk is that it has to be worth it. If you're going to risk your time, effort, and hard-earned (or borrowed) money, you have to really want to do it. "You have to have a burning need, because otherwise you won't have the necessary dedication and commitment to see it through," says Mary Jane Ryan. Most successful women agree. They also realize that every choice involves risk and that every risk is an opportunity. This allows them to approach risk taking positively, with the following principles in mind:

- Know your tolerance for risk
- Understand the risk and its consequences
- Look at the long term
- Don't be afraid of the "Impostor Syndrome"
- Call on your past experience
- Trust your intuition
- Have a fall-back plan
- Use networking

Know Your Tolerance for Risk

"One of the things that makes women unable to make decisions is perfectionism."

—Cheryl McLaughlin, Owner, The McLaughlin Sports Performance Group

Just as there are all levels of risk, there are all levels of comfort with taking risks. Some people know they won't be able to sleep well at night, for example, if they've invested their life savings in a high-risk venture. They tend to focus on the possibilities for loss. Other people look at the potential for extremely high returns on the same venture and decide that the gain is more than worth the worry they might feel. Neither attitude is necessarily "right"—there are lessons to be learned either way—but it's important to understand your own tolerance for risk. You can push past some fears and focus on gain, but going beyond that tolerance point may be too much. The key is to know where your tolerance ends and your terror begins. As Muriel Siebert, the first woman to own a seat on the New York Stock Exchange says, "Look, there are times when you want to do something, but if you can't feel you can take the risk of failure, then don't do it."

Women in particular sometimes find risk taking and decision making uncomfortable, especially if they are required to act quickly. For managers in a fast-paced business environment, this discomfort can be a serious problem. In order to accept responsibility for making immediate decisions and taking risks—complete with their resulting consequences—it's essential to know your underlying beliefs about risk taking. Consider these questions:

- What risks have you taken before?

- Did you feel confident about them?

- What kinds of risks keep you from sleeping at night?

- Do you base your decision making on research and intuition?

- Do you approach risks optimistically?

If you have taken risks and seen positive outcomes from doing so but still feel hesitant about risk taking, other issues may be affecting your decision making. One of the most insidious for women is perfectionism—the belief that everything we do has to measure up to some impossibly high standard and that we must never make mistakes or fail. Perfectionism is a paralyzing trap that keeps us from stretching beyond what we perceive as safe. As perfectionists we will only do what we know how to do. We never want to look foolish, and we will never trust our own instincts. Instead, we stay focused on satisfying external standards of perfect behavior.

Successful women know they can learn from their bad decisions as well as from their good ones. In fact, sometimes they can learn more from the bad ones. Women who see themselves as human—and who expect to make and learn from mistakes—accept themselves and their decisions. Risk taking becomes less overwhelming and they are freer to take necessary actions.

"When women get stuck [and can't make decisions], they have to recognize why they're stuck," Cheryl McLaughlin observes. "One of the things that makes women unable to make decisions is perfectionism. Women who choose to excel in some way have known that they had to work harder for their credibility than men. Before they come out with an idea, service, or product, they feel it has to be perfect. Perfectionism, no matter what the profession—a businesswoman or an athlete—will kill them. Yet perfectionism is part of American culture. Today, with all of the options open, women are supposed to be successful not only socially but in the classroom, as an athlete, in business, and in everything they do. But there's no way they can do it all."

Cheryl has found that the antidote to paralyzing perfectionism is her passion and commitment to her goals. "I have always had a feeling that if there was something I needed to do, there was no way I could not do it. I had a passion and a sense of what I needed to do, and I didn't care what anybody thought." Cheryl also had role models of women who didn't follow the norm and who were successful. "My grandmother was the first woman to own and operate a gold mine. A number of her friends were women 'before their time.' I had a connection with women who told me early in life that I could do whatever I wanted to do." And none of them told her she had to be perfect.

Carol Decker, a publishing consultant who has been a successful sales executive for the likes of *Business Week* as well as publisher for *Lear's* suggests that a healthy attitude is the basis for good risk management and for creating teamwork. "Attitude is everything. It comes down to two things. First, don't do anything you're not enthusiastic about. Enthusiasm moves others into action. Second, be positive. I see it at home, I see it with my staff. The whole idea is trying to encourage people to take risks. If you say to them, 'I know you can do it, just try it,' they will. Attitude filters down from the top of a corporation, from the CEO to the mailroom."

Understand the Risk and Its Consequences

"I saw how many clients came in. I saw the potential. I *knew*."

—Suzanne Newman, President, Suzanne Newman, Inc.

Successful women know that all risks are not created equal. Although they may see risks as opportunities, they nevertheless take the time to analyze them and consider the consequences of taking (or not taking) action. They look at timing; the upside and downside (also known as the risk-reward factor); and what will be required in the way of money, effort, time, and commitment. They gauge what the risk involves and what it will mean to them. They factor in the intangibles, like passion and drive. How much do they want the results? Are they willing to do whatever it takes to see the action through?

There may be times when taking a risk may make sense to you but not to others, especially friends or family. Suzanne Newman took a risk that she felt confident about, although her parents vehemently disagreed. Suzanne clearly understood the nature of the risk and was willing to live with the consequences.

One afternoon in 1985, Suzanne Newman was shopping in New York City with a girlfriend. "By coincidence, my friend and I walked into a little millinery store on 59th Street, not far from where I lived. A lady in her late seventies helped my friend with a hat." Suzanne looked around the hats lining the walls, the boxes, the ribbons, the veils, and watched with fascination the way the milliner transformed her friend's look and mood.

"I was extolling the owner's talents when the old woman turned to me, gently tapped me on the shoulder, and said, 'My dear, my shop is for sale.' From that minute on, I could think of nothing else. I had never been in business before, and I had never thought about hats—it had never even occurred to me! It was almost like an electric shock went through me and I said to myself, 'This is what I want to do.'"

Suzanne, then in her late thirties and recently divorced with a young daughter, returned to the shop later to discuss terms. She spent many days there, watching the customer traffic and observing how things were done. Although she and the owner tried to make a deal, Suzanne found negotiating terms difficult. "I realized that the owner was having a hard time letting go. She knew that she needed to sell her shop because she was getting old and couldn't cope anymore. But as much as she wanted to sell it, she didn't want to let go. Finally she agreed to carry the loan herself. I didn't have the money. Even though I owned the shop on paper, she worked with me for a year and taught me how to run the business and how to make hats, which came to me quickly."

Suzanne's parents couldn't believe her decision to own a millinery shop. "Are you crazy? Who wears hats? Nobody wears hats!" But Suzanne's observations of the store and her own instincts told her that it was the perfect business for her. She was resolute. "I saw how many clients came in. I saw the potential. I *knew*."

Today, at Suzanne Millinery and Fur Hats located in a larger space on Madison Avenue, Suzanne creates unique hats to suit her clients. Her straw and ribbon creations are known worldwide and are worn by Princess Diana, Lady Brook Astor, Barbara Bush, Bette Midler, Meryl Streep, Glenn Close, and many others. Suzanne admits, "I have achieved tremendous satisfaction from what I do. Apart from the profits, I have the pleasure of achieving, having done something I wanted to do. To this day, I'm grateful for the deal I made with the store owner, because without it I wouldn't have been able to experience this feeling of satisfaction."

Suzanne is glad, too, that she recognized the risk she was taking and dared to take it. She took into account her need to work after her divorce and her desire to have a place where her daughter could come after school. She weighed the risk-reward factor by observing the shop's earning potential and working with the shop owner to learn the business. And she creatively developed a way to purchase the business that supported her belief in her decision and her determination to make it work.

Look at the Long Term

"I always try to think of myself as if I were older. Twenty years from now, am I going to be happy with the decisions I'm making now?"

—Lauren Hefferon, Owner, *Ciclismo Classico*

Although it can be very difficult to step back in the middle of a decision or a risk-taking situation and think about long-term effects and larger contexts, to do so is essential. Short-term, crisis-mentality thinking can lead to larger problems later on. If, for example, you pull in an investor as a partner to generate quick capital, you may find you don't agree about the work or what constitutes success. You solved the immediate financial problem but ended up with others that were equally serious. Taking time to look ahead makes for sounder decisions and a more balanced approach to risk.

Lauren Hefferon, owner of *Ciclismo Classico,* a Boston-area-based bicycle-touring company that specializes in Italian trips, says, "I always try to think of myself as if I were older. Twenty years from now am I going to be happy with the decisions I'm making now? If I am, fine. If I'm not then I should consider other decisions. In college I never thought about the future. My business has made me think more in terms of a time line, what could happen and what couldn't happen based on my decisions. I realized that I really had control."

Lauren learned much of what she knows about risk taking from observing other successful businesses. "I believe in models," she says. "The women I know who have fears about taking risks are the ones who are floundering from one thing to another. They have a lot of great ideas, but they're just scared. Fear is a big obstacle for many people. My fear is the opposite: What if I don't do this? I know I'll regret not trying. I just think, 'What do I have to lose?' So what if you're poor for a while? So what if you fail? That's how you learn. I would hate to have regrets. Life is too short. Besides being a fun thing to do, biking has taught me always to look at the road ahead, to keep my focus forward."

Don't Be Afraid of the "Impostor Syndrome"

"For the first six or eight months I felt very insecure—it was the "Impostor Syndrome"—would people find out? When people started asking for *my* opinion I got more confident. I realized that the things I took for granted that everyone knew, everyone didn't."

—Michele McCormick, Principal, MMC Communications

Even when we know that risk taking is an essential part of career self-reliance and life in general, we may still feel awkward in new situations. We know we need to stretch ourselves, but when we push beyond our comfort zone we feel uncomfortable and vulnerable. Psychologists label this fear the "Impostor Syndrome." "Impostor" here has negative connotations that go beyond deceiving others. It encompasses a fear of not being good (or skilled or knowledgeable or experienced) enough—and even worse, being found out. People afflicted with this syndrome lack confidence in their skills, even if their qualifications and education are outstanding. They find themselves obsessively overcompensating for their perceived deficits. Successful women learn to go ahead even when they feel like impostors, knowing they will gain confidence and whatever else is required along the way. In fact, feeling like an impostor becomes a healthy way to expand their comfort zones, take risks, and be creative. That's what Michele McCormick did—and the results have been impressive.

When Michele first opened her public relations business, she was full of self-doubt, even though she knew her experience working in other public relations agencies and as a freelance writer made her more than qualified. "For the first six or eight months I felt very insecure. It was the "Impostor Syndrome"—would people find out? When people started asking for *my* opinion I got more confident. I realized that the things I took for granted that everyone knew, everyone didn't." As she worked to build her agency, Michele expanded her experience and her sense of herself. She says, "The underlying benefit of having my own business is that it enhanced my self-confidence." Within three years Michele's company ranked in the top twenty-five PR agencies in Sacramento.

Michele had been a freelance writer during the years her husband was transferred all over the world as an Army officer. She had held jobs as an editor of an overseas English language newspaper, a tour director in an Army travel office, a radio news producer for an all-news station, and a fundraiser for charitable causes. "Some of the principles I learned from my many other jobs became very important lessons for my business: Get paid when you perform, sell every article, and persuade people to talk to you. I learned a lot about a variety of topics." Michele got over her fear of the Impostor Syndrome when she realized and gave herself credit for all the knowledge she possessed. "Before I started my business, I hadn't realized how much my accumulation of skills played into what I do every day in PR."

Realizing that the Impostor Syndrome is a natural part of many job and career changes may help make it seem less awkward. When you feel like an impostor, it's important to recognize that it may be more feeling than reality. You have the experience, skill, and background to succeed in a new role; your self-confidence just hasn't caught up yet. That's when it pays to remember that the Impostor Syndrome is a temporary (and often brief) stage, uncomfortable but necessary as you adjust to new circumstances and challenges. Successful women are willing to live and learn from this awkward syndrome because they trust their abilities.

Call on Your Past Experience

"I feel that, through my various business endeavors, I have shown that I can 'own my own future' in a predominately male industry."

—Claudette Weber, President, Brero Construction, Inc.

There never was and never will be a formula for successful risk taking, yet each of us has acquired skills that can give us the confidence to take risks if we acknowledge those skills for what they truly are. Think of how Michele McCormick's past experiences ended up coming into play in her PR business. In fact, calling on past experience is one of the best ways around to build the confidence required to take risks. You may be surprised to realize how much you've done and know. Claudette Weber made past experience her most valuable ally as she learned to become a risk taker.

At age sixteen Claudette Weber got married and dropped out of high school, had three children, and was divorced by the age of twenty-one. During that same period, she worked and got her high school diploma through night school. Before starting Brero Construction she also started and owned or partnered in several businesses: a jitney bus service, a helicopter school, a restaurant, and a paint manufacturing firm. She refers to herself as a "classic entrepreneur." She entered the construction industry in 1961 as a receptionist, and over the course of working for three firms, moved on to payroll clerk, secretary, bookkeeper, project manager, controller, and vice president. The owner of the last firm she worked for, Chuck Cunningham of Cunningham Construction, encouraged her to start her own business. The idea grew on her until 1980, when she started Brero Construction with $2,500 and a Volvo station wagon. She decided to focus on the public market and to specialize in institutional and commercial construction, including schools, hotels, and light rail stations. Her contacts and experience with bonding companies and bankers assisted her business development. Claudette carefully selected which projects to bid on so that growth could be planned and project management controls set in place.

Today, with $16 million in annual sales, her company is the largest woman-owned building construction firm in the United States, according to the Women Construction Owners and Executives Association. It is also the fifth-largest Hispanic-owned building construction company. Claudette's awards include National Woman Contractor of the Year in 1988, *Inc.*-Merrill Lynch Entrepreneur of the Year in 1991, and the 1993 Woman of Achievement Award presented by the *San Jose Mercury News* and The Women's Fund.

Claudette's long apprenticeship learning the construction business gave her an immense amount of what she calls "field experience." Without it she might not have had the confidence to risk starting her own company, given the competitiveness of the industry and her own lack of a college education. She is proud of what she's done. "It's the same feeling a writer gets from writing a book. It is a wonderful sense of accomplishment and a wonderful sense of permanence. You have something to show for your work."

Trust Your Intuition

"In terms of trying to decide whether to publish a book or not, ultimately we go on instinct."

—Mary Jane Ryan, Partner and Executive Editor, Conari Press

In risk taking, experience usually plays a key role. We recognize similarities or differences in sizing up situations, opportunities, or challenges, and we decide what to do based on what our experience has taught us. Intuition and instinct, however, play an equally important role. We have all learned a valuable lesson about intuition at one time or another when we ignored a "gut feeling," especially in matters concerning people—hiring personnel, dealing with clients, or trusting a money manager.

Trusting your intuition may allow you to recognize opportunities more readily than someone who loses time and momentum pondering every angle of a situation. It can also help keep decision making from becoming overwhelming. With every opportunity there is a right moment to take action toward a certain purpose. Women who trust their intuition are ready to capture that moment.

You may already use your intuition more than you realize. Perhaps you decide to take a new approach to a project at work. You have a hunch that something different and daring is needed. When you present your idea, you discover the fresh approach brought increased creativity and enthusiasm from your team and ultimately led to better results. Or you decide to take an alternate route to work. You don't know why, you just feel like it. Later you discover you avoided a huge traffic jam on the regular route.

Successful women like Mary Jane Ryan believe that confidence in their intuition grows with experience. Although intuition plays an enormous part in her decisions about which books to publish, Mary Jane knows she must also stay aware and react to the marketplace. "If you had told me five years ago that we would be publishing books on spirituality, I wouldn't have believed it. But we have responded to the marketplace very successfully." What works for Mary Jane this year gives her clues to what will work next year, but she knows that past publishing successes alone will not guarantee future triumphs.

Have a Fall-Back Plan

"I thought it might be a struggle, but I wanted to know the worst that could happen to me if it didn't work. Then I prepared a safety net."

—Claudine Fletcher, Owner, A Quality Journey

Successful women are risk takers, but they are not foolhardy. They know there always has to be a "Plan B" for every "Plan A"; that is not negative thinking but simply good sense. Preparing a fall-back plan may be vital to accommodating high levels of risk and maintaining a positive outlook. It's part of seeing the big picture.

Claudine Fletcher of Walnut Creek, California, knew her days were numbered at the corporate training company where she worked when her boss told her she wasn't a team player. An earlier incident had seeded her imagination with what she could do if she lost her job. "I had a career speaking for other companies, and I had given speeches to service groups. After one talk a man from the audience came up to me and asked, 'How much do you charge?' I said to myself, 'Charge?' I had no idea they paid people to do this. I laugh now, because I quoted $50." She charges more than twenty times that today.

Claudine never used to think about fall-back plans. When she was young, she thought everything would always be open to her. That changed when Claudine lost her hearing at age twenty-two and consequently her job as a registered nurse. As she went through a series of personal crises her self-esteem suffered. It took her eight years to overcome her depression and learn the skills to handle her new way of life without hearing. Some of those skills she learned in Weight Watchers where she went from client to employee and eventually to lecturer, leader, and trainer. With those skills she joined the advertising firm of Manning, Selvage and Lee to make public appearances and give media interviews on behalf of Weight Watchers International.

Though Claudine had acquired great skills in speaking and training, she feared going out on her own as a speaker. Her advice? "You have to have the courage to risk. Have a cushion behind you so you're not petrified, but take the risk." She had been saving money to create a nest egg for herself, but she also formulated a fall-back plan. "I thought it might be a struggle, but I wanted to know the worst that could happen to me if it didn't work. Then I prepared a safety net. My sister worked for the government, and I asked her if she thought I could get a government position as a fall-back job. She thought I could."

Claudine's business grew rapidly from referrals and repeat business. "Sometimes I get an engagement because people have heard that I don't hear. It's their idea of a 'gimmick.' If it is, it's a costly 'gimmick' to have. However, most of my jobs come from my speaking. People appreciate what I have to say and tell others." And one of the things she tells others is to bolster their courage to take risks by formulating fall-back plans.

Use Networking

"You need to develop relationships on all levels. You never know who you will be working for or with. I think it's something that is important to learn early."

—Kate Coburn, Vice President
Retail Leasing and Marketing, Rockefeller Center

Kate Coburn learned early that a team of supporters and resources can make risk taking much less intimidating. Effective networking helps in gathering information and in getting advice or contacts. It also provides successful women an effective means of advancing career and business opportunities.

How do you start a business or promote a product if no one knows about it and you have very little capital to advertise? This was the problem Ali Lassen faced when she founded an image consulting company in Los Angeles in the mid-1970s. She wanted to get a business going, but she didn't have the contacts to get it up and running quickly. Later, when she started Ali Lassen's Leads Clubs in 1978, she was in her fifties, going through a divorce, with three of her six children still living at home. The idea for Leads Club was born from her frustration. "Leads Club has one purpose: to generate quality leads and referrals for its members. Our target market has always been the smaller-business person; 61 percent of all people working are employed by small businesses. But they generally don't have a large public relations and marketing budget. Small-business people need to rely on other means."

"In the late 1970s, no one knew what the term *networking* meant," Ali explains. "Most networking opportunities were just for men, so I started out having meetings just for women. Many of the women entering business had proper schooling and had spent time in the corporate world but were finding out that there was a very distinct glass ceiling. Many of them took the risk to go into business for themselves. They were underfunded, and they couldn't get loans. They needed this sort of exposure."

Skillful networking can yield contacts, resources, and information. Do you want the name of a good resource? Ask someone. Do you want to know where to find the best office equipment for your business? Ask other business owners what they use, whether they like it, and why. Networking is simply asking questions or sharing information, and everyone does it. But successful women know how to parlay that natural give-and-take to the next level. They become networking experts because they know the power of an introduction: "So-and-so kindly gave me your number." Networking is the key that opens the doors to all kinds of information—both for and about yourself. No businesswoman needs to go it alone. Joining groups and organizations is a friendly and inclusive way to learn and have people learn about you. Of course, you are ultimately responsible for letting people know about you and your business.

If you're in a corporate job or own a business, if you're in a transition or feel stuck in a job, networking is especially important. You can build contacts and relationships by joining clubs, associations, professional or community groups, or specialized-interest groups. The result of joining associations and forming relationships is support, referrals, and friends.

Jamie Walters, owner of InnoVision Communication in San Francisco, built her network by joining a professional organization, the International Association of Business Communicators (IABC), whose members come from the fields of public relations, employee communications, graphic design, printing, and marketing communication. For Jamie, joining IABC ended up serving more than one purpose. Besides helping her get her business going, it helped her to refine her people skills. She explains, "If you're basically shy or an introvert by nature, the only way to get over that is to repeatedly put yourself in situations where you're talking to people. Today, it seems natural to me to be out talking to people, but it hasn't always been easy. Before, when I thought I didn't want to go into a meeting, I did anyway, and I was glad. I learned a good rule: If you make yourself the host at a meeting and look for opportunities to make others feel comfortable, it makes it easier. It works like a charm. The person who says, 'I can't go into a room and talk to somebody I don't know,' needs to know that she can go and be a fly on the wall for a while. You don't have to go to meetings and be a master extrovert and a master networker the first time." Indeed, taking the risk to put yourself out there at a networking meeting is good practice for other risks, especially if you're just starting out in a career or business.

The successful women in this book know that risks and decisions are far too important to be left to chance. They confront them promptly and directly to ensure the best outcomes. And they don't wait around for things to happen: They *make* them happen. There is no book or program called *Risk Taking Made Easy.* That's because it's not easy. It is, however, a part of our everyday lives. Our attitude toward taking chances often determine our overall success. Successful women will tell you never leave risk to chance. They get ready for risks, get the mindset they need, and *risk!*

Kate Coburn's Guide to Becoming a Networking Ace

1. Get involved early at whatever level you can.

2. Don't just join an organization. Become active and serve on committees.

3. Develop relationships and take them one step further. Have breakfast, have lunch, have dinner outside of the normal meeting. Get to know people apart from the organization. Know them as people. That's crucial.

4. If you're involved in an organization, make sure that the people in that organization know that you're there as a resource and will respond quickly to them. In Commercial Real Estate Women, we like to say that if someone gets a call from a member, that phone call is going to be answered quickly because there's a mutual respect among members.

5. Accept the responsibility in membership and networking to help others. It's very much a do unto others as you would have them do unto you.

6. Follow up promptly when people ask you to do something. Put yourself on the line. Make the phone call.

---

7. Be a giver and be of service. Avoid the kind of thinking that says if I do something for you, you will have to do something for me in the future.

8. Market yourself in networking, not on your skill level but on your integrity and on your commitment. When you have a job, that's what you bring to it. It is assumed that the skill level is there. Integrity and commitment are what set you apart.

9. Send notes that acknowledge and thank people for even the smallest thing. Let them know that you appreciate what they've done.

Successful Decision Making: An Assessment

We can't and don't always make perfect decisions, but by reflecting on the following questions—the same questions many successful women use in assessing a situation—we may find the process easier.

1. Do you have a positive attitude toward decision making? What other things are happening in your life that might affect your decision-making ability?

2. Do you take time to gather information before you make decisions, or do you just react? Don't rush decisions, even if you have to make them quickly.

3. How urgent is your decision? Do you have some time to decide? Create a time line for making your decision and implementing it. Don't procrastinate.

4. If you think about a decision before you go to sleep, how do you feel about it in the morning? Sometimes an obvious answer comes when you let yourself work on it unconsciously.

5. Who will be affected by your decision besides yourself? Is it appropriate to discuss it with that person?

6. Is the decision one you would be proud to tell your boss, your children, your mother?

7. When you take action, do you monitor it to make sure the action is getting the results you anticipated?

8. Are you willing to change your action plan if you find you need to, even if it means a degree of personal or professional embarrassment?

9. Are you willing to have the buck stop at your desk?

10. Are you relentless in trying to create a win/win solution?

Commandment Seven

When Someone Says "You Can't," Say "Watch Me!"

N o one who is successful gets where she wants to go without encountering obstacles of various shapes and sizes. They're simply part of the landscape. Some come from outside; products of family, friends, co-workers, a tough business environment, or societal expectations. Others come from within. Your worst critic can be the woman who looks back at you in the mirror telling you you can't or shouldn't do something and playing your personal 'stop tapes' in your mind. That's normal. As we've seen throughout this book, it's your *response* to obstacles that is important. The creative, positive will to engage any obstacle and overcome it can be cultivated, usually with dramatic results. For some of us, that comes naturally. For others it has to be developed, often to counter the expectations our society places on women.

"Other people may put their 'stop-tapes' on you. They may tell you your idea may never work, or that it's already been done, or that they tried it and it didn't work for them. Do it anyway."
—Karen LeCocq, Sculptor

Career counselors have observed that in the past women tried to make it in the world of business by adopting the dominant male model of behavior and success. They wore power suits, learned and played by the men's rules, and assumed that success lay in climbing hierarchical ladders. They worked long hours to prove to themselves and to others that they could be successful.

Even when they succeeded, many women felt that something was missing—the expression, perhaps, of a different model of working and living. Women are widely considered to have a "diffuse awareness"—the ability to do multiple tasks and to look at all aspects of a situation. In considering a decision, men tend to react to content and facts, women to relationship and context—where it fits in the big picture. This dissonance between their own experiences and the dominant business model has made women doubt their own judgment and ability at times, bringing the "Good Girl Syndrome" into play. Many women have been afraid to try something if it's not in the rule book, if it's not the "right" way to do things. When they try to find a successful model and emulate it, they sometimes discover that they have to duplicate it in order for it to work. If they're not prepared with their own contingency plan, they can't respond at a moment's notice to something that's *not* in the model.

The antidote to overreliance on rules is self-confidence—a self-confidence born of experience and the positive attitude we've emphasized throughout the book. It also comes from taking on obstacles, from learning how to overcome them and how to compete in the business world on our own terms. Cheryl McLaughlin, sports psychologist and owner of the McLaughlin Sports Performance Group, sees business competition as similar to competition in sports. She explains, "Competition in sports means that you're willingly choosing to participate in an activity where you put obstacles in the way of your success. Essentially, it's a problem-solving activity. Your opponent's job is to send you a lot of problems, and your job is to figure out how to solve them, then send a bunch of problems back. If you look at it in that way, the questions become: How well did I solve the problems today? How well did I even know what the problems were? Once I knew what they were, did I have the knowledge or skills to know what to do?"

Cheryl's take on competition can be extended to any kind of obstacle. Facing obstacles is a combination of defiance—"just watch me"—and the attitude that says obstacles are problems to be solved, not insurmountable barriers. The women in this chapter have much to tell us about how we can learn to take an obstacle and turn it into success.

Karen LeCocq: Absolut Courage

"I feel a woman should go with her ideas, no matter how crazy she may think they are at the time."

—Karen LeCocq, Sculptor

One of the most common obstacles women face is that inner critic and naysayer, a person who is all too ready to sabotage their success. Had Karen LeCocq listened to her self-defeating thoughts, she would have missed the unusual experience that led to her acceptance and success as an "Absolut Artist."

Karen is a painter, sculptor, and photographer who read an article about Michel Roux, president and CEO of Carillon Importers and the creative genius behind the Absolut Vodka Signature ad campaign in the early 1990s. He had commissioned such artists as Andy Warhol in ads that read: "Absolut Warhol." Karen decided she wanted to be one of those Absolut Artists, even though she knew that Roux was receiving hundreds of solicitations from other artists every week. So she set out to do it. "I got out all of my *Art in America* and *Art News* magazines and looked up each Absolut artist ad. I visualized an "Absolut LeCocq" ad being one of them. I went out and purchased the four varieties of Absolut vodka so I could construct four sculpture pieces around them." What she calls her "self-stop tapes" were playing full blast, telling her, "That will never work; people will think you're crazy; you'll spend a lot of money and once again you'll end up with nothing." But Karen recognized those thoughts for what they were: internal obstacles that could be ignored.

In 1993 all of Karen's pieces were purchased by Carillon. She became one of three Absolut Artists that year, joining such well-known figures as Keith Haring, Ed Ruscha, Kenny Scharf, and Ginny Ruffner. The "Absolut LeCocq" ad appeared on the back inside cover of *Art Forum*, the international art magazine, as well as on the back cover of twenty national magazines, including *Conde Nast Traveler, Harper's Bazaar,* and *Spy*.

Karen says now that she does her art because "I believe in it, and because I believe in myself. Of course, there are times I don't believe in myself—when all that's in my head are negative thoughts from the many people who have told me that I was crazy, that my work wasn't good. I feel money is the reward an artist receives when she begins getting recognition. When and if it comes, it gives you validation in the real world. Until then, and even after that, you have to learn to validate yourself."

Karen adds, "I feel a woman should go with her ideas, no matter how crazy she may think they are at the time. I would encourage anyone with a burning desire to do something to just go for it. You don't want to wake up when you're in your nineties and realize you never even tried for your dream."

Eunice Azzani: Obstacle Buster

"Yes, there are obstacles, but let me create the strategy to remove them rather than believe there is no way around them."

—Eunice Azzani, Vice President and Partner, Korn/Ferry International

In the course of her career as a corporate recruiter at Korn/Ferry International, where she is now a partner and vice president, Eunice Azzani has learned the importance of using her unique qualities to create her success, even when that meant doing things in ways that didn't fit the dominant business model. She says that she used to think her Texas accent was a disadvantage; now she believes it has been helpful in bringing a "down-home" quality to her interactions with people, who find it a refreshing change from the formality and rigidity that permeate the business world. Some of her colleagues disagree, even feel she should not be so open with her clients, but Eunice says, "I think I am successful precisely because I am who I am. People are drawn to someone whom they perceive has maintained the realness, the courage. When you're different, if you're not part of the corporate model, or you don't look and act the role, people are always in effect saying don't be who you are, you have to be this way. I'm convinced we have really destroyed a lot of creativity in our nation because people are trying so hard to be something they're not that they can't shine."

Eunice applies her no-nonsense approach to confronting obstacles with great success. She advises women to "know what the obstacles are and create a strategy to overcome them. Most people don't approach life strategically. Not that it all has to be long-term planning; you have to be able to shoot from the hip and be flexible. But rather than fall into the trap of 'Can it be done?' get into the mindset of 'What's the strategy I need to do it?'"

She tells a story about a partner in the Korn/Ferry office in Seattle. "He kept saying, 'The market up here is really bad, we'll never be able to do it.' I looked at him and said, 'You know what, I don't think you'll be able to do it. But that's because you don't believe you can.' The minute you stop believing you can do it, it won't happen. I'm just stating the obvious, but I find that people get off track, because someone says 'There aren't any jobs, or aren't any of this or that, for success you have to look a certain way, act a certain way.' There are people who make things happen regardless of those constraints."

From her long years of advising job seekers and from her own experience, Eunice has come to believe that women need to be encouraged to do whatever is necessary to achieve the success they want. "I like to tell women that I break the rules, that if I hadn't I'd be nowhere. The rules weren't set up to assist me and you in

155

corporate America. And frankly, I wasn't part of making them, and that's okay. My definition of success is doing what you want and making a difference. It's about adding value. My personal mission is to make a difference for women." Eunice Azzani continues to leap past obstacles in her own work and on behalf of others as a lead member of Korn/Ferry's Diversity Program, whose purpose is to identify and track key women and minority executives. Her message of authenticity and self-confidence is a key ingredient in her success.

Confronting Obstacles from Inside and Outside

Karen LeCocq successfully overcame her own barriers—the thoughts that threatened to keep her from fulfilling her vision. Through her talent and her tenacity she joined the elite club of Absolut Artists. "To be in art and remain in art, you need to possess a driving force that makes you create art no matter what people say, or how many critics pan it, or if it never sells." But in Karen's case it did. Eunice Azzani believes that a crucial part of overcoming any obstacle is remembering your passion. She says, "When people tell me I can't do something, I think, 'Hide and watch!' Some of it is getting back in touch with what drives you, what motivates you, what energizes you, what builds you up instead of knocks you down. I call it passion."

Successful women like Karen and Eunice have learned that obstacles can be overcome if you keep five simple but compelling principles in mind:

- Address the source of your obstacle

- Keep your sense of humor

- Ignore the naysayers

- Follow your passion with conviction

- Remember your past successes

Address the Source of Your Obstacle

"To be successful in a sport or a business, women must take *direct* action. They need to be in charge and, at times, unyielding in their opinions and decisions. The difficulty for many women is dealing with negative reactions from others when they show the direct side of themselves."

—Cheryl McLaughlin, Owner, McLaughlin Sports Psychology

The key to overcoming any obstacle is understanding it fully: Where does it come from? Is it an external obstacle, like lack of funding or other people's opinions? Or does it come from within, from doubts or fears or lack of confidence? Or, as in many cases, is it an external obstacle that is being made worse or more difficult because of the way you are thinking about it? Karen LeCocq counters her inner obstacles with action and persistence. Eunice Azzani obviously learned how to overcome hers early on. Both bear witness that learning to overcome inner challenges is an integral part of facing the outer ones. "One of the things to do is depersonalize those inner obstacles," suggests Eunice. "Step back and say, 'Can I get in touch with the things that I feel I'm good at doing? Can I get back to where I feel confident and powerful and important?' Instead of these messages we get: 'We can't. There aren't any jobs. You can't do this. That's not going to happen. Never, never, never.' There are a lot of those messages that we constantly get and many people get so many of them they start to believe them."

Experience is invaluable. In fact, there's no better antidote to that most-common of obstacles, lack of self-confidence. Successful women have found that the best way to develop self-confidence is by *doing* things. Mary Jane Ryan, owner of Conari Press, published her first book before she had any experience in book publishing. From the success of that book she got the self-confidence to develop her publishing company. Sometimes the lessons from an experience aren't the ones you expect, but each one makes you more willing to take other chances.

Athletic activities are a great way for women to develop self-confidence. Sally Edwards, founder of Fleet Feet, Inc. (a chain of franchised athletic shoe stores), a member of President Clinton's Council on Physical Fitness, and a trustee and officer of the national nonprofit organization Women's Sports Foundation, believes that women are changed for the better by their experiences in sports. "Once a woman enters a snowshoe race, or finishes a triathlon, or rides her bike a hundred miles, that accomplishment empowers her to be able to accomplish things in all aspects of her life." Of course, we all don't have to turn into superathletes in order to build our self-confidence. But the experience of "going for it," of putting ourselves out there to learn how to meet obstacles head on, builds confidence in other areas of our lives as well.

Another inner obstacle many women face comes from being socialized to get things done indirectly rather than directly. Fear of not being liked or accepted if they're too aggressive about their own interests can make them less than effective in taking risks or making decisions. Sports psychologist Cheryl McLaughlin remarks, "To be successful in a sport or a business, women must take *direct* action. They need to be in charge and, at times, unyielding in their opinions and decisions. The difficulty for women is dealing with negative reactions from others when they show the direct side of themselves."

When you know the source of an obstacle, you're much better equipped to confront it with self-confidence. Knowing the source is the first step, but then you must take action. That may mean ignoring your "stop tapes," as Karen LeCocq calls them, or believing as Eunice Azzani does in your own distinctive approaches to solving problems, achieving goals, and realizing your dreams and passions. Dealing with barriers that come from within prepares you to overcome outward obstacles—negative comments from family and friends, pressure from traditions and society, and fear of dealing with institutions such as banks and regulatory agencies. It can also see you through other, more personal challenges.

Some obstacles are more challenging, certainly, than others, but they are part of everyday life. How we react to them sets the tone in our business and personal lives and affects our ultimate success. One thing that bolsters many successful women in difficult situations is that they keep their sense of humor.

Keep Your Sense of Humor

"A sense of humor is the most important thing of all . . . . Humor can dissipate really stressful situations."

—Debi Stebbins, President and CEO, Seton Medical Center

Obstacles are, of course, serious business. There's no doubt that they often feel like a matter of life and death. But in reality they usually aren't. Keeping your sense of humor in the middle of a problem or crisis can keep that crisis from overwhelming you. Laughter not only relieves stress, it puts things in perspective, a gift that in itself may help you solve the problem—and provide some great stories to tell later. It can also allow you to go on generating the energy and commitment you'll need to keep going.

Debi Stebbins, President and CEO of Seton Medical Center, says, "A sense of humor is the most important thing of all. You have to laugh a lot in a job. Humor can dissipate really stressful situations. It's really helpful if you can insert humor in really tough negotiating situations or if you're going toe-to-toe with people."

Having a sense of humor doesn't negate an obstacle's importance, but it does bring it into perspective. Successful women recognize its power to give balance and sustain them through difficult situations. Carol Decker, former sales executive at *Business Week, Reader's Digest,* and *The Atlantic Monthly,* former publisher of *Lear's* and now a successful publishing consultant, has often called on her sense of humor to propel her career, handle difficult bosses, and encourage her staff and friends. "We all get punched at, rejected, you name it," Carol says. "We hear things about us that aren't true. Or someone tells you that what you're doing doesn't work, isn't right, but you know it's right. You have to come back, especially entrepreneurs who are trying to start things on their own. But you can't take it all too seriously. Remember Bobo—the blow-up clown (punching bag) with the sand bottom? Bobo has a smile on his face and he always bounces back. I have friends who have started out alone in a business and they usually call their businesses 'So-and-So and Associates.' I send them a Bobo and he's the associate. You look at that clown face and think, 'Oh, what the heck, I'll make that call one more time.' Make it a game to always come back. Think, 'They're not going to believe I have the guts to call back again,' but do it. Just do it. Have fun with it."

Carol adds, "Business is not life-threatening. Climbing a Grand Teton where a slip is a 3,000 foot drop—that's life–threatening. The definition of success is happiness. Whatever you're happy at doing you're successful at. If you're not happy then you're not successful. It affects your work, your family, your friends, and your community. People know when you're happy."

Ignore the Naysayers

"Don't tell me I can't, because I'll do it even if I don't want to. I see the gloom-and-doomers, as I call them, all the time. There are always people out there who will give you advice based upon their own fears."

—Eunice Azzani, Vice President and Partner, Korn/Ferry International

Dealing with our own internal critics can be tough enough at times, but handling those who don't seem to care about our success can also be daunting. As Eunice Azzani says, there are always plenty of "gloom-and-doomers" who are all too happy to tell you why you can't do something. Some of these naysayers have faces we know—colleagues who envy us, parents who'd rather see us doing something else or who tell us that we're working too hard, even friends who seem to want to make their fears our fears. Other naysayers are much more impersonal and diffuse—the kind of conventional wisdom that tells us "It's never been done that way," or, "*You* can't do that!"

Whether it's other people's opinions, society's expectations, or life circumstances that create the barrier, successful women know that you must respond with courage; you must follow your own inclinations. "When people come in and sit down with me," Eunice Azzani says, "I tell them, 'I believe you can do anything you want to do.' The key is talking about what you want to do and what you are good at doing, because what you're good at doing is usually what you enjoy doing. Then you ask yourself, 'If this is what I want to do, the next key question is how do I do it? Not whether I can or not.' That's where people get bogged down. They ask the question, 'Can I?' and they go out and check with people and they hear, 'Oh, you can't do that.' Because everybody is answering for themselves, not for that person. This is what amazes me: Why do we give that up to other people? Why do I believe someone else?"

Carol Decker agrees. "In order to ignore naysayers, you have to first believe in yourself. In order to believe in yourself, you have to be honest with yourself and face up to weaknesses. You also have to have fun along the way."

Diane Jacobs, the cake artist we met in chapter 3, believed in herself, but she thought others wouldn't because she was young, African-American, and female, and had no business training. When she started her own cake-art business, Diane had to ignore many naysayers. Diane says, "I had an accountant who thought I should get a warehouse in East Los Angeles because the location I picked in the city was too expensive. He figured I could get a truck and deliver. Yet, I was always told that the first thing to consider about going into business is 'location, location, location.' I knew no one was going to come to East LA to buy a cake." Diane also had problems with contractors. One tried to boss her around and even yelled at her in the county planning office. "I thought, '*I'm* going to pay *him,* I don't have to deal with this.'" The second contractor she interviewed wouldn't return her calls until she wrote him a caustic letter. "He didn't think I was for real. Some of it was my age, some of it my race, and a lot of it was being a woman." Diane overcame the naysayers around her through her belief in her own abilities and her passion for what she wanted to do.

Follow Your Passion with Conviction

"I think that personal conviction is truly a key to leading one's life successfully."

—Emily Sano, Curator, The San Francisco Asian Art Museum

Perhaps one of the most insidious traps for women is trying to make decisions that will please other people. The successful women in this book either knew or have learned that it's nearly impossible to please yourself *and* other people when it comes to making major decisions about your work and your life. Compromises are possible, but not when they cut to the heart of your passion and joy. Faced with others' expectations and demands, some women, like Emily Sano, have had to defy parents and tradition to stand by their own convictions.

Emily Sano was born in California one month before her family was forced to move to an internment camp for Japanese-Americans in Poston, Arizona. "When World War II was over in 1945, my father was among a group of people who took jobs as day laborers on a cotton plantation in Arkansas. After about two years, most of the Japanese left, but my father was an adventurous man and wanted to try cotton farming himself. He started with a mule and fifty acres—both the mule and the land were rented. It was sharecropping, but my father was quite successful."

Emily left that rural town when she entered Indiana University. "My father encouraged me to go into the sciences, thinking it was the secure route. I almost flunked German and calculus. I wasn't good at either. I thought, 'This is not my calling.'" When she spent her junior year abroad in Tokyo with the Stanford language program, many of her friends were art historians. "They always had so much to do: they had museums to see and temples to discover. I also found that their gossip was interesting—who bought what and what the auction prices were."

When Emily returned to the United States to finish her senior year of college, she won a Woodrow Wilson Fellowship that allowed her to go anywhere she wanted for graduate school in any field. "I chose to study art history at Columbia University in New York. My father was devastated by my choice."

Nevertheless, Emily finished her master's degree in art history and went on to continue her course work for her Ph.D. "By this time my father was so upset, he cut me off. I was not permitted to go home for two years. It was a grim time."

After graduate school, Emily went on to the Kimbell Art Museum in Fort Worth, Texas. She describes a moment of great success there: "The Kimbell Art Museum is the second-wealthiest museum in America. I was able to do anything I wanted to do. I installed an exhibit called 'The Great Bronze Age of China,' which was an enormous blockbuster in north Texas. We had more people per day than the Metropolitan Museum of Art in New York."

Some time later Emily extended her distinguished career by coming to the Asian Art Museum in San Francisco. Despite her success as a talented and sought-after curator, she felt a great deal of sorrow because she couldn't follow her father's wishes. But she was also determined to define her success according to her own passion. "I thought my father was unreasonable. His conviction was contrary to my innate sense of justice," says Emily. "He was concerned about financial security. I, too, was interested in security, but I never felt a compulsion to be rich. I think my father felt that if I didn't go into a science or a related field—which was exceedingly secure—I should have at least gone into business or government. It reflected a certain ignorance about American society and the possibilities for an educated person. Science or business was not the *only* way to live life. My major conflict with my father was that I just didn't believe that his opinion was well-informed—and therefore just. I felt I would somehow manage." And she certainly did.

"I believed in the role that art played in culture and that one could understand about people's attitudes, the quality of their minds, the quality of their character as a people through art. I thought it was worthy to pursue that professionally. That's why I was ultimately prepared to stand up to my father's objections and proceed." Emily's passion for her work and her belief in herself were what gave her the strength to stand by her convictions and overcome a difficult—and painful—obstacle.

Remember Your Past Successes

"Someone made a comment, 'If you had a bank across the street, Shirley, you could do anything you wanted, but you can't here.' A light bulb went on in my head. I called a friend of mine and said, 'Guess what we're going to do? We're starting a bank!'"

—Shirley Nelson, Chairman of the Board, CEO, Summit Bank

One of the very best resources successful women have found for overcoming obstacles is their own experience, achievements, and contacts. Past successes provide insights, knowledge, and a sense of how things should be done—if we have the confidence to count on them. Shirley Nelson decided her experience and success in banking were enough for her to take a very bold action.

During the time Shirley worked in a bank in Oakland, California, she closely observed her customers—mostly doctors—and from that developed strong ideas about how a bank could be better run to serve their needs. As a bank manager she didn't have the clout to change that bank, but when an off-the-cuff comment in an altercation sparked her imagination, she found another way to put her ideas to work.

Shirley explains, "I had an uncomfortable experience with the administration of the bank where I worked. We were fighting over a $20 salary increase for an employee of mine. Someone made a comment, 'If you had a bank across the street, Shirley, you could do anything you wanted, but you can't here.' A light bulb went on in my head. I called a friend of mine and said, 'Guess what we're going to do? We're starting a bank!'"

Shirley called on her past experience and her successes as a manager. "I felt I was left with no alternative but to start my own bank, and, honestly, I didn't perceive it to be a big challenge, except for dealing with the regulatory agencies and obtaining the necessary approvals. It took about two years to do the required economic studies. During that time I assembled a group of people in the community to serve on the Board of Directors. Each person represented a different constituency—a doctor, a lawyer, an accountant, a real estate broker, a small business owner, an auto dealership owner, and a developer."

Despite her confidence, the obstacles Shirley faced were not trivial. Most of them were external, stemming from the male model that dominated the banking industry. "In 1979, I realized that there were only about 14,000 people in the United States who could claim the title of president of a bank—and about 99.999 percent were men. I was also aware that at that time, as a woman, I would never be approved as president by the regulatory agencies. So we opened with a man as president, but after ten months I assumed the role of president and CEO and learned, along with the board, how to run a bank."

Shirley noted that at that time, most banks headed by women did not succeed. She says, "A male bank executive from my former employer actually called the market maker of our stock and told him that I would fail in less than two years. Another gentleman put forth the prophecy that since I didn't have a college degree, I would fail. I've since been awarded an honorary Ph.D. in Public Service from John F. Kennedy University in Orinda, California, and, of course, the bank is still thriving. I did find the Old Boys' Club alive and well in this industry, but I have since experienced somewhat of an acceptance into that club. I think that acceptance really followed the bank's performance."

Shirley's perception of her obstacles is the interesting message in this story. Considering the external roadblocks she faced, it was her experience and self-confidence—what she knew about banking, both as an industry and as a business—that carried her through. Without the internal barriers of fear and doubt, she was free to do what naysayers told her she couldn't. Her belief in herself made others believe in her, too. "At the time," she says, "it was inconceivable to me that we wouldn't become wildly successful."

What we learn from successful women and their mindset toward obstacles can help us understand and overcome our own obstacles. We might also have to admit that the first one we have to tell to "Watch me!" is often ourselves. Traditions, society, physical setbacks, and our own doubts can make our goals more difficult to reach, but reach them we can, beginning with the right mindset and ending with the appropriate actions.

Eunice Azzani's Obstacle Busters

1. Believe you can do anything you want to do. The minute you stop believing you can do it, it won't happen.

2. Talk about what you want to do, what you are good at. What you're good at is usually what you enjoy doing.

3. Depersonalize obstacles—especially internal ones.

4. Identify what drives, motivates, and energizes you, what builds you up instead of knocks you down. This is your passion.

5. Listen to your instincts, but do your homework. It is a process of discovery.

---

6. When you determine what you want to do, think *how* to do it, not *whether* you can do it.

7. Identify your obstacles, inside yourself and outside.

8. Create a strategy to overcome the obstacles.

9. Trust yourself.

10. Be careful whom you're trying to please. Whatever you do, let it be *your* choice—and make it an informed one.

11. Be able to tell your story well. Jazz it up and feel good about it.

12. If you want to be important, act important.

Assess Your "No-To-Naysayers" Acumen

1. Do you tend to play it safe—or to take chances or break the rules? Do you suffer from the "Good Girl Syndrome"?

2. Do you feel resentful of others or frustrated by "the way things are?" Are you willing to change things?

3. Have you clearly and fully identified your passion?

4. Can you stick to your convictions but stay open-minded and open to change?

5. When confronted with comments from naysayers, do you consider whether they know what they're talking about? It's your situation, so follow your instincts and stand by your convictions.

6. Have you clearly explained to others what you want? Your clarity helps dispel their fears and objections.

7. Have you mentally prepared yourself to go it alone or with a different group of supporters than you originally imagined?

8. Have you listed your past successes, large and small, to keep focused on your abilities and confidence?

9. If you are trying to please other people, have you also asked yourself whether you are pleasing yourself?

10. Even if you disagree with the naysayers, can you listen to them and determine whether there are some elements of truth in what they're saying? If so, learn from them.

Commandment Eight

Become Financially Savvy

The successful women we've met so far have definitions of success that are as individual as they are. Some emphasize intangibles like making a difference or finding meaning. But all of us know that financial knowledge and security are the basis for feeling successful. They are also a source of freedom, allowing us to expand our lives in ways not possible if money is lacking or if we feel defeated by financial matters. Successful women know that being financially savvy is essential, whether they are in a corporate setting or working on their own.

> **"Money is a *very* important subject."**
> —Muriel Siebert, President, Muriel Siebert & Company, Inc.

Being financially savvy does not just mean having business-related knowledge. It also means managing your personal finances, both short- and long-term, to achieve independence for yourself and to give you and your family the kind of life you want. As we'll see in this chapter, the key ingredient in financial know-how is taking charge—from managing or avoiding credit card debt to saving for retirement to understanding the larger financial context of the business world around you and how you fit into it. None of us can count on an employer, an advisor, or anyone else to take care of our financial well-being, now or in the future. Regardless of what your life experience has been or how you feel about money, it's important to become financially informed and resourceful.

Women play a major role in our economy. According to recent estimates from the National Foundation for Women Business Owners (NFWBO), nearly eight million businesses in the United States are owned and operated by women, while women-owned firms provide jobs for an estimated 18.5 million people, or 1 worker in 4, generating sales of nearly $2.3 trillion. That's a substantial contribution to the economy. By the end of the 1990s women are expected to own half of all small businesses. The key to the continued and increasing success of women in the economy now and in the twenty-first century is a concerted effort to become more financially sophisticated and to get an even firmer grip on the way we manage our money and our business affairs.

In interviews for this book, many successful women remarked that they knew little about business or finance when they started out. Significantly, all ended up learning—sometimes the hard way. The most dangerous thing some had done to the health of their careers or businesses was blindly handing over their financial matters to advisors or accountants. The fact is, mastering the rules of managing and handling your finances, both in your personal and your business life, is crucial. Even if you don't own the business where you work, as a valued employee you need to know how your efforts contribute to the bottom line. Women who know their value to the company— and let their superiors know they know—position themselves for advancement.

Muriel Siebert: The First Woman of Finance

"You have to decide how you're going to prepare for your retirement or your children's schooling or whatever. You need discipline. You have to be honest with yourself. There are all kinds of ways [people and things] to get advice on what you need to do."

—Muriel Siebert, President, Muriel Siebert & Company, Inc.

Muriel Siebert has built her entire business life on an aggressive and creative approach to money—its management and its uses. Called

"The First Woman of Finance," Muriel is known for many firsts: first woman to own a seat on the New York Stock Exchange, first to head one of its member firms (her own Muriel Siebert & Company, Inc.), and the first woman Superintendent of Banking for the State of New York. Those firsts, beginning in the late 1960s, did not come easily or without obstacles, but Muriel has prevailed, largely through her own talent, persistence, and financial savvy.

Muriel says, "Money is a very important subject." Yet she realizes that it is not an area that comes as easily to others as it does to her. "I found in college and after that I have a talent: I can look at a page of numbers and they light up and tell me a story. Business was a natural place for me to be. In my first job I was a security analyst and was studying companies and writing reports. My accounting knowledge was very important in my ability to find stocks through cash flow or for whatever reason."

Although Muriel does not think all women need her depth of understanding in money and finance, she advises all of us to take the responsibility for learning about those subjects in our professional and personal lives. "You have to decide how you're going to prepare for your retirement or your children's schooling or whatever. You need discipline. You have to be honest with yourself. There are all kinds of ways to get advice on what you need to do."

The first step to developing this kind of discipline is taking responsibility for your financial education. Knowledge of financial issues, in turn, positions you for personal and professional success. Muriel suggests looking into stock brokerage seminars, continuing education courses, financial planners, and software packages, all readily-available resources. Software programs for managing personal finances, although not set up as educational tools, help you learn by doing. Especially good are "Quicken," produced by Intuit, and "Managing Your Money," by Meca. For small businesses, "Quick Books" by Intuit and "Mind Your Own Business" by Bestware provide a helpful format for handling business finances. The Internet also offers helpful forums on business and finance.

Throughout her career Muriel has seen creative risk taking as an integral part of financial savvy, always looking to make the moves necessary to advance herself. She says, "Some risks I had to take because men were being paid twice as much as I was. Somebody would offer me more money and I would move." One of Muriel's risky firsts was on May 1, 1975—Wall Street's May Day, when a new federal law abolished fixed commissions for brokers. When Muriel announced that her company would become a discount commission brokerage, the reactions from Wall Street were hostile. Her long-time clearing house dropped her instantly, and her firm faced Securities and Exchange Commission (SEC) expulsion in sixty days if she could not find another house to clear her transactions. She wrangled a thirty-day extension, signed up another clearing house just before the deadline, and led her company to dramatic success in the new world of discount brokering.

Her five-year stint during the late 1970s as superintendent of New York State's Banking Department also led to a number of risks—but risks mitigated by her profound understanding of an industry that was then in deep trouble. To prevent bankruptcies and failures, Muriel forced banks to merge and persuaded stronger institutions to help weaker ones. She arranged millions of dollars in federal financing to make the new mergers viable. And she took over the floundering Municipal Credit Union, which serves New York City employees. Within a year-and-a-half she had turned it around with the help she garnered from executives on loan from other banks.

Her latest business venture includes the development of "Siebert OnLine," a new proprietary software that delivers brokerage services to clients—free of charge—through a personal computer. And she recently teamed up with a company that she can take public, a challenge that she says will be very stimulating.

Muriel has a clear sense of the kind of advice that will help women with their financial know-how, regardless of their role in business—in corporate positions, in their own businesses, and in their personal lives. Read to the end of the chapter for her nine "musts" of financial success.

Alison Becker Hurt: Cooking Up Financial Savvy

"The weirdest things happen when you're raising money. People you didn't expect to invest become irate because you didn't ask them. Then others, who promise and promise to invest for days on end, suddenly disappear and you never talk to them again."

—Alison Becker Hurt, Owner, Alison on Dominick Street Restaurant

Alison Becker Hurt had run two different restaurants for five years before she decided to start her own. The turning point for Alison was the realization that she "didn't want to work for anybody and do all the work for them anymore." With the responsibilities she carried at each restaurant she managed, she felt "they might as well have been my own." That realization prompted her to educate herself in raising start-up capital and mastering the other skills she needed to become a financially savvy businesswoman.

In 1989 Alison opened Alison on Dominick Street in what she calls "the middle of nowhere in Manhattan." Before she opened, she spent a year learning about her financial needs, raising money, and looking for space. She exclaims, "The weirdest things happen when raising money. People you didn't expect to invest become irate because you didn't ask them. Then others who promise and promise to invest for days on end, suddenly disappear and you never talk to them again. I had somebody put money in and then want it back. This is the kind of information women should know about raising money."

Eventually, Alison decided to form a limited partnership. This meant that she was the general partner, remaining in control of the daily operations of her business, while the other investors' liability was limited to whatever they had contributed. "I went through a lawyer to set it up," Alison says. "I think it's a smart thing to do, especially the first go-around." Alison believes this kind of partnership is especially helpful to those who want to own their own business but don't necessarily have the collateral to qualify for institutional loans. Later, when Alison had a track record with her restaurant, she applied for conventional loans using the restaurant property as collateral.

Over the years Alison has learned the importance of becoming more financially savvy—and confident. She says, "The IRS isn't something to be scared of, because it's more than happy to work with you, once you get over being scared of it. The same thing with bankers." Alison, who has recently acquired bank financing, believes that women fear banks because of the possibility of rejection—but only because they don't know how it all works. "If you go in and try to borrow money and the loan officer turns you down, and that's your first experience, you're afraid to go to another bank. But if you were taught to expect that, to know that it may take you forty tries to get a loan, then you'll know what to expect." She has also learned to view success and failure in a different way. "I always figure if you fail, you fail. It's easier once you realize that failure is not necessarily bad. It doesn't mean that you're a bad person; it's just something that didn't work. If you're smart and you're willing to start all over again, you can always work your way back up."

Mastering the Rules of the Money Game

The money game may seem to be one thing or another depending on whether you are starting a business or working in a corporation, but in fact there are many basic similarities. Whether you run your own business or department or are just starting out in a company, it's important to know what constitutes acceptable profit margins, how to interpret daily and weekly sales reports, how to understand profit and loss statements, and how to forecast budgets and cash flow. You can't make good decisions in any business setting if you don't have a firm grasp of the basics; nor can you participate at higher levels and advance your career if you can't speak the language of money and finance.

How do you go about gaining financial know-how, especially if it seems a foreign and intimidating subject? Muriel Siebert, Alison

Becker Hurt, and other successful women know it is simply a process of increasing your sophistication through experience and of actively educating yourself. You can't learn it all overnight, nor do you have to go it alone. Here are five important suggestions that can serve as the basis for developing greater financial skill and expertise:

- Understand the big financial picture
- Take charge of learning what you need to know
- Make sure you get paid what you're worth
- Research and write your own business plan
- Set solid financial goals

Understand the Big Financial Picture

"I wondered where I could go to get technical assistance. I didn't know where to look. I found out later that there were many resources at the Small Business Administration, and had I known about them when I had my own business, it would have been very helpful to me."

—Betsy Myers, Director of Women's Initiatives and Outreach,
The White House

Have you ever been in a situation, especially one involving financial matters like taxes or cash flow or profit-and-loss statements, where you just couldn't make sense of them? Did you feel you might be missing some essential ingredient? Did you feel like you just didn't get it, even though you understood the individual numbers on the page? If that's happened to you, it may be because you are missing the big picture, the business context, or the financial relationships that for some, as Muriel Siebert put it, "light up and tell a story." Successful and financially-savvy women have educated themselves not just about specific accounting practices but also about the larger context of finance and the environment in which they're doing business. They know that lack of interest in financial matters and resources can sabotage a great business idea or a promising career.

Before her current position as White House Director of Women's Initiatives and Outreach, Betsy Myers was Assistant Administrator for the Office of Women's Business Ownership at the Small Business Administration (SBA). Betsy's experiences with her own insurance and financial-planning business enabled her to understand the problems women business owners face. In fact, she says, she found out later that there were many resources at the SBA—resources available to all business owners—that could have been very helpful had she known about them. One is knowledge about raising capital for a small business—a major obstacle for many women. With so many women funding their businesses from their personal credit cards because they are unaware of other sources, this is no small issue.

During her tenure at the SBA, Betsy helped establish an easier way for women to get loans. "In the PreQual Program, we reversed the steps of the loan process. Instead of a woman going to the bank first, she would come to SBA first and we would pre-approve the loan. That was a huge success. When I joined the SBA and saw the statistics—52 percent of women business owners use credit cards and 18 percent use personal resources—I was appalled that 70 percent of women can't get capital. Many women-owned businesses are service businesses without collateral. Banks don't traditionally take risks and make loans for small amounts."

The SBA not only offers a variety of loan programs, it guarantees loans made by private lenders. You must still produce a business plan and qualifications for a loan to receive support from the SBA, but the guarantee often helps you get a better loan package with lower interest rates, longer repayment periods, and reduced monthly payments. An applicant for an SBA-guaranteed loan usually needs to have one-third of her own money in the business, as well as collateral for the amount being borrowed. And the SBA is only one source of capital; there are many others, including an alliance between the not-for-profit Women Incorporated (WI) of Sacramento, California, and

The Women's Business Development Center in Chicago. This alliance provides its 10,000 members access to its $150 million loan pool with loans ranging from $25,000 to $2.5 million.

The point is to expand your vision. Before you pull out your credit cards, take time to research what other sources of capital are available. When you approach raising capital in a businesslike manner, financial institutions and private lenders will see you are serious about your future success—and that you know how money works. Other sources of funds include limited partnerships (as Alison Becker Hurt did), personal savings, life insurance policies, credit unions, and, in some cases, venture capital companies. Your choice will depend primarily on your individual circumstances and the nature of your business. If you don't know the best or right way to go about getting funding, seek the advice of a banker or a financial advisor.

If you're an entrepreneur, understanding the big financial picture and the business and economic environment will help you know what you need and how to get it. If you are in a corporation, this understanding will prepare you to make a conscious contribution to the bottom line and to make more successful strategic and tactical decisions. No matter where you work, becoming financially informed and resourceful is essential in managing your career and achieving your goals.

Take Charge of Learning What You Need to Know

"The same problems with money happen in your business as in your personal life. Some businesses don't grow because the owners aren't clear about money."

—Glinda Bridgforth, President, Bridgforth Financial Group

Just as each woman's career, work situation, and life are different, so will her needs for information and expertise vary. Consultants don't have to worry about inventory the way retailers do; a managing editor at a publishing house doesn't need to know the same financial concepts and statements as a stock broker. But what every woman has in common with every other is the need to *be in charge* of knowing enough—perhaps more than enough—about the financial aspects of her business to ensure her success. As more and more women start their own businesses, rise in corporations, and position themselves to affect the bottom line in companies, the need to become financially savvy has never been greater. And as Muriel Siebert says, women must take responsibility for educating themselves about money.

The first step in becoming financially savvy is becoming *interested* in money. That may sound a bit strange, but some women would prefer to let others deal with money and finance, in part because they feel they don't know enough. Since some women may also have emotional conflicts or issues about money, it's important to understand how such problems can sabotage their personal and professional financial situation. Glinda Bridgforth takes a particular interest in this subject.

Despite her successful track record in banking, there was a time when Glinda Bridgforth had a hard time applying what she knew professionally to her personal money problems. Her story illustrates that even sophisticated businesswomen can get into financial trouble in their personal lives. After fourteen years in banking, Glinda was burned out and decided to take a short leave of absence that turned into two years. She says, "When I took the leave I had terrible feelings of failure. Everyone else could handle the stress, so I thought there must have been something lacking in me, since I couldn't deal with it. I fell into a depression. My personal life had problems as well; my marriage was deteriorating." To elevate her mood, Glinda spent money on herself, but that strategy didn't last, since she was living on one-third of her former income. "I went to a financial counselor because I was overwhelmed. On the first visit, the counselor said, 'You could be a counselor yourself, Glinda.' She was looking at my banking experience and my level of expertise." Through the difficult times that followed, as Glinda got control of her budget and credit, she decided that she had learned so much about personal financial management that she wanted to teach other people.

Glinda's message is that our attitudes toward money do not just materialize out of nowhere. They are very much influenced by our parents' and families' perceptions and our own experiences. She's had mature, well-educated women tell her they "don't do money" and don't want to have anything to do with managing their financial affairs. Money had somehow become attached to emotional conflicts or serious problems that made them want to avoid dealing with it completely. Whatever your situation, it's important to recognize the emotional component of our behavior with money.

Glinda sees money management as having two different components: the emotional side and the checkbook and budget side. "I have my clients do their emotional inventory of money first. When they understand their beliefs, they can become clear about money. I think it's important to look at everything from mind, body, and spirit—not just bottom line, dollars and cents."

Dollars and cents are not to be discounted, however. "Doing your emotional money inventory is important, but doing your spending plan is, too," Glinda adds. "You need to know the financial needs of your personal life style and your business setting. Do a detailed breakdown of what you need to survive and thrive. Devise a spending plan that falls between what you ideally and realistically want to spend. Be conscious of *your* needs."

There are plenty of ways to learn about finances that are less costly than hiring a financial advisor like Glinda, including brokerage firm seminars, community college courses, continuing education night classes, and public libraries. It's also a good idea to start building a personal library of books on money and finance. The information is available for you to become financially savvy, but you have to take steps to acquire it.

Make Sure You Get Paid What You're Worth

"People have to trust themselves, do research about what is reasonable to charge . . . . Once they've established that, they need to be conscious about how they feel. I started by charging what I had paid another counselor. About three months later, I felt that I was worth more."

—Glinda Bridgforth, President, Bridgforth Financial Management Group

If your inclination is to take less than you think you're really worth because you think it will bring you more business or get you a job, don't. You may soon end up having to raise your prices to make your business profitable. Or you may feel so undervalued in your company that you decide you have to change jobs to earn more money. Sometimes that's the only way to get paid more, as Muriel Siebert found out by changing jobs early in her career, but it should be an intentional decision, not a by-product of taking less than you're worth.

The main reason any corporation, company, small business, or sole proprietorship exists is to make money. It's also the main reason most of us work. Successful women know that it's up to them to make sure they get paid what they're worth, regardless of the awkwardness they may have felt at one time about how much to charge for their time and expertise. This is especially true for women who have never owned a business or who start over in a new field. Glinda Bridgforth says that what she charged for her financial services evolved as she became more self-confident. "When I first started, I went with a lower fee. I think people have to trust themselves, do research about what is reasonable to charge, and learn what is the high end and what is the low end of the pricing scale. Once they've established that, they need to be conscious about how they feel. I started by charging what I had paid another counselor. About three months later, I felt that I was worth more. It was another three months before I had the guts to increase my fees again."

If you're thinking of pricing yourself low to get new clients or to get your foot in the door of a new company, realize that there's a fine line between getting ahead by charging less and being considered less valuable *because* of the lower amount. People tend to assume that they get what they pay for, and if your service or product is too inexpensive, they don't value it. When you value your time, others will, too.

Caterina Rando, a business coach and owner of PowerDynamics in San Francisco, has found that to be true not only with her clients but personally. Caterina says, "One of the things I hear in my business start-up groups is that some women business owners fear people won't pay enough for what they do. What they're doing is creating a self-fulfilling prophesy. If you believe it has value and you project it in that way, then people will pay for it."

Sometimes women don't know how valuable they really are—especially if they have been with one company for a long time—until they go out in the job market. This was true for Judy Vredenburgh before she became a vice president at the March of Dimes. Judy explains, "I did very well at Abraham & Straus. I moved up to Merchandise Vice President in 1984. Then a man was moved in over me into a position I thought I deserved. I believe I was taken for granted because my husband was a tenured professor in New York and I would not leave the area. In 1987 I decided to go out into the job market and pursue it, even though I had never even thought about doing that before. That experience made me realize how marketable I was."

Judy Vredenburgh adds that, in corporate settings, "It's important to demonstrate how your work contributes directly to the profits of the organization. It's easier if you're in a job where there is a greater connection, but even if you're not, you have to constantly point out your connection to the bottom line. That's how you'll be valued. Have confidence and position yourself where the action is."

Research and Write Your Own Business Plan

"You need a business plan. If you can't do it yourself, you have to hire somebody to do it. A bank is not going to loan you money on an idea."
—Muriel Siebert, President, Muriel Siebert & Company, Inc.

Women starting businesses often don't write a business plan for the same reasons they use their credit cards instead of applying for a loan. Ignorance of financial resources and realities leads them to try to make it without going through the necessary processes. Without a business plan, you'll have a hard time getting others (such as banks) to take you seriously, and you may have more trouble succeeding in your enterprise.

The women in this book who failed to write a business plan remember having no idea how to answer the financial questions the plan raises. These are the very women who recommend most strongly that you write a business plan *before* you open your doors. As they found out the hard way, financial preparation saves time and money. Writing a business plan *yourself* helps you think about financial questions, plot your strategic course, and identify where capital can best be spent. Even after you've started your business, the plan is an important operating tool that helps you evaluate whether you're on track, where you've made the right (or wrong) assumptions, and what adjustments need to be made.

A business plan asks all the right questions—the questions that will have a bearing on your success in the enterprise. It forces you to think about the big picture of your company, including the four basics: the product, the market, the financing, and the people running it. It tells lenders and investors:

- Why customers would want your product—what benefits and features distinguish it from the competition.

- What your market is: who benefits from your product, who would want to buy it, and how you would reach those people.

- How your business will grow, including a cash flow forecast that shows how the business will be financed, how you will spend the money, and how the loan will be repaid.

- Who will run your business. If you will be the sole proprietor, it describes your background in a related field and the present skills you will apply to the new business. If you have partners or other key members on your team, it describes them as well.

The business plan is also part of a loan application used by the loan officer to evaluate your financial background, credit history, experience in the kind of business you propose, understanding of the market, and education. When you go to a bank for a loan, says Muriel Siebert, "You have to have a very good plan. You just can't go in there with an idea. You have to have a potential financing plan and where you're going to get your business from. You need to have enough reserves and enough capital to last through the start-up phase. Some people think they're going to break even in six months, and maybe they need a year or more. Nothing ever goes exactly the right way. You'll find a lot of small businesses close for that reason."

Shirley Nelson of Summit Bank also stresses the value of a serious business plan. "Most people who put together a business plan on their own pull numbers out of the air without showing where they got the information. You have to be able to sell somebody on why your business is going to work. You have to prove that with some statistics. Statistically, the ratio of losses on loans to women are lower than for men. Women work harder at paying a loan back."

A business plan provides you with more than financial figures and a marketing plan. By preparing one yourself, you get a feel for the financial needs of your business. First-hand knowledge is best, because it takes the mystery out of the process and provides you with realistic information.

Set Solid Financial Goals

**"When I set my goals at the beginning of the year, I put them in catego-
ries. At first, I thought I would write my goals in a notebook. Instead, I
drew the categories on heavy paper and put them on my wall . . . ."**

—Glinda Bridgforth, President, Bridgforth Financial Management Group

Much of what we've talked about in this chapter has been geared
toward the business and career side of financial management. But as
Glinda Bridgforth made clear, being financially savvy means taking
charge of both personal *and* professional matters. A major component of independence and self-reliance is planning and setting concrete financial goals. Successful women know that financial goals are
much more attainable when you write down specific action plans for
reaching them.

Glinda Bridgforth used to write her goals in a notebook and keep
them in a drawer, but she heard that goals were more effective if they
were seen daily. "When I set my goals at the beginning of the year, I
put them in categories. At first I thought I would write my goals in a
notebook. Instead, I drew the categories on heavy paper and put them
on my wall, but I hadn't yet filled in the details. Finally, on a Sunday
night I filled them in and on Monday morning my phone started ring-
ing. I got eight new clients that week! There is something extremely
powerful about writing goals down and putting them up where you
can visualize them. I think it helped me both on a conscious level—
to get up to make a phone call—and on a subconscious level when
they were in front of me. My business has increased 43 percent from
last year. I attribute it to putting my goals in a visible place."

Glinda advises her clients to do the same thing, regardless of
whether they are in business for themselves or working in a corporate
setting. "We identify goal categories: the number of clients they want
to work with per week or the sales they want to achieve, and then
devise action plans to achieve those goals. We do personal goals as
well. If you don't have that balance, then this isn't going to work, and

you aren't going to be happy. However, if you focus too much energy in personal areas, then your business or career is going to suffer. I believe in focusing on balance."

The ultimate goal, most successful women agree, is the financial independence that gives you the freedom to make choices based on your longer-term goals and desires, not on financial necessity. C.J. Hayden, owner of Wings Business Coaching in San Francisco, developed her company with the express purpose of helping women create financial independence. "In order to become economically equal, women must be economically independent. That means 'undependent.' Women have to make their own way or there will never be any kind of equal footing. As long as a woman is financially dependent on someone else—a husband, a parent, or an employer—she remains economically unequal. That doesn't mean that everyone has to be self-employed, but it does mean that they need to know that at any moment they would know what to do if they lost their job." C.J. believes that becoming economically independent is a goal every women can and should set for herself.

The most important aspect of becoming economically and financially independent is saving—saving on a regular and consistent basis. Betsy Myers of the White House Office of Women's Initiatives and Outreach recommends six months liquid savings—ready cash. Others advise a year. The exact period doesn't matter. The point is to use cash—not credit cards—as your safety net. When Betsy worked with her clients at the SBA, she asked them how much credit card debt they had. The average was around $10,000. Betsy herself admits, "I got up to $20,000 in debt on my own credit cards for my business. It happened slowly. Pretty soon it was $5,000, then $10,000, then you have a couple bad months and before you know it, you are paying 18 percent interest. I was there myself. I saw what it did to my cash flow. In a way, I'm glad I experienced this because I can see how easily it can happen."

Muriel Siebert also emphasizes saving as a way of life, especially as it relates to preparing for retirement. "I think you should take every kind of retirement plan available. If you're eligible for an IRA, open it and make sure you contribute. Do a 401K. You have to find out what kind of retirement vehicles are available to you, either at your current job or as an independent person. Most brokerage firms have reports on that kind of information. Then you have to fund it to the best of your ability. Because if you miss a year in an IRA, when you go to retire thirty years later and that account has compounded at 8 to 10 percent a year, you will have lost a nice chunk of money."

Successful women have learned the importance of personal and professional financial savvy. It's no longer just the province of accountants, financial planners, bankers, corporate departments, or other experts. With the rapid increase in women-owned businesses, and with more women rising in corporate upper management, the next step is for every women to become aware of the vast information, much of it free of charge, and to use it. It's another form of self-reliance—and the key to women's greater independence and autonomy.

Muriel Siebert's "Musts" for Economic Independence

1. Acknowledge that money is a very important subject. Since they don't teach basic financial things like mortgages and credit cards in high school or college, learn them yourself.

2. Take personal responsibility for knowing about finances— both in your personal life and in your business.

3. Be honest with yourself. Decide what strategies you're going to use to prepare for your retirement or your children's schooling, to expand or fund your business, or whatever you need to do.

---

4. Educate yourself. There are all kinds of ways, including talking to people who can tell you how much you need to know. Read books and magazines, take courses, talk to experts, read the financial section of the newspaper.

5. Start investing somewhere. You don't have to pick stocks; there are mutual funds in which you can invest as little as $50 every three months without fees.

6. Make saving a routine. I tell people that they should save as much money as they spend on clothes every month—as much as the most expensive dress every month.

7. Be disciplined. When you get a bonus, don't just take it out and buy the things you'd like; put a piece of it in your investment account.

8. Take advantage of every kind of retirement plan available, then fund it to the best of your ability. Don't miss a year.

9. Know you have to take care of yourself financially. Today people have Social Security and Medicare, and they can squeak by, but it's not going to be the same twenty or thirty years from now. You cannot expect the government to take care of everybody.

Ten Ways to Begin Acquiring Financial Savvy

1. Keep abreast of financial news on television, in newspapers like *The Wall Street Journal* or *Barrons,* and on the radio.

2. Find the right banker even before you need one. Angie Coffee, Senior VP and Regional Manager of CivicBank of Commerce in Walnut Creek, California says, "If you don't personally know a banker, check with other business people in your community

or in organizations you attend. Ask them who they like. Banking is a people business."

3. Get an introduction to your prospective banker. "The *best* kind of first meeting with a banker is to be referred by an existing client of the bank," says Shirley Nelson, owner of Summit Bank in Oakland, California. "Set up a meeting with a banker at the highest level you can, and first get to know him or her. Discuss your business, and your needs, then allow the banker to determine how your request can be handled at the bank."

4. Assess your collateral. Collateral includes real estate, stocks and bonds, saving accounts, accounts receivable, and even your insurance policy. Many women don't possess enough collateral to balance the risk the bank must take to grant a loan.

5. Be prepared to be scrutinized for what Angie Coffee calls the lender's Five C's:

   Character of person

   Collateral

   Condition of economy

   Credit rating

   Capacity to repay the loan

6. If you work in a corporation, introduce yourself to the key financial people in your division and learn how they look at the budgeting process, sales forecasting, and other financial functions.

7. Learn how capital expenditures in your department are determined. Know who is involved in the decision-making process. Understand how your group spends its budget and how it contributes to the bottom line.

8. Ask to see your company's financial reports—daily sales reports, monthly or quarterly profit and loss statements, monthly and annual budgets, and quarterly and annual reports. Learn how to interpret them.

9. Learn the acceptable profit margins and how they were created for the products or services your company or division offers.

10. Compile financial information about your competition that relates to creating new channels of distribution or entering a new market. Take an active role in contributing information that may contribute to the financial health of the company. Pay attention to events and trends in your industry that affect your company's financial health.

Commandment Nine

See Mistakes as Road Signs, Not Road Blocks

I t's very unlikely that any of us who've made the inevitable mistakes in our business lives received a pat on the back and encouragement to learn from them and move on. For most of us, mistakes are embarrassing. We can't help feeling that we've fallen short of our own and others' expectations of perfection, and the negative reactions of our colleagues and co-workers reinforce those feelings. And yet most of the successful women in this book have learned to take a different approach to mistakes. First of all, they know they're going to make them, so they don't fear them. Second, they realize it's better to take action and risk making a mistake than to "play it safe." When they do make mistakes, they ask themselves, "What can I learn from this so I can do better in the future and become more competitive and more valuable?" They don't take mistakes lightly; they don't ignore them or hope that they will miraculously disappear; but they understand that mistakes can call attention to issues and teach lessons that might not otherwise

> **"I think an effective leader has to take risks, and if you're really taking risks in meaningful ways, you are going to make mistakes. The key to success is to recognize them as mistakes, learn from them, and don't repeat them."**
>
> —Debi Stebbins, President and CEO, Seton Medical Center

surface. Successful women don't want to make mistakes, but they are willing to risk them because they know mistakes are part of achieving success.

The women we'll meet in this chapter have made all kinds of mistakes in every conceivable area of their business and career lives, from hiring people who didn't work out to delegating too much or not enough to being ignorant of the ramifications of some business decisions. They are still highly successful, because they not only recovered from those errors, they used them to learn how to do what they do even better.

Deborah Stebbins: Good Rx for Mistakes

"To be effective and learn from mistakes you have to be willing to embrace change. That's true of success in general. Managers or leaders must not only embrace change but also be the standard-bearer for change."

—Debi Stebbins, President and CEO, Seton Medical Center

When Debi Stebbins was seventeen and in her sophomore year at Stanford University, she had aspirations to become a physician. She was advised, however, that her very good grades might not be good enough to get her into medical school. Because she still wanted to be in medicine, she started working at the local Children's Hospital in the summers and got to know the hospital administrators there. The director, who became her mentor, suggested she get into hospital management. For a while Debi wondered whether her decision not to go to medical school might have been a mistake, but now she believes it opened the right door for her. "I'm not a fatalistic person," Debi says, "But I do think some things happen to you for a purpose. Maybe that's another way to deal with mistakes or disappointments. Not that you don't control your own destiny or influence it, but sometimes disappointments and mistakes happen, and something better is going to happen as a result. That's how you get through the toughest ones."

After receiving her master's in public health at the University of California at Berkeley, Debi took an administrative position overseeing the nursing department at Alta Bates Hospital in Oakland. She was there fourteen years, the last six as CEO for ambulatory or outpatient diversification. Today Debi heads Seton Medical Center in Daly City, just south of San Francisco. Her nine years there—including the last two as CEO—have increased her understanding of what it means to be a leader in the difficult health care environment we face today. In the process she has adopted a philosophical approach to mistakes. "There have been many mistakes that I've made in my career, or bad decisions, but I like to think that I was able to turn most of them around. Philosophically, the way I look at mistakes is that if you don't make any, you aren't doing something right. You're not doing enough. I expect the people who work for me to take risks because I think an effective leader has to take risks, and if you're really taking risks in meaningful ways, you are going to make mistakes. The key to success is to recognize them as mistakes, learn from them, and don't repeat them. I'm of the school of thought that if you repeat the same mistake, it's really your problem. You're missing in your perception if you're not picking up on that."

Debi continues, "One mistake I made in the last three years was hiring a senior management person I had some doubts about. In this case I picked up on a lot of strengths, which this person did demonstrate, but also some potential liabilities. I made the trade-off because I hoped that I could turn the liabilities around. In fact, I couldn't, and ultimately had to terminate the person. Sometimes we wait too long to try and rehabilitate people." Debi finds that keeping someone who isn't working out well hinders the entire staff, but the issues go beyond that.

"From that experience I learned that it's very important to your success as a woman and as a manager to surround yourself with the best people you can find. Some people don't want to hire anybody who might be nipping at their heels, but in fact you want somebody who can step into your slot and keep the place running if you aren't there tomorrow. You only do that by hiring the best you can find. Then you have to allow them to make mistakes, and you need to act as a mentor."

Mentors have played an important part in Debi's career, especially in helping her learn how to avoid potential mistakes. "A good mentor of mine told me this early in my career: 'You have to read your audience. You have to listen. Never personalize criticism.' That's so hard to do, but so important. My mentor often said, 'Try to put yourself in the other person's shoes, get into their head about why they're acting the way they're acting or being concerned about what they're being concerned about.' That advice has been helpful to me, especially in dealing with physicians who are acting as independent practitioners. You don't have any official control over them, but they control 90 percent of the organization's expenses by the way they manage the treatment of patients. So my working relationship with physicians is very important to me. The advice from that mentor has really served me well, though it's harder to do at some times than at others."

Debi says that accepting change is an important part of success—that and learning from your mistakes. "Managers or leaders must not only embrace change but be the standard-bearers for change. Part of learning from your mistakes is being able to change, being able to analyze your strengths and weaknesses and the lessons from a mistake. That means making the change in yourself or in the situation."

Sue Swenson: Focusing on Results

"I don't want to look back and say, 'I wonder what if.' I don't want to think, 'Something could have been different if I had just stuck to my guns and my beliefs.'"

—Sue Swenson, President and CEO, Cellular One

Sue Swenson didn't come to be president and CEO of Cellular One—which reports half-a-billion dollars in revenues—by being afraid to make mistakes. Sue started her career at Pacific Bell's Telesis organization in the management development program, working in the business, operations, and marketing departments of several California locations. The management style she developed creates an atmosphere where teamwork and communication are important values for everyone. But she didn't always know what would work best when it came to hiring, motivating, and managing employees. In some ways the toughest situations have taught her the most. Of one of her early jobs in particular she says, "I learned a lot about myself in that job: what I was made of and how much I believed in what I was doing. It was a real test, because my style and my approach were so different from the environment in which I worked. It was a real opportunity for me to stick with it to determine whether what I was doing really had an impact. It was a great time for me, because I learned that what I did made a difference."

Sue always seemed to connect with the people in the organization a bit more personally than many other managers did. As she put her values into practice, she learned that she could make decisions independently and produce the results the corporation wanted. Being a little bit different was, of course, a risk, but Sue says, "I don't want to look back and say, 'I wonder what if.' I don't want to think, 'Something could have been different if I had just stuck to my guns and my beliefs.' You have to look at yourself in the mirror every morning. You have to be true to yourself and true to the people who work with you."

As Sue sees it, mistakes can take many forms and reach different levels and still be valuable to individuals and to the corporation as a whole. She views customer complaints, for example, not as a problem but as quite the opposite. "We get customer complaints, like all companies do. You can have two attitudes toward them. You can say, 'What an annoyance this is. Don't these customers know that we're doing this for them? Don't they understand our process and procedures?' Or you can say, 'This is really a gift.' If you take complaints this way, they are like little gems to make your business better. It's almost like free consulting. These so-called mistakes can help you see the frailties in your process and your procedures."

She says the same applies to any work situation that is not going the way you want it to. "The trick is not to get so completely worked up about it that you avoid it. It's like when you're a kid learning to dive and you hit your head on the diving board. You've got to get up and do it again, but hopefully next time you'll do it better based on what you learned."

Sue's communicative and team-oriented management approach is important in creating an environment where people can move on after a mistake. "To the degree that people are encouraged, not discouraged, from trying to do something again, the environment is crucial. You want people to learn and to integrate that attitude into their thinking. They need to be encouraged by those around them, unless they are just so self-motivated that they'll try it on their own. Whether by their supervisors or their peers, people need to be encouraged so they grow. Otherwise you will have people pulling inward and not trying to do things. That completely squelches creativity." Sue believes that her role is to try to help others based on her and her group's experience so that they avoid having to go through the same problems. When you learn from your mistakes, you're much better equipped to reach the goals you've set for yourself.

The Wisdom of Mistakes

Debi Stebbins and Sue Swenson understand that the goal of life is not to avoid mistakes but to use them to their advantage, to let them teach valuable lessons. The biggest mistake, in fact, is to arrange your life so that you try to avoid errors and problems. If you do that, you may never take any steps toward achieving your dreams, and you may never master the skills and experience you need to find the success you want. If you had been unwilling to make mistakes, you would never have learned to walk, to ride a bicycle, to cook, to use a computer, to create a sales strategy, to start an initiative, or to hire a new employee. The biggest mistake you can make is not to try. Remember, you have to take that first step. As wildly successful women know, it's not the mistakes that create problems, but the way people respond to them. Mistakes can be either teachers or destroyers; it all depends on attitude. The wise advice of women who have learned this lesson contains four important principles:

- Assume that mistakes are useful teachers

- Avoid the really big mistakes

- Learn to recognize warning signs

- Move on after a mistake

Assume That Mistakes Are Useful Teachers

"I always look at the glass as half full. I always ask, 'What can I learn from this?' So that I either do it better or I avoid it next time."
—Sue Swenson, President and CEO, Cellular One

Approaching mistakes positively goes a long way toward taking the sting out of them. Try asking a few objective questions after the fact to zero in on what there is to be learned. What were you trying to accomplish? What didn't work? At what point did the problem occur? What caused the gap between what you wanted to happen and what happened? What key people can you consult with to help you understand what went wrong? Is there anything else you need to know to help you proceed differently in the future? Keep in mind what you do well so that you can put mistakes in perspective.

Cheryl McLaughlin, owner of The McLaughlin Sports Performance Group, is a pioneer in the industry of sports psychology. She has thought a lot about how the behavior of women in sports corresponds to their behavior in work and careers. The athlete's ability to keep the right mindset, she says, is what allows her to do well at her sport. Cheryl never talks about winning or losing. Instead she focuses on how well the athlete did her job, understood the issues, and knew where to get help. She believes the same applies in business.

Cheryl finds that the most successful athletes have "an air of invulnerability" when they go into a competition. That doesn't mean that they will have a perfect performance. It means they feel and believe that no matter what happens they'll find a way to handle it. "It's challenging to have them take a look at themselves without feeling so vulnerable that they feel fragile. There's a readiness issue. First, they have to educate themselves about what competition is, what it's not, and what issues it forces them to face." The kind of confidence they gain from this process allows athletes and business people alike to feel ready for whatever comes their way—and to keep going and winning regardless of minor setbacks.

Pat Beals, owner of Teetot & Company, which manufactures Halloween costumes and dress-up clothes for the consumer mass market, expects mistakes to teach her valuable lessons. She says, "When I finish a project, a meeting, or an appointment, I always take time to review what I did and to decide what I could have done better. But I'm equally aggressive about telling myself what I did really well. The right stuff deserves at least equal time and attention to what I did wrong, if not more."

Avoid the Really Big Mistakes

"People make mistakes in hiring when they employ someone in their own image, and not for the job that they want them to do. Those mistakes are often made by employers who haven't written job descriptions. They really don't know what they want."

—Maureen Hochler, President, Hochler Associates

Although it's important to recognize that mistakes can be great teachers, that doesn't mean that everything has to be learned through trial and error. Identifying the biggest potential pitfalls and strategizing ways to avoid them is essential to success in any line of work.

Successful women figure out how to avoid the "big mistakes"—costly errors involving employees, money, and time management.

Avoiding Mistakes with Employees

As anyone who has ever managed knows, hiring, managing and sometimes terminating employees are among the most important responsibilities of any business setting. Bringing the right person in can add great value to any enterprise; hiring someone who doesn't fit the job or the organization can lead to all kinds of problems. There's a lot at stake. Effective management can make the difference between an organization that is fired up and highly competitive and one that seems preoccupied with its internal problems. For the very small business, having the wrong person in a job can be so distracting that it may seriously jeopardize that business's existence.

The best preparation for avoiding employee problems is to be aware of four basic issues in hiring, managing, and firing:

1. **Understand your own business style.** Knowing your own style can help you anticipate possible mistakes. Do you like to jump into things? If so, do they usually work out? Do you rely a lot on your intuition, or do you prefer a more methodical approach? How you work and relate to people affects whom you attract to work with you. By understanding yourself and your personal business style, you will be more successful in hiring.

2. **Be clear about your position as the employer.** It's important to communicate what you expect from employees and how you want to relate to them. Some people don't know how to react to a woman boss; either they want a closer relationship than is appropriate (a mother figure or a friend) or they have difficulty taking direction. When you are clear about your own position, you and everyone around you will feel more comfortable. Women managers may be known for their inclusive style,

but successful managers realize that teams still need and want a leader.

3. **Choose the people you work with carefully—especially when it comes to business partners.** Maureen Hochler, president of Hochler Associates, says, "People make mistakes in hiring when they employ someone in their own image and not for the job they want them to do. They think, 'He talks right, he walks right, he looks and acts just like me, so, gee, he'll be great.' I think the biggest problem in hiring is when nobody has set up clear descriptions."

Katie Smith, principal of Mulberry Neckware, a $12-million tie business, agrees. "The most important thing you do in business is hire the right people. At one point, when our business really took off, the challenge was handling that growth, which meant hiring great people when we were under pressure. The trick was to define the different functions into job descriptions—then relinquish control of those tasks. We trained people and then let them go so that we could stay focused on the big picture. Our employees are entrepreneurial and they care about the company. We have nine people in management, and if I were gone for eight weeks, I know the company would do well in my absence." Maureen Hochler agrees. "If you hire everybody like yourself, you set yourself up for everybody wanting to do the same things. You want to hire people who want to do what you don't want to do."

Sue Swenson says that she uses the interview to tell whether the applicant has something to say. To her that indicates that "when they come in on the job, the energy is going to be about doing what's right, not about self-promotion. Some people try to present an image of trying to be exactly what they think you'd like. I don't want people who are just telling me things I want to hear. We have a business to run. We have people to grow and develop. I want people of character, substance, and opinion. That's what people in the organization look up to. They don't look up to people who act like chameleons."

If you are considering working with a business partner, here are a few tips for making the relationship successful. First, be sure you really need a long-term partner. Bringing in a partner only for financial reasons, for example, can lead to difficult work relations at best, and at worst can harm the business. Make sure the reason for the partnership is crystal clear.

Next, determine whether you share a similar philosophy about the business. Explore how well your work styles and skill sets match. Strong and enduring partnerships are more likely to be formed when you agree about the scope of the business, how it will grow, who will perform what functions, and other important business issues. Equally important, however, is a compatible approach to the issue of balance between work and personal lives. Many women do what Cheri Comstock and her partner Jackie Larson did. Now the owners of The Focus Group in Chapel Hill, North Carolina, both women quit high-paying corporate jobs to form a partnership because they wanted the flexibility to work around their children. The partnership wouldn't work if they did not agree on the scope of the business or the amount of time each was supposed to devote to it.

Finally, put your agreements in writing. When you are considering a partnership, think about how you can ensure that it will be run amicably and fairly, and put that in writing. Partnerships work for people in different ways, but they work best when all expectations and conditions are clear and there is a written escape clause.

4. **Manage with the "big picture" in mind.** Working with and directing employees on a day-in, day-out basis, like hiring, is a matter of paying attention to the right priorities. Women

sometimes have a difficult time in particular with employee discipline, especially if it appears to be leading toward firing. Katie Smith, of Mulberry Neckware, says that for a while, she suffered from the Mother Teresa complex—repeatedly giving chances to people who didn't do their jobs. She's not alone in this problem. Katie now says, "When you have a bad apple, get rid of him as soon as possible. Keeping people on when you know they aren't right can destroy the whole atmosphere of the office. Legally, we have to be careful, but sometimes we are too careful. You have rights as an employer. Your other employees resent it when you let a bad apple stay on. Hiring is not too magical: you have to have good judgment about people."

Maureen Hochler adds a few suggestions and caveats about firing an employee: "When you fire someone, you can get sued if you haven't followed your own policies and procedures, and if you haven't documented everything. If you've prepared people and you've let them know what your standards are, and you've documented everything, then they understand what's happening when you terminate them. It's the surprised one that will come back and get you. Yet most people won't sit down with employees and tell them that they aren't doing a good job, because they are afraid to confront."

Avoiding Mistakes With Money

One of the biggest mistakes successful women warn against is not being involved in or savvy enough about their financial matters. Financial statements measure the pulse of your business or organization. If you choose to have someone else manage them, know and understand what they're doing. When women delegate control of their money to financial advisors, accountants, or partners in business, there's a potential for disaster.

Glinda Bridgforth of Bridgforth Financial Management believes that "Most people begin to work with a bookkeeper or an accountant when their business starts to grow. But what is important to ask yourself is 'Am I completely turning over control of this and not monitoring it?' I have talked to many people who have had problems with their bookkeepers. It took one woman three years to realize her bookkeeper had embezzled $65,000. I have clients who have accountants handle their books, and when they receive the profit-and-loss statements, they don't have a clue what they mean."

Sandy Gooch, founder of Mrs. Gooch's Natural Food Markets, thought her biggest mistake in developing her business was "trusting too much in people who said they knew business—how to do the accounting or operations. I didn't trust my gut enough to know they weren't truthful. I wanted certain relationships with people to work out so much that I didn't heed my intuition." Sandy advocates not only trusting your gut but also learning every aspect of your business—especially the finances.

Using Delegating to Avoid Mistakes in Time Management

One of the most common mistakes women make at all levels and in all kinds of organizations is that of trying to do everything themselves. Sometimes they are working on their own and they believe there's no one else to do it. Sometimes they simply haven't learned how to structure work processes and procedures so that they can share responsibility and concentrate on what they do best. Not knowing how and when to delegate can sabotage your other efforts to achieve success. On the other hand, it is equally important to avoid the opposite mistake—that of getting rid of only what you don't want to do.

Remember the three W's of delegating: when, what, and whom.

- *When* you should delegate depends on how you're spending your time on the needs of your company. If you can't get out to meet potential clients because you have to write orders or monitor every detail of every report that comes out of your department, you are shortchanging your business. When the work you've identified as central to your success is not getting done, delegate. You can hire temporary help if you aren't ready to hire permanent employees.

- *What* you should delegate is relatively simple to determine. Identify the tasks that are easiest for someone else to do, retaining those that you enjoy most and that contribute most to your success. Many women delegate the paperwork that bores them—often financial statements, orders, and payments. Be very sure, however, that you delegate only what you understand yourself. Delegating repetitive jobs often works best because you can tell the employee exactly what you expect. If you believe that no one can do what you do as well as you, you may be right, but it will slow you down. Good delegators know that others may be able to do certain jobs as well as they can or better.

- *To whom* you should delegate is a question that is easier to answer in theory than it is to put into practice. Find competent people and make your expectations and requirements very clear. Jan Dutton, owner of PaperWhite, a lace clothing and linen manufacturing firm, learned a valuable lesson about delegating early on. "At first I assumed others could read my mind, and that they were as committed to the product as I was. I had a very hard time understanding that they weren't. I could remember every detail, but they couldn't. Assumptions set everyone up for frustration and disappointment. It doesn't allow for growth." The best way to provide an entrepreneurial atmosphere in a business is to delegate effectively—describe what needs to be done, show employees how it was done before, and suggest that they figure out a better way to suit them. Keep in touch with their progress, but stay out of their way.

Managing your time takes more than delegating, however. Business consultant Judy Stewart uses something she calls the 80/20 Rule.

"The 80/20 rule suggests that you should concentrate on the most important issues or items and forget the extraneous. In retail, 80 percent of the business will be done on 20 percent of the items. In your personal life, you may have fifteen things you need to do today, but if you do the top three—the most important three—it takes care of 80 percent of it."

Avoiding the big mistakes in hiring and managing employees, paying close attention to financial matters, and delegating wisely to make the best use of time allow successful women to run their companies rather than spending their time putting out fires.

Learn to Recognize Warning Signs

"I had a lot of red flags and warning signals—in blaring lights—but I didn't pay attention to any of them. I had to fall flat on my face. I realize now that it was inevitable that I would fall."

—Jan Dutton, President, PaperWhite

The next-best thing to avoiding mistakes is to recognize them and take action to correct them as soon as possible. Most major mistakes are preceded by warning signals. We often don't heed these signals, however, because we're too busy or preoccupied or simply unwilling to confront them. Successful women, especially in corporate settings, learn to set up systems for identifying warning signs so that they can deal with problems before they turn into serious headaches. Sue Swenson at Cellular One uses employee-satisfaction surveys to measure how well their organization is measuring up to their team agreement about how they're going to operate. These surveys have not only led to a stronger team, they have also helped the company achieve higher levels of success more quickly, because, as Sue says, "no energy is spent in unproductive activity or thought."

"I'm a big believer, especially when you're in an upper-level position—whether you're running your own company or running a business working for a corporation—that you must develop your own network of trusted advisors, both internal and external to the organization," says Debi Stebbins, CEO at Seton Medical Center. "I don't mean a gossip mill. I mean a group of people who don't formally report to you but whose opinions you trust and respect. For example, a few physicians watch out for me and are willing to come to me and say if they've picked up something that is an early warning sign. They are people I can count on to be out there picking up the drum beat when things are going awry. I think that is a good deterrent to getting further into a mistake, if you have that kind of good feedback."

When presidents and managers don't listen to others, they set themselves up for future problems. Debi adds, "When you're in a conflict situation—which is sometimes when mistakes arise—you have to be careful not to get too entrenched in your position. Maintain some flexibility. Don't be too dogmatic. That's sometimes a failing I see in less-experienced leadership people. They want to get in there and show that they can take command of the situation. They don't take the time to really listen to other people and pick up the cues. It was harder to be flexible earlier in my career when I was much more insecure. You get intimidated by people who criticize you and think, 'Oh, I must be wrong if they're saying this.' Instead I've learned to listen and understand that I've got a viewpoint on this and they've got a viewpoint and the solution may be somewhere in the middle."

Knowing when to listen is a key issue in heeding warning signs. Jan Dutton, owner and President of PaperWhite, now a several-million-dollar company, found out the hard way that she needed to develop her ability to see and heed the warning signals that told her that her business was in trouble. Jan's business ran on sheer guts and inspiration during the booming 1980s. Jan says, "The growth was always there, but the business had no foundation. It was so easy to develop because the timing was great. It was also bad luck because we never really had to sell. We just created beautiful things that we thought were ordained to be and that people would always have the money to buy. We had tons of inspiration. But we got carried away with that inspiration and got into a lot of trouble." She says she was running her business in an emotional rather than strategic way. "I have incredible determination. If I tell someone I'll do something, I'll do it. Determination is an asset for most people, but it can be a liability too, because in order to do that you put your blinders on to many other things. I can convince a lot of other people to do things, but you can't listen well that way."

Nine years later, Jan's lack of attention to business matters severely damaged her business. "I had a lot of red flags and warning signals—in blaring lights—but I didn't pay attention to any of them. I had to fall flat on my face. I realize now that it was inevitable that I would fall. Although I believe in the emotional aspect of business, it has to be tempered with basic business principles. I don't think I did as much of that as I could have in the beginning."

One of the major problems, Jan says, was that "we were always catching things just in time. That continued to happen on a bigger and bigger scale until it became normal. You start to think your way is the only way, but in reality, you constantly have to evaluate. That's what I would do differently—constantly assess situations with the attitude: 'Can we do it better?' I didn't always have that attitude. I'd think let's do more, let's do this, let's do that." Today, Jan has recovered from her earlier "fall" and even from a more recent disaster when the roof of her office fell in after heavy rains and destroyed her files and computer equipment. Jan says that event gave them the opportunity to get new computers and software programs and streamline the business. They recreated their files over several months but made the business run more efficiently. This successful woman has determined to learn from her past mistakes and move on. She won't make the same mistakes again—and she believes she'll be much more likely to see the new ones coming and avoid them.

Move On After a Mistake

"If you make a mistake, admit it. It's the most empowering thing you can do."

—Debi Stebbins, President and CEO, Seton Medical Center

When it comes to making mistakes, one of the most important principles to be learned is not to let them linger and torment you or hold you back. Sometimes that's hard to do. Perhaps we have set impossible standards for ourselves or we don't like to admit that we've made an error. But hanging on to being right (when you're not) or assigning blame or being so embarrassed that you have a hard time going forward can only diminish your success. Successful women react to mistakes quickly and decisively. They take responsibility for them, analyze what can be learned from them, and use the lessons they learn to reach even greater levels of success.

As Debi Stebbins recently told a class of graduate students in Health Care Management, "If you make a mistake, admit it. It's the most empowering thing you can do. Go in to whomever you're worried is going to be judging you by that mistake and fall on the sword. Say, 'I wish I had done this differently, but I learned why I should have done it differently. And next time I will do it differently.' There is something about people seeing you as being a fallible human being that makes them want you to succeed more. I have been in situations where I have argued with people, reflected on it, and thought perhaps I wasn't completely right. When that happens, I go back to that person and say, 'I thought about it more. I wish I'd handled that differently. This what I think I should have done. Now let's move on.' Time and time again, those people are my best allies in the future. They realize, 'This woman's just like me. She's real.'"

Mistakes are road blocks only if viewed as such. The wildly successful women in this book believe that "mistake" is synonymous with "learning opportunity." Whatever word they use, successful women use mistakes as the road signs on their way to success.

Sue Swenson's Secrets for Focusing on Results

1. Understand yourself and your personal values.

2. Be true to yourself and to the people who work with you.

3. Adopt a "Let's figure this out together" approach to problem solving. Connect with people in the organization. Treat them with respect and dignity, as you would want to be treated.

4. Do what you think is right for the business. Be willing to make decisions independently.

5. Create an atmosphere where people can be independent, where they believe it will be worth the risk if they try something different.

6. When developing a team or hiring people, look for people with substance, not form—people who are willing to say what's on their mind and not just tell you something they believe you want to hear.

7. If someone has an opposing position, listen to it and know why they have that opinion.

8. Determine whether what you're doing really motivates people in the organization.

9. Encourage others not only to move past mistakes but also to analyze them to see what went wrong and how the same problems can be avoided in the future.

10. It's okay to have fun at work. "Work" and "fun" are not incongruous.

Do You Know How to Avoid Mistakes in Hiring, Firing, and Managing?

1. **Hire the best person you can afford.** Publishing consultant Carol Decker says, "I believe in hiring people who are smarter than I am. People who have new insights, or energy, or experience. Why would I want people who only think what I think? I want people who are interested and smart. With some of the people I hired in the last ten to fifteen years, I thought, 'I'll be working for these people one of these days.' Somebody told me a long time ago always to be kind to people on your way up because you might be passing them on your way down."

2. **Hire people with a sense of humor.** Sue Swenson says, "I hire people with a sense of humor. We work really hard, and you have to have fun."

3. **Have written standards and company policies.** Set up clear expectations through written human resource policies and job descriptions. With clear standards and a fair performance review system, employees will respond better to feedback about their work, even in cases where they may be in trouble.

4. **Keep the lines of communication open to create teamwork.** Carol Decker says, "We try so hard to prove that we can do it that we tend to isolate ourselves and work alone. Then we come back and say, 'Look what I've done.' I think if you come for help and have open discussions early in the game, you could cut the task time in half. It's a team. You need good communications."

5. **Don't hire friends.** There are always exceptions, but generally it doesn't work to have one friend be the boss and the other the employee. Decide whether you could fire that friend and keep your friendship before you consider hiring her.

6. **Listen to your intuition when hiring.** Someone could have the best credentials, experience, skills, and recommendations, but if you don't feel comfortable for any reason, don't override your hunches.

7. **Don't hire someone at the first interview.** Do the background research, no matter how much of a hurry you're in. Better to hire temporary help than to act too quickly and spend months dealing with the consequences.

8. **Provide training.** For the employees, the benefits of training include: greater job satisfaction, fresh challenges, preparation for advancement, and enhanced feelings of value to the organization. Training also increases their ability to be "career self-reliant." The benefits to the company are better trained and more innovative employees.

9. **Praise in public, criticize in private.** This is an old rule of management that never needs updating.

Commandment Ten

Enjoy Your Work and Your Life

The successful women we've met so far are serious when they talk about their work, their goals, their values, and their definitions of success. They've all accomplished great things, in many cases despite daunting odds. Yet most of them have told me that they also want to enjoy what they do, that having a good time, even having fun, is a major part of the success equation. Having a good time takes a number of forms, from designing and developing creative products or services to pleasing their customers to figuring out ways to keep their businesses growing to working with other people. It's not so much *what* these successful women do but *how* they go about doing it that makes their work enjoyable and fun for them.

What factors make work enjoyable? As we'll read in this chapter, passion, a positive attitude, and a sense of excitement and adventure—and fun—are the things that make work more than "just a job." There's no mystery in the fact that the rewards of work,

> "It's a win/win situation for everyone. The consumer is happy, my employees are happy, I've attracted a wonderful team of professional colleagues, the business is growing, and the product is good—that's really fun. It's hard to beat."
> —Nancy Mueller, Founder and President, Nancy's Specialty Foods

tangible and intangible, are greater when women are truly engaged in what they're doing. Nor is it a surprise that other talented people are inspired to work with and for women who are having a great time and enjoying high levels of success. Whether it's better customer relations or breakthrough products you seek, you're more likely to achieve them if you're energized by a passion for what you want to do, the leavening touch of humor, and the ability to enjoy the challenges you face.

Nancy Mueller: The Joy of Quiche

"I'm at a point in my life that I could sell the business, fold up camp, and sit on the beach for the rest of my life. However, building the business is stimulating and challenging—and I'm not ready to retire. The fun is in achieving objectives, and the excitement is in building the brand."

—Nancy Mueller, Founder and President, Nancy's Specialty Foods

Nancy Mueller started her business almost twenty years ago out of her kitchen in Palo Alto, California, and she's still having fun with it. "Nancy's Specialty Foods is the largest manufacturer of quiche in the country, probably in the world," she says proudly. "We produce thirty tons of quiche a day—200 million quiches a year!" Along the way to this impressive level of success, Nancy has enjoyed the entire process of creating a product and learning how to grow and run her business. She's faced her share of challenges, but always with good humor and a sense of adventure.

Nancy began in the food business after a short stint as a pharmaceutical research and development chemist at Syntex Corporation in Palo Alto, California. During that time she was one of the founding members of the Bay Window Restaurant, which gave all its profits to a charity called the Family Service Association. Eventually she became its business manager. But Nancy discovered that she wanted to own her own for-profit business. "I wanted to look back at the end of ten years and have tangible evidence that I had accomplished something."

In 1977 Nancy decided to package and sell the hors d'oeuvres that were so popular at her annual Christmas party with family and friends. "I didn't know whether my idea would be successful or not; actually you never know. I studied the marketplace, determined the price the consumer would pay, and worked it back to see whether it was a good business equation. It seemed to be." She began with hors d'oeuvres and then expanded to both entree-sized and individual quiches that were prebaked and microwavable.

Today Nancy has surpassed her initial dreams many times over. "Your goals grow along with the opportunities. The passion comes from the challenge and the excitement of growth. If we had the same sales for three years in a row and could see no opportunity for growth, I think it would become discouraging—even if we were profitable and life was easy. It's no fun when there aren't challenges. I believe that it's the *process* of achieving the goal that's exciting—the climb up the mountain. Once the goal is achieved, it's time to create new goals. Then you're into the process of achieving it again, and the passion stays."

Nancy adds, "I'm a widow, and I'm at a point in my life that I could sell the business, fold up camp, and sit on the beach for the rest of my life. However, building the business is stimulating and challenging—and I'm not ready to retire. The fun is in achieving objectives, and the excitement is in building the brand. I have a story on the back of my packages that tells a little about how I started the business and asks the customer to comment on our products. I get wonderful letters from people speaking to me very personally about their enjoyment of the product. It's very stimulating. It means that I've satisfied their needs, and that this is a business equation that works. It's a win/win situation for everyone. The consumer is happy, my employees are happy, I've attracted a wonderful team of professional colleagues, the business is growing, and the product is good—that's really fun. It's hard to beat."

Jenniefer Kirk: Tales of Folly and Fun

"The whole thrust of our company is fun. Our product is fun. It's pure whimsy and fantasy designed to make people happy, and make people smile. That's really what this company is all about."

—Jenniefer Kirk, President of Sales, Kirks Folly

Jenniefer Kirk and her siblings Elizabeth, Helen, and George formed their company, Kirks Folly, in 1979. Today, they offer a collection of high-fashion jewelry and hair accessories, watches, gift items, and picture frames—more than 3,000 items. The fantasy designs incorporate fairies, angels, pixies, stars, and moons and are sold through their showroom on Fifth Avenue in New York City as well as through national department stores, specialty stores, and QVC, the television home shopping network.

Jenniefer says, "Our mission statement is to be a leading fashion design organization dedicated to capturing the imagination and dreams of our customers. We're a family business and we try to extend that family feeling into the whole business world—our feelings toward loyalty, dedication, quality workmanship, and fantasy."

Jenniefer didn't start with a mission statement, however. The business started with a chopstick. "My younger sister, Helen, turned a plain wooden chopstick into a work of art. She decorated chopsticks with shells and rhinestones to be used as hair adornments. I thought they were very unusual, and I felt that I should sell them. I took them to Bloomingdale's because it was the best store in the country. When you don't know anything, you don't know that you don't just walk into Bloomie's. But that's what I did. That's how the business began—not from a plan or an idea, just an item that I thought was very beautiful and salable—and that I felt compelled to sell."

Jenniefer interested the buyer at Bloomingdale's during her first appointment. "I told her that nobody was going to understand what to do with the chopsticks, so the buyer asked my sister and me to come into the store and sell them ourselves. We went into the store on a Saturday and set up a lovely case with all the chopsticks. It was great fun. We were very friendly and showed the customers how to put the chopsticks in their hair. We made up hairdos as we went along. At the end of the day, we asked the buyer how we did. She answered, 'I'll buy all you can make.'"

That summer Bloomingdale's gave them a $16,000 order. "At that point we had to decide either to stay where we were, earning a little money, or learn to produce in quantity and go after this as a big business," says Jenniefer. "We invented a way to mass produce, and the next year we sold $1 million worth of decorated chopsticks. However, it wasn't that easy, because we knew nothing about business. It was done with 100 percent tenacity. If you can go into a business with that kind of attitude, you have everything to gain. That's why I encourage people to start from ground zero and take little steps. Even then you make mistakes, but I believe in learning the hard way."

In 1991, after years of modest growth Kirks Folly went on QVC. Now they have the opportunity to show their collection to more people, more dramatically. "On TV, the picture of the item is enlarged to twenty times its size. I explain how each little piece was made and the inspiration behind it. For me, it's the ideal platform for my merchandise. The show reaches forty million people."

No matter what size their company is, Jenniefer wants her customers to have a good time with Kirks Folly products. The Kirks Folly newsletter, *The Angelic Herald,* describes the events they sponsor, such as the Fairyland Costume Ball and a fantasy Caribbean cruise, and the newest pieces of jewelry and when they'll be available through QVC. The QVC shows are fun events, too, complete with colorful costumes and fanciful themes such as the "Kirks Folly Renaissance Faire" and "Romance Land."

The fun that Jenniefer and her siblings promote has won them a following. "We get the most incredible response from our customers. These people really love what we do. In the old days I'd just hear from the people when I went to stores. Now, since television, I hear from people every day about how our jewelry makes them happy.

We're all on the same wave-length and we understand each other. My business has broadened my life, my mind, and my spirit by 350 percent!"

The Art of Enjoying Your Work

The stories of Nancy Mueller and Jenniefer Kirk—like so many others in this book—are filled with a clear and pervasive sense of enjoyment of their work. These women aren't having fun every minute of their lives, but they relish the challenges and opportunities they see in their businesses. They radiate a kind of enthusiasm and joy that haven't traditionally been associated with work, at least the way we usually think of it. These successful women have mastered the art of enjoying what they do by offering services and products they're proud of, creating work groups that enjoy each other, meeting and overcoming difficult challenges with integrity and energy, and injecting personal and professional meaning into their daily lives at all levels. Their ability to enjoy their work and succeed at it revolves around just a few straightforward principles:

- Define and enrich your work
- Challenge your creative side
- Nurture your own growth
- When you outgrow your work, start anew
- Create great incentives and teamwork

Define and Enrich Your Work

"Your work is most enjoyable when it's an expression of your own creativity. Take what you like most about your work and put your personal touch on it."

—Connie Garcin, Principal, Connie Garcin and Associates

We've read how the challenges in a job or a situation expand the definition of the work and make learning about it part of the pleasure.

Successful women give their work their personal stamp, allowing their personality to set the tone for their business or for the group they manage. They are willing to look for what intrigues them in any job to set the stage for growth and further enjoyment. For Connie Garcin, finding what really interested her and becoming an expert in it not only made her job more enjoyable but also led to an entirely new career.

Connie Garcin was a management trainee with Smith Transportation Company when she heard that there was a position available as safety director. Although she had virtually no qualifications for it, she thought it might be interesting, so she took it on the condition that if she wasn't doing it well within sixty days, she would return to her previous job. Fortified with her journalism background, she began asking questions about safety of everyone she could in the industry. She found out that there were many safety problems. Industrial injuries were at an all-time high, and so were the freight claims.

To learn more about the industry and its safety problems, Connie immersed herself in the business. She took an active role in the California Trucking Association, volunteering to work—among other things—on the planning committee of the statewide safety congress. As she studied the issues, Connie drew conclusions about what would make a difference in safety at Smith Transportation. Since the drivers were all union and making top dollar, she suspected that money would not be the motivator she sought. Instead, she figured out how to motivate safety by developing a program that recognized exemplary drivers with the safest driving records. In her first year as safety director, the payouts for worker's compensation claims dropped by almost two-thirds, saving the company $150,000.

Connie's unique approach to the challenges of her job focused on safety as a "people program." If it had involved trucks rather than people, Connie says she would probably have been bored. But people excited her then and still do. Today, with her own consulting firm, she is known as an expert in the field of drivers' safety. "When people come to me for advice about starting a consulting business I tell them to do only what they feel passionate about. What are they experts in? What is the essence of the job that makes them feel alive? I wanted to go into journalism. Somewhere along the way, though, I realized that it wasn't the writing that interested me, it was the people. People are people whether they are the CEO of a company or a truck driver. Even today when I meet with a client, I interview him using my journalism skills; then I go back to my office and compile my notes, and from that I can write a proposal, because I understand the client as a person and the people issues—the safety issues—he faces. When people know what interests them, they can get more out of any job. If I hadn't gone into the trucking industry, I would probably have used my journalism techniques and interest in people very well someplace else. Excitement in any job springs from identifying your strengths and what you enjoy and developing them in the work you do."

Connie isn't using her journalism background in the way she thought she would—or in any kind of a predictable way. But by finding a way to put her real passion into her work, she has enriched it and made it her own.

Challenge Your Creative Side

"You must be happy with what you do with your eight-or-so hours a day at work. Some go to work to make a living. Others work to fulfill creative needs—they're the ones who find personal satisfaction by pursuing their passions."

—Ruth Heine, Owner, Custom Color Service

Even if you're a highly committed and passionate business owner or member of an organization, you will probably find that the way you define your work, your values, and your goals will change over time. Women who've devoted themselves to becoming experts in a field often find themselves adding new creative dimensions to their work to keep up their enthusiasm and engagement. Ruth Heine, a photographer who has owned Custom Color Service in Boston for fifteen years, keeps her "fun factor" alive by staying challenged creatively.

Ruth learned the art of photography from an old-line portrait company. After ten years there she decided she was feeling creatively stifled and wanted to strike out on her own. She knew she was good at taking pictures, so she turned to the photo-finishing end of the business and found her interest in her business expanding. "I like control from start to finish—take the photographs, develop the film, set the picture on paper, and do the presentation. Over time the technical end became more satisfying than the photo shoot. I enjoy doing the airbrushing and experimenting with the processing by using different temperatures from what's recommended by the film manufacturers. Sometimes I vary the timing or the paper I use. I enjoy the whole process, from meeting the client, listening to his needs, coming up with a variety of ideas, and executing the project. I'm passionate about every single aspect. If you're not passionate, you don't do a good job."

Ruth tries to challenge her creative side in every aspect of her business, not just the aesthetic side. She says, "People need to be creative and feel personally satisfied. To find that satisfaction you need to try a number of different things, and if needs be, start at the bottom in a new venture." In business, she has found, "It's easy to fail in today's world if you haven't done what you promised. Most importantly, you must be happy with what you do during your working hours. Some people do well financially, but feel empty."

Ruth has decided to refocus the direction of her business to set new creative challenges. She means to keep her work fresh and engaging. "I'm forty-seven years old," she says, "And I love doing photography. However, I'm at the stage where I've done it, and know I'm good at it. I need a new challenge, so I took a travel agents' course. For years I didn't take my camera when I traveled, because I needed the break from my profession. But I see that what I'm doing now will evolve into something new and challenging. I plan to combine my love for travel and my photography."

Sue Scott, president of Primal Lite, Inc., agrees that creativity is everything. "This company is based on innovation and creativity." Named Entrepreneur of the Year by the San Francisco Chamber of Commerce in 1990, Sue believes in continuing to challenge herself creatively. With a degree in sculpture from the San Francisco Art Institute but no business background, Sue launched Primal Lite, Inc., in 1986 when she was thirty-three. Her first business idea—making dinosaur lamps—showed disappointing sales, and she had to rethink her business. A native of the Southwest, Sue found inspiration from her two favorite icons, the trout and the lizard. In 1988 Sue introduced Bunch-A-Lizards and Mess-O-Trout, which became the first of her series of unusual plastic shapes lit with miniature Christmas lights. They were an immediate hit.

Today, her decorative strings of light sport everything from black and white cows, lobsters, pizzas, cacti, trout, lizards, and laundry. She designs unique lighting not only for the gift industry but also for mail order catalogs, lighting stores, and even feed and tackle shops. "My definition of success is feeling like you're putting yourself on the line. It's taking a chance. It's stretching yourself beyond the limit."

Nurture Your Own Growth

"When you're put to the test, it's amazing what you can really do."

—Kris Bondi, Independent Consultant for Kaiser Permanente

Keeping yourself fresh and engaged at work can sometimes be a matter of finding projects—either on the job or in your personal life—that allow you to grow personally. A particular project can provide enriching experiences that wouldn't otherwise be available, especially if it means putting on a program, serving on a committee, or volunteering for an organization you believe in. And it's possible that what you learn with the project can have benefits for your work as well through new contacts, additional knowledge, and a heightened sense of your customers.

Some women look outside their work lives to find the challenge they need to grow. Kris Bondi, who had recently been laid off with 112 other managers from Tosco Oil Company, increased the hours she was volunteering at the Red Cross. "I had been involved in the Bay Area Disaster Task Force of the Red Cross for a long time and was part of a group of 135 public-affairs specialists who respond to local major disasters. When I lost my job at Tosco, I volunteered for out-of-area assignments for the first time. A couple of months later, Hurricane Marilyn hit St. Thomas."

Kris sees her two weeks on St. Thomas as a great growth experience. She felt she had accomplished something significant. "When you're put to the test, it's amazing what you can really do. Ninety percent of the homes were severely damaged or destroyed. Telephone poles looked like snapped twigs. Boats were on the side of the hill. The people were so wonderful; they took it in stride. It made me appreciate what I have." The benefits of volunteering extended beyond Kris' appreciation for what she could accomplish and for what she had. Before leaving for St. Thomas she had interviewed with Kaiser Permanente, a health maintenance organization in Oakland, California, and had asked that her second interview be postponed until her return. The human resource director, impressed by Kris' involvement with the Red Cross, saw her commitment as a strong point. It set Kris apart from other applicants, and she won a contract with Kaiser upon her return.

Another case in point is that of Marilyn Smith. Marilyn had done extremely well in the real estate business for many years, but she found she wanted something more. The challenge came in the form of reviving The Mountain Play in Mill Valley, California, which had declined in popularity. Marilyn says, "I started with absolutely no framework. I had no budget to follow, no artistic staff, no office. I really started with just an idea."

The Mountain Play, first performed in 1913 in an amphitheater on Mt. Tamalpais, began as a morality play and later evolved into everything from Indian legends to Shakespeare. In the early 1900s audiences either hiked the six-and-a-half miles from Mill Valley or rode the railroad to get up the mountain. Marilyn explains her enthusiasm for the play: "When my husband and I moved to California when he was in medical residency, I went to one of the Mountain Plays. I was a new transplant from the Midwest, and the experience of seeing the outdoor amphitheater for the first time made its mark on me. The theater, styled after a Greek amphitheater in Sicily and a true 'Wonder of the World,' gives everyone a similar reaction on first view. With minimal research, it became apparent that this theater, only forty-five minutes from San Francisco, was only being used one day a year. I was offered the opportunity of being a presenter for this amazing arena."

Marilyn did not come to this project without experience or knowledge. She had been a school teacher and had produced children's musicals for the Marin Symphony. Now, Marilyn says, "This is my twentieth season, and it's been a thrill that's hard to describe. It's wonderful to see how much the theater means to everyone from business groups to family gatherings. I am proud of what The Mountain Play has become."

Creating your own project or taking on initiatives at work—whether being the employee to work with the United Way or the one to prepare a special presentation—enriches your work experience. Remember Audrey Oliver from chapter 3? On her own Audrey created the concept for a coloring book that was used in a pilot program for the Denver public school system. That project advanced her career, increased her community participation, involved her in writing national policy, and eventually made her a recognized authority in minority procurement policies. A simple idea, a small project, may lead to enriching and expanding experiences in your career.

The successful women we've met in this book see taking on unusual and varied projects and challenges as quite normal. They know that in every experience where they have to stretch their abilities and their minds, they grow personally. It's part and parcel of feeling successful and having fun.

When You Outgrow Your Work, Start Anew

"I was proud of my shop and I loved it, but I had had enough. I was ready for a change."

—Julie Lopp, Executive Director, Life Plan Center

For the women in this book, challenge plays a central part in their success and enjoyment. If they weren't learning and growing, if they felt as if they had learned all they could in their chosen career, they searched for new challenges and found the courage to make necessary changes. Julie Lopp is a successful woman who actively sought a change in her life, but it took courage and planning to make it happen. And she found that those changes were neither immediately evident nor easy.

Julie Lopp was in her early thirties when she divorced and had to support her two young children. With the advice of her parents, who had gone into the candy store business in Wisconsin after she was grown, Julie opened a candy store featuring old-fashioned fudge in Virginia City, Nevada—a ghost town and tourist attraction. "I thought I could teach during the winter in Los Angeles and work the summers at the candy store in Virginia City. It seemed like a reasonable strategy. I negotiated a little corner of a store, and my father gave me a line of credit for three months and provided the pots and pans for candy making. I rented out my house to a professor in Los Angeles, put the kids in my little station wagon, and drove to Virginia City."

Julie made it through the first summer by working day and night. Business was so good that she hired a store manager and returned to California to teach school that fall. Over the following twenty-five years, Julie supported herself and her children—and saved much of the earnings from the candy store in Virginia City—while living and teaching in Los Angeles and visiting her store in Nevada for a few days every month. When Julie's children finished college, she felt that it was her time to change her exhausting work schedule. At first, however, she felt stuck. "Over the years, the store was so successful that it became my 'chocolate handcuffs.' I realized that to change my future, I either had to eat them or break them, and I didn't want to do either. I was proud of my shop and I loved it, but I had had enough. I was ready for a change, but I didn't know where to go, or how to make that change."

After attending a career- and life-planning seminar, Julie set herself the goal of figuring out what she wanted to do. "I knew I could get off of my little pad if I believed there were other stepping stones out there. I didn't want to leap off a cliff saying, 'Oh well, heaven will take care of me.' I wanted a tether. But my biggest fear was that I wouldn't take the leap of faith, that running the candy store would become my destiny. I feared that I would forever be disappointed because I hadn't taken that leap."

Eventually she developed a vision that allowed for gradual change, growing her business but decreasing her financial dependence on it. After six years of downsizing, Julie sold her business and continued her search. "I still had to figure out what I wanted to do. I knew that I missed people and ideas and that I loved the world of work. I thought of becoming a career counselor. I especially liked my own age group, my peers, so I narrowly defined that I wanted to work with people over fifty and help them find careers or volunteer work to have a work life that they loved."

Someone suggested that Julie explore career centers and go to conventions. "I kept hearing about Life Plan Center in San Francisco, a career center for people over fifty founded by Gladys Thacher. I went to the Center and told Gladys of my interest. She said that their executive search team was looking for an executive director." Based on the variety of her work experiences, her management abilities, her availability, and her enthusiasm for the challenge, Julie won the position of executive director. She won't have to feel any regret—she had the courage to take the leap into a new career.

Create Great Incentives and Teamwork

"I'm structuring my company so that people can grow in it—so that it's not just 'Sabrina Horn' that the clients are buying. I firmly believe that when people feel—and are—important, they have a greater sense of commitment and belonging to the company."

—Sabrina Horn, President, The Horn Group

Rewards of all kinds are important to everyone in an organization, no matter how big or how small. They can range from the kind of personal recognition for performance that Connie Garcin instituted at her employer's trucking firm to cash bonuses to the satisfaction of collaborating with a well-chosen team on a successful new product or service. In many cases, a welcoming and enjoyable work atmosphere can also serve as an incentive, since it can greatly enhance the quality of life in the organization.

Sabrina Horn, owner of a Silicon Valley public relations firm The Horn Group, has a vision of a company where people can grow and will want to stay. Sabrina wants to work in an atmosphere of camaraderie and respect—a place where people enjoy working. "I'm structuring my company so that people can grow in it—so that it's not just 'Sabrina Horn' that the clients are buying," Sabrina explains. "I firmly believe that if people feel—and are—important, they have a greater sense of commitment and belonging to the company. I would love to create an environment that's different from traditional PR agencies where the average life span of an employee is only two years. We have been in business five years and we've only lost two people out of twenty. Plus we have grown at least 80 percent a year."

Sabrina carefully considers the structure and running of her company to ensure employee involvement. "The management approach we take is to grow from within, rather than from bringing in people from the outside. We also practice participatory management, which does not mean just giving 'lip service' to everyone who has an opinion, but giving everyone a vote. The caveat is that employees have to understand the consequences of that vote. If they have a problem, they need to come to me with three potential solutions to that problem. Then we can figure out what works best."

Sabrina believes that The Horn Group has set a new standard for incentives in her industry. "We have a mentor program. If people have problems at home or at work, they can go to someone within the office. We've also provided trust funds for all employees' children and match up to $1,000 a year for every child. We have a 401K where last year we matched thirty-three cents on the dollar. We have full health care, dental and vision benefits, and a maternity leave program. It's a female-run business, and I understand women's needs. I think it's the right way to do business, particularly if your product is a service provided by people. If, in the long run, I can raise the bar for the industry, I would feel that I'm successful as a businessperson."

When you enjoy your life and work, you can face challenges with less fear and more creativity to make room for personal as well as professional growth. Those who work for and with you will also benefit from your spirit of enjoyment. Competency is a given for successful women, but those who really relish their lives and work take pleasure in the experience as well as the achievement. When they're having fun, everyone else will, too.

Linda Paresky's Advice for Enriching Your Work

When Linda Paresky met David, her future husband, she had no idea that they were destined to take the travel industry to new heights. But in 1965, motivated by their love of travel, they embarked on their journey with three graduate degrees from Harvard (her MAT, his Law and MBA) by opening their own travel agency, Crimson Travel. At that time, 85 percent of Americans had never been on an airplane. After thirty years and two mergers, first with Heritage Travel in 1988, then Thomas Cook in 1989, Linda became Co-Chairman of a $1.2 billion corporation. When it was acquired by American Express in 1994, the company had 400 offices, 4,000 employees, and sales of $2 billion. Today Linda is Senior Vice President of American Express Travel Services.

After ten years in the travel business, Linda used her ingenuity and training in education to solve their problems in finding qualified and trained personnel. In 1975 she opened the Travel Education Center, which today has expanded to four states—Massachusetts, New Hampshire, Illinois, and Maine—and graduates more than 600 future travel agents annually.

When I asked Linda to tell me how she managed to combine her love of travel, her love of education, and her love of family into an exceptionally successful career, she gave me these ten points:

1. Choose a field you enjoy and people you enjoy working with, because you will spend a lot of time with them!

2. Listen to your customers. A complaint is an opportunity for continuous improvement and organizational learning; an unmet need is an opportunity for a new product or service.

3. Treat customers, vendors, and employees with honesty and integrity.

4. Create an environment that empowers everyone in the organization to have a sense of ownership—for internal and

continues

external customer satisfaction—and unleash the creative potential of everyone in the company.

5. Change the paradigm from command-and-control management to a supportive-leader model.

6. Model the values you espouse.

7. Achieve a balance between work, love, and play. Set personal and organizational goals.

8. Be prepared to work long and hard.

9. Give back to the community. Make a difference.

10. You'll need a big dream to sustain you and a penchant for action to get you there.

A Sure Way to Have a Great Time: Make Your Customers Happy

Successful women know that one of the best ways to enjoy their work is to create excellent customer relationships. Jenniefer Kirk has a great time with her customers in person and on QVC. Nancy Mueller enjoys producing and selling more and better quiche than anyone else. When customers are satisfied, everyone in the organization can feel satisfied, too. It motivates them to produce even better products and services that will continue to serve customers' needs. Knowing what customers like and will buy can also spark creativity and lead to new ideas. Jenniefer Kirk and her siblings started with decorated chopsticks and today offer a whole fantasy world and thousands of unusual products.

1. **Great customer relations start with happy employees.** Every employee who answers the phone reveals the mood of the company to the person calling. Customer service starts with the internal customer. Creating an atmosphere where listening

and being helpful matter will carry over into all aspects of the business—especially customer service.

2. **Great internal communication creates great customer relations.** Great communication and respect within a company has a ripple effect. Sue Swenson, President of Cellular One, says, "I derive my success from seeing a team of people work well together. This has an incredible impact on the organization, starting with the employees and emanating out to the customer. That's what makes the business successful. It's the focus on the people so that no energy is spent in unproductive activity or thought. That's success to me. And then everything else flows as a result of that."

3. **Keep your customers in mind when you develop your product or service.** What benefit will your clients and customers derive from what you do? Keeping focused on the benefits helps keep you focused on the enjoyment of your enterprise.

4. **Ask for your customers' comments.** Nancy Mueller and Jenniefer Kirk place enormous value on the feedback they get from their customers and use it to create new products and improve existing ones. As Sue Swenson says, complaints are a gift. Use them to improve your product or service.

5. **Keep your customers informed.** Many companies send monthly or bimonthly newsletters. Send special notices of changes, new employees, new products. Copy news articles about your company for your customers.

6. **Look at customer complaints as free consulting.** Value the input from customer complaints. Talk to the customer to learn all the details of the situation, listen, and ask whether he or she has a suggestion. As Sue Swenson reminds us, "[customer complaints] point out the frailties in your process and your procedures."

7. **Take personal responsibility for mix-ups.** Don't pass the buck. Take interest and take action. Tell the customer what you personally will do to help out. Then do it and follow up with the customer as soon as possible.

8. **Go the extra mile—and dollar.** Even if it costs you extra money to settle a problem, consider that you're spending it on PR. It's money well spent. One unhappy customer tells more people than you can imagine.

9. **Know your customers.** If you don't have the opportunity to meet your customers in person, get to know them on the phone. Pay attention when they mention events in their stores or stories about their children. Know their payment history and thank them if they have a good record. Work *with* them.

10. **Involve your customers in your company.** Some businesses invite good customers to sit on informal "boards of advisors." Others, like Kirks Folly, involve their customers in special events, parties, and cruises. Invite customers to join in the fun.

Commandment Eleven

Give Back to Keep the Cycle of Success Going

One of the most impressive aspects of researching this book was the generosity of the women who contributed. They felt that if what they had to say would help other women, they would gladly take part—and suggested others who had interesting and meaningful stories. From the very beginning, even before this book had found a publisher, the women interviewed gave generously of their time and their insights. They didn't say, "Call me when it will count." Their enthusiasm for this project made it count and helped make it possible.

> **"It's most important to pass along to others on their way up what your wonderful supporters gave you: confidence, moral support, and the hope to actualize your dreams."**
> —Angi Ma Wong, President, Intercultural Consulting and Training

As the book developed, women kept saying that for them, success included "giving back." Many who had risen to the tops of their companies or built thriving businesses believed strongly in helping other women, especially those who were just starting out or struggling to create their own success. They genuinely desired to make a difference by passing on what they had learned from their experiences. They understood, too, that giving back would bring them a great deal of personal satisfaction. As Claudette Weber, owner of Brero

Construction, told me, "Giving back isn't sacrificial, because the feelings that you get from it are a bonus to you."

Giving back can take a number of forms. It begins with the realization that each of us can make a difference and that we all have something worthwhile to share, regardless of our current level of expertise. For women just starting out, being able to talk to others in the same situation and brainstorm solutions to common problems can sometimes be a way of giving back. For more experienced women, giving talks and volunteering in professional, community, and school organizations or signing up to be a mentor can provide opportunities for helping others. Successful women get back as much as they give when they serve as role models, inspiring and encouraging other women, promoting values such as self-reliance, offering practical advice, and effecting change.

Judy Vredenburgh: Giving Back in a Second Career

"While I loved the opportunity to achieve career success and financial independence, I knew early on that I would go as far as I could and by age fifty pursue a career that would allow me to give back in a socially meaningful way."

—Judy Vredenburgh, Senior Vice President for Revenue Development, March of Dimes

Many of the women in this book have spoken about the importance of integrity, good relationships with customers and colleagues, and other values that improve the quality of life and work. Judy Vredenburgh, a woman who found great success in women's clothing retailing, espoused those values too. During her long career with a number of national retailers, she says, "I believed the whole time that I was selling clothes that I was helping women, that I was giving the customers good value, trying to do it in a very ethical framework." At some point, though, she realized that, even so, her main contributions were in selling clothes and providing shareholders value. That was fine, but Judy found personal pleasure in sharing what she had learned along the way to help other women rise in the ranks of corporations. Her long-term plan was to have a second career that would allow her to use what she had learned in business to help society.

Judy began her retailing career in the training program at Abraham & Straus, part of Federated Department Stores, because it looked as though it would quickly allow her to operate fairly autonomously with a high level of responsibility. A big part of her personal motivation, Judy says, comes from her need for economic independence. "I did very well as a merchant. I loved being responsible for sales, margins, and inventory turn. But as I rose through the ranks in retailing, I also wanted to make it possible for women to do things that they couldn't do before: to hold significant line positions. Because of my own experience with being married and having a child, I also wanted organizations to see that just because a woman was pregnant didn't mean that she couldn't do the job or was not going to come back to work. Retailing has historically been dominated by women, but at low levels. It's only been recently that women have aspired to middle management, then upper-, then upper-upper management positions, not to mention wanting to include being married and having children."

During her retail career in women's clothing, Judy worked for a number of major firms, taking increasingly more responsible positions, some of which involved mergers and turnarounds in difficult situations. As CEO of the Chess King business, a young men's specialty apparel chain with five hundred stores nationwide, Judy saw herself in a high-risk, high-gain situation, and possibly her last step in retail. She says, "My boss and I disagreed with the general direction of the turnaround. I did my strategic research and started to get results, but we didn't have a meeting of the minds and parted company. After a short time, they sold the business."

It was at this point that Judy had to decide what she wanted to do next: go back in the job market and run a new business or start a second career. She took some time to recuperate from her frantic sixty-to-eighty-hour work weeks, and after much reflection, decided it was time to enact her long-term career plan. After following her own investigations, volunteering her skills in strategic planning work for Big Sisters in New York, and joining their board of directors, Judy found that the world of not-for-profits was right for her. "In the nonprofit world I found people motivated largely by the desire to do good. And I learned that my skills were complementary to those of the educators, social service providers, policy makers, and scientists who were drawn to nonprofits. I brought them my external customer orientation, as well as my deeply held understanding of what focused priority and goal setting can bring to an organization's ability to creatively accomplish results. What I was really looking for was an opportunity that would provide the intrinsic satisfaction of helping others not as fortunate as myself."

Judy put together a resume and started networking. She eventually took a job as Senior Vice President for Revenue Development with the March of Dimes. Although she had no background with nonprofit fundraising, Judy knew she could apply her corporate knowledge in new ways. "Our president, Dr. Jennifer House, wanted some fresh thinking coming into the organization and took a chance with someone with no bias toward traditional fundraising or the usual March of Dimes approach. When I was hired in 1993, the revenue had been flat. But we've turned that around. We had an excellent 1994 and 1995, and 1996 will continue to be excellent. We basically took our traditional methods of making money and energized them. We diversified and developed innovative ways to bring in funds and new audiences." The change and revitalization Judy brings to the March of Dimes are possible because of her extensive experience in business—and her willingness to give back in the not-for-profit arena.

Judy is enjoying her new role helping people through the March of Dimes just as she had helped women climb the corporate ladder in her previous jobs. "I have a fabulous job. I have an opportunity to be in a job that has measurable results that are important to me, and yet the point of all this effort is to fund meaningful programs that improve people's lives." Judy also contributes her time once a month to lead a group of women entrepreneurs and help them on a one-on-one basis to become more successful. She facilitates the group of small business owners, who serve as each other's informal board of directors and consultants. They discuss staffing, finance, marketing, and sales issues. Judy says she gets her satisfaction in this group from helping each woman entrepreneur maintain economic freedom. Judy Vredenburgh is finding meaning, sharing her knowledge on several levels, and enjoying her role in keeping the cycle of success going.

Gladys Thacher: Smoothing the Transitions of Later Life

"People in this time of life are not driven by ego. They have tremendous good will that they want to share."
—Gladys Thacher, Founder and Chairman of the Board, Life Plan Center

Some women contribute to others' success by creating organizations that help solve problems they find particularly troubling. By working out solutions to these problems for themselves, then extending their knowledge to others, these women provide valuable and much-needed services. Gladys Thacher has done this. Having confronted the challenges of career and transitions throughout her life, she has drawn on her experience to create a series of nonprofit organizations that help people find strength and value in themselves by analyzing their own skills and finding rewarding work.

Gladys originally became interested in the career development problems of young people when she was working in a halfway house in the late 1960s. She wanted to understand why her young clients did not feel empowered and why they struggled to return to the community. Using her counseling training, she started an organization in her living room called Enterprise for High School Students. It was a place for fourteen-to-eighteen-year-olds to figure out what their skills were and to find jobs.

When Gladys was asked to join the Smith College alumnae board, she realized another need. "It was the 1970s and the beginning of the Women's Movement. Since women with liberal arts degrees often couldn't see what their skills were, we wrote to all of the alumnae and asked what they had done in life, and if they would be willing to talk to other women." Gladys originally thought that women from Smith College would be inclined to help only other alums, but she found that women of all backgrounds wanted to help as many women as they could. Today the organization she founded, Alumnae Resources in San Francisco, helps men and women with their career development and workplace transitions.

When Gladys learned that many of the older clients of Alumnae Resources weren't getting their particular needs met, she realized from her own experience that people over fifty-five had different kinds of transitions. "I found that at age sixty-one I was at a major life transition," Gladys explains. "The landscape ahead of me was significantly different from what I had traversed before. It contained an ingredient that I call 'the significance of aging'—the limitations of life. I knew I needed another way of negotiating my way. I needed to do some self-reflection to find out what held real meaning and value to me. It was up to me to make the kind of life that had integrity, where everything else would flow from that integrity." From that experience Gladys started the Life Plan Center.

Gladys believes that older people have lives full of meaningful experience but that society has no role for them. "Instead of their golden years, older people see years of great anxiety. They wonder how they will fund their old age. Yet what cuts deeper is the fear that nobody will want them or need them once they are not identified with a job. This is a very troubling time, and these older people need the support of others who are in similar situations."

Life Plan Center offers that support with information about careers, peer counseling, and classes, helping people over fifty-five reassess their view of life and their roles. "They must dig down and discover what values they need in life, no matter what they do. It's a time to redefine who they are apart from their jobs. Over the years they push aside getting to know what they want because of outer pressures. People fifty-five and older feel transitions most strongly and need to look at this third stage of their lives as an adventure. Each person is faced with a yawning gap of security about his identity, what his future holds, and what he wants to do." The program is structured so that peers share their knowledge about how to meet life transitions successfully.

Gladys has recently gone through another transition in her own life, turning over the presidency of Life Plan Center to Julie Lopp (whom we met in chapter 10). She is still giving back, however, through her role as chairman of the board and role model for others.

Completing the Circle

For Judy Vredenburgh and Gladys Thacher, the way to give back was to lead not-for-profit organizations providing valuable services to their clients. But there are many ways to give back to each other and to our communities. Efforts great and small, from giving an informational interview to volunteering to serve on a board of a philanthropic organization or someone's company can all help improve the world around us and contribute to each other's success. Remember these principles:

- Share what you know to help others succeed
- Believe that each person can make a difference

- Learn to be a good mentor

- Participate in organizations that further others' success

Share What You Know to Help Others Succeed

"Sharing knowledge empowers other women. You never know who you'll inspire. One thing you say or do might give hope and encouragement to someone who needs it."

—Angi Ma Wong, President, Intercultural Training and Consulting

Sharing your knowledge and experience is not something reserved solely for women who've reached the top of their fields. We can all help each other along the way as we accumulate insight and expertise. That's not just a practical matter, either. Helping others yields rewards in the form of personal satisfaction and meaning, both so much a part of how many women define success.

Angi Ma Wong agrees. "Knowledge is no good unless you spread it around." A diplomat's daughter, Angi was born in China. In the course of her career she has started and run four diverse businesses. She is an Asian marketing consultant, a publisher and award-winning author, and an expert in feng shui, the ancient Chinese art of placement that harmonizes your environment with the natural energies of the earth for health and prosperity. In 1995 Angi was named one of the Outstanding Los Angeles Business Women by National Association of Women Business Owners and nominated by Ernst & Young and Merrill Lynch for *Inc.* Magazine's Entrepreneur of the Year Award.

"Share what you do best and be generous with your expertise and enthusiasm," Angi says. "Whose life will you change today because you were kind, generous, giving, compassionate, or a good listener? I believe that you must always remember—and keep in touch with—the people who helped, mentored, and believed in you. Show your family, friends, and business associates your appreciation. Use your God-given gifts for the betterment of yourself, your family, your community, your country, and the world."

"Sharing knowledge empowers other women," adds Angi. "You never know who you'll inspire. One thing you say or do might give hope and encouragement to someone who needs it."

Claudette Weber, owner and president of Brero Construction, feels the same way. Her interest in providing information and assistance to women who may wish to enter the construction industry has led her to help form the California chapter of Women Construction Owners and Executives, as well as the Women's Hispanic Business Council of Northern California. "When I can motivate somebody or get her enthused, I get absolutely charged. That's the best thing to keep me going." Claudette also gives speeches and seminars at universities and at national conventions in the construction industry and for Chambers of Commerce. She volunteers her time speaking to YMCAs, YWCAs, and business councils. She has found many avenues to share her knowledge and keep the cycle of success going.

Her latest activity is as an invited member of the American Leadership Forum (ALF), an organization with just five chapters. The California group of twenty "movers and shakers" includes, among others, a supreme court justice, a mayor, the head of the David Packard Foundation, the head of the Red Cross, and several CEOs of electronics companies. The ALF concentrates on helping members give back to their communities in ways that will affect larger social issues such as crime or education. "Each year the group comes up with a very specific project, such as adopting a high-school class in a tough neighborhood and trying to keep them out of crime. A lot of us are at a stage where we have become successful, and now we're saying, 'I need a new challenge.' Then you become more communal. Although it's time away from your business, it's giving back—it's gaining in every single thing you do. It's absolute magic."

Believe That Each Person Can Make a Difference

"I had never done fundraising in my life, but I had good administration skills. When we did our first event, I really liked what I did."

—Miriam Israels, Board Member, Citymeals-on-Wheels

Sometimes the problems that confront us seem so large and so over-whelming that it is hard to believe one person can make a dent in solving them. As successful women know, however, problem solving is the same process whatever the problem. Whether it's in business or out in the community, each person can contribute ingenuity and creativity to finding a solution. It all begins with the belief that individual action can make a difference. Together, those individual contributions add up to positive results. Miriam Israels took her belief in making a difference, plus administrative skills developed over her years in education, to add to the quality of many lives through Citymeals-on-Wheels, a New York City program that provides hot meals for the home-bound elderly.

When Miriam Israels returned to New York after her husband died, she brought with her twenty years of experience in administration at the Bi-National Center, an educational organization in Mexico devoted to teaching English. At age sixty-four she had been gone from New York so long that she had lost touch with most of the friends she had known before she left. She wasn't sure what she was going to do, but she knew she wanted to find a way to give back to the community. "I went down to the Mayor's Volunteer Center to learn about my city. I worked on different assignments, fully expecting to volunteer two days a week for a couple of years."

"I was interviewed by the director of Citymeals-on-Wheels, and instead of going out to another assignment, I worked directly under her supervision. She wanted a source library, and that was my first big project for her," says Miriam. Eventually Miriam's administrative skills were recognized, and she was kept busy full-time for fifteen years raising money that provided food to shut-ins in New York City.

"Citymeals-on-Wheels is a wonderful program that had been going on for years, funded by city, state, and federal money. We still deliver 20,000 meals daily in the five boroughs of New York."

Of starting over in New York and finding her role in Citymeals-on-Wheels, Miriam says, "It was the luckiest thing that could have happened to me. I've met many interesting people—all the restaurateurs in the city helped us get started. My experience with Citymeals-on-Wheels has made me feel that I am doing something worthwhile, and I'm giving something back. I think how lucky I am. I have no children. I'm on my own, and here I am able to help other people." Miriam retired from Citymeals-on-Wheels in 1993 when she was seventy-nine but remains active in the organization through her participation on its board.

Learn to Be a Good Mentor

"I've never imposed my values or my ideas on the people I mentor. I've always found out what they wanted and showed them how to get where *they* wanted to go."

—Ollie Stevenson, Principal, Career Transition Services

Besides participating in community groups, as Claudette Weber does, or working for nonprofits like Judy Vredenburgh and Miriam Israels, there is much that women can do individually to help others succeed. Sometimes it's as small as a thoughtful note of appreciation or encouragement or an answer to a question that may save a colleague hours of research. Mentoring offers another way for women to help others become successful, individually or in a group.

Most successful women know the importance of finding mentors—those wise and trusted counselors and teachers who know the ropes in business and are willing to listen, support, and advise you on whatever issues are most important. Women who seek mentors often find them through friends, trade associations, the Small Business Administration, the Service Corps of Retired Executives (SCORE), and business organizations such as American Woman's Economic Development Corporation (AWED). However, women develop new ways of matching women with mentors all the time. Local chapters of women's organizations such as the National Association of Women Business Owners (NAWBO), YWCAs, and chambers of commerce have entrepreneurial groups and mentoring programs.

Jenniefer Kirk of Kirks Folly has benefited from her participation in organizations and from the one-on-one consultation she has with her mentor, an executive in the insurance business. Jenniefer sought help from the American Women's Economic Development Corporation (AWED). She says, "I'm in the Executive Roundtable group for women who own businesses with over $1 million in sales. We meet every month. It's been a great source of strength for me. I joined it specifically because I didn't have the tools I needed to grow the business properly. I wanted to learn from others. I found that I was not alone in my problems; everyone had the same problems, some bigger, some smaller. It made me take action on things a lot faster when I had the support and input of other people. Decisions that used to take six months now take six days, and I feel good about them."

Of her mentor she says, "When we really felt down and out, or when we got crazy, we could call him. He'd sit down with us and listen. He always made us feel good and capable. I would encourage people to find someone experienced in business who can look at your problem. A mentor can look at something that looks to you like an overwhelming hurdle and show you how easy it is to handle and tell you that you can do it. I meet with my mentor once a month, and I always look forward to it."

Ollie Stevenson also knows the secrets of good mentoring. She runs her own consulting business, Career Transition Services, in Beverly Hills, California, and is a Senior Consultant and Master

Trainer for Drake Beam Morin, the largest career consulting firm in the world. Her latest book, *101 Great Answers to the Toughest Job Search Problems* (Career Press, 1995), draws on her experience as an African American and her expertise as what she calls a "job change expert." She travels across the country counseling, speaking, and conducting workshops in job change techniques to major companies including Atlantic Richfield Company, Lockheed, IBM, and Xerox. Ollie sees the difficulty people often have when they try to mentor others, and she believes that people must be careful and respectful. "I've never imposed my values or my ideas on the people I mentor," says Ollie. "I've always found out what they wanted and showed them how to get where *they* wanted to go."

Ollie gives an example of projecting personal values on others. "Recently, one of the men attending one of my workshops had applied for a job, and the company asked him many questions that seemed intrusive. For instance, the company wanted his last performance reviews. A couple of the women in the workshop said, 'Oh that's terrible; if I were you, I'd rethink working there.' I was watching him and he wasn't saying anything." Ollie told the women, "You don't understand that *he* wants that job—*you* don't. If you want to help him, you need to suggest to him ways he can accomplish his goals, not tell him what you think he should do based on what you would do."

Ollie continues, "Sometimes when I meet someone I think they have potential to do something fabulous—from my point of view—but that doesn't matter if it's not what they want. At some point in time they might get where I think they should go. But for it to work, the impetus has to come from within the person." Mentoring is one situation where both people get a great deal out of the exchange. The mentor is giving back, and the person receiving the help is being empowered to achieve greater levels of success.

Participate in Organizations That Further Others' Success

"I want to provide a place that's fun to work, where people can enjoy what they're doing and feel like they're doing a good job. I want them to grow as individuals, and make a decent living, then return to the community twice what they take out of it."

—Brenna Bolger, President, PRx

As we've seen, successful women are often enthusiastic participants in community-based organizations. They know such activities create multiple benefits—recognition for themselves and their businesses, a way to share what they know to help others, and a stronger community.

Brenna Bolger, president and CEO of PRx, a public relations firm in California's Silicon Valley, has designed a company she says "provides a place that's fun to work, where people can enjoy what they're doing and feel like they're doing a good job. I want my employees to grow as individuals and make a decent living, then return to the community twice what they take out of it." Brenna teaches her clients that being involved with the community is not only good for business, it's a *requirement* of business.

Brenna has gone even further. She has formed a nonprofit organization, 20% Plus by 2020, to address the scarcity of women in high-ranking positions in government and in corporations. "The day of the Anita Hill announcement I decided we [women] couldn't go on doing nothing," says Brenna. "I founded 20% Plus by 2020 to see that women make up 20 percent of Congress, 20 percent of the top corporate management, and a third of the federal judiciary by the year 2020." In the last six years 20% Plus has focused on a program Brenna envisioned to help young girls. Called SPEAK UP, the program works with seventh and eighth graders to give them better speaking skills. Brenna says, "My belief is that the reason women start to fall behind in the board room is the way they act in their school rooms and the way they act in their first jobs. I don't believe most women are verbally strong enough or confident enough. They don't express their ideas as powerfully as they need to. They tend to be a little apologetic. They speak tentatively. If we can give young girls more belief in themselves, then maybe, just maybe, we will see more of them in board rooms in the years to come."

A year after the founding of 20% Plus, as California and the rest of the nation headed into the recession of the early 1990s, Brenna turned the reins of the organization over to a young woman who had hit the glass ceiling at a major statewide bank. She turned her own attention back to PRx and to launching a regional economic rejuvenation movement to help keep companies in Silicon Valley. Joint Venture: Silicon Valley (JVSV) attracted thousands of women and men who were convinced that business and government could work together with education and the capital markets to preserve the best of California's environment and fix the many "broken parts" that were driving businesses out of the state. In concert with the San Jose Chamber of Commerce and Stanford Research Institute, JVSV developed a slate of twenty-one initiatives for bettering the economy and attracted corporate contributions of more than $1 million during its start-up phase. Brenna has again turned the leadership of the organization over to someone else in order to focus on her business, but she has other new community projects in the works.

The women we've met throughout the book have invaluable advice to share about what success means and how we can get there. Of course, by now we know that there are no "secrets." Every successful woman has defined success on her own terms, whatever her work setting. Yet, for all the diversity represented in these chapters, the women we've met share an enthusiasm, a positive attitude, a flexibility, and an alertness to possibilities that is truly outstanding. Perhaps most admirable is their willingness to share what they have learned with the rest of us. They encourage us all to have faith in ourselves and, in turn, to keep the cycle of success going by giving back and sharing our knowledge in the service of those who come after us. None of us have to reach a certain stage in our lives or in our businesses to qualify. When successful women all help each other, the tide of that success will not only lead to higher levels of achievement but also to more engaging work, more personally satisfying lives, and a better world.

Angi Ma Wong's Golden Rules for a Successful Life

1. Life is not a dress rehearsal, so don't waste it on worry, guilt, or regrets. Every day is a gift, so make it count.

2. Know and be true to yourself and what you love, care, and feel passionate about. It is important to know your own strengths and overcome your weaknesses. You are what you think you are. Visualize in your mind what you want to be and, yes, you can do or be anything you choose.

3. The world is full of good people who are able and willing to help you if you would only ask them. "To know the road ahead, ask those coming back."—*Chinese proverb*

4. Listen and learn, learn, learn from everyone around you. Others have valuable information for you if you let them teach you.

5. Be willing to work harder than you've ever worked before, but stay focused on your goals and dreams. Success is getting what you want; happiness is wanting what you get.

6. Don't let anyone else define success for you. Surround yourself with happy people even though they may not be as knowledgeable. You can always train someone, but you

cannot buy loyalty or a positive attitude. These attributes will contribute much to your environment.

7. Be humble. Everyone in the world knows at least one thing more about something than you do.

8. Share what you do best and be generous with your passion, expertise, and enthusiasm. Like planting seeds, you never know what great things may come from something you said or did. Whose life will you change today because you were kind, generous, sharing, compassionate, or a good listener?

9. Start each day joyfully and with a heart of thanks to whichever power you believe in for all the blessings that you have that day: family, friends, shelter, food, clothing. Forget about comparisons with others. There will always be those who have more than you.

10. Be good and kind to yourself. Instead of beating yourself up over your mistakes, learn from them, move on, and don't look back. See problems and setbacks as challenges that build character and make you a stronger person.

11. Step back and see the big picture. It will help to keep things in perspective. What difference will this make in a week, a month, a year, or five years from now?

12. It is essential to your health and prosperity that you make time to nourish your mind, body, and soul daily. Maintaining balance in your life and recharging your inner self are critical for being effective in all that you do.

13. When you are feeling bad, do something for somebody else or give something away. This simple activity will help

continues

you realize that there is always someone less fortunate than you whom you can help. It shifts the focus away from yourself.

14. Decide what you value and want most in life and what you are willing to sacrifice to attain or achieve it. The time may not be right for that job, man, child, or promotion, but its time and yours will come. I tell people that God never closes a door without opening a window, and I have found that the view from the window is almost always much wider and better.

15. Enjoy and savor your successes, great and small. You deserve them.

Ways to Keep the Cycle of Success Going Strong

1. **Plan to make a difference.** Making a difference doesn't usually happen by accident. Make it happen. Brenna Bolger of PRx says, "I want to know that my life wasn't spent idly and that I did something to make life better for other people."

2. **Take your daughter (or someone else's) to work.** Support national events sponsored by women's organizations such as the Ms. Foundation and its "Take Your Daughter to Work Day." You don't have to wait for that one day, however, to introduce young people to your business.

3. **Engender the spirit of giving back in others.** Ali Lassen says, "Success is feeling good about what you're doing. St. Paul said when you are blessed with life, you need to give back. I was

blessed with help from others and a tremendous variety of experiences, and a desire to share that with people."

4. **Make people feel good and capable.** Carol Decker suggests, "When someone comes forward with a new idea that's a risk, if you say, 'Oh, I think you can do it,' they're going to do it."

5. **Grant informational interviews.** If you are swamped with too many requests, schedule a seminar or an open door day and invite interested people to come at the same time.

6. **Volunteer your time.** Help others and help yourself. Kris Bondi of Kaiser Permanente says, "I don't think I have done volunteer work thinking I'm going to get something out of it. And yet, every single time I volunteer I get something out of it."

7. **Choose which organizations interest you and get involved.** Your interest and your expertise go a long way to help others. Sally Edwards says, "I'm dedicated to developing programs and opportunities for women in sports, and so I have been a trustee and officer of a national nonprofit organization called the Women's Sports Foundation in New York."

8. **Teach others yourself.** Make opportunities to teach others by speaking at schools and organizations.

9. **Start programs to help others learn.** Education is the key to self-reliance. A program can work at any level, from local grass roots to national. Laurie Clark, who heads the Grace Family Vineyards Foundation, says, "There is a wealth of students who go untapped. They can too easily become part of the mass of people who settle into mediocrity rather than try to rise above it."

10. **Make yourself available.** Be known as a woman who makes time for others. Jenniefer Kirk says, "I have people call me out of the blue and say 'I love what you do; can you just help me here?' There wasn't a person I'd turn down who wanted information. I always say, 'Of course,' because people were so kind to me when I got started. It goes around."

National and Women's Business and Professional Organizations, Associations, and Resource Groups

9 to 5: National Association of Working Women, 238 West Wisconsin Avenue, Suite 700, Milwaukee, Wisconsin 53203. Hotline: (800) 522-0925. Phone (414) 274-0925. A nonprofit organization offering information on job survival issues, workplace policies, and discrimination.

Alumnae Resources (AR), 120 Montgomery Street, 10th Floor, San Francisco, California 94104. Phone (415) 274-4700. Fax (415) 274-4715. Alumnae Resources is a nonprofit career development organization offering career planning and job search assistance.

American Business Women's Association (ABWA), National Headquarters 9100 Ward Parkway, P.O. Box 8728, Kansas City, Missouri 64114-0728. Phone (816) 361-6621. Fax (816) 361-4991. With more than 2,100 chapters, the ABWA offers business education and seminars around the country. This nonprofit organization for working women has 90,000 members. Membership includes a subscription to ABWA's *Women in Business* magazine.

American Society of Women Accountants (ASWA), 1255 Lynnfield Road, Suite 257, Memphis, Tennessee 38119. Phone (800) 326-2163 or (901) 680-0470. Fax (901) 680-0505. The ASWA is a society for women in all fields of accounting. It provides members with professional development, job referrals, career counseling, and leadership training opportunities through regional conferences and offers a bimonthly newsletter.

American Women's Economic Development Corporation (AWED), Headquarters: 71 Vanderbuilt Avenue, Suite 320, New York, New York 10169. Phone (212) 692-9100 or (800) 222-AWED. West Coast Office: 100 W. Broadway, Suite 500, Long Beach, CA 90802. Phone (310) 983-3747. Fax (310) 983-3750. AWED is a nonprofit organization that offers management training and business counseling.

An Income of Her Own (AIOHO), 1804 W. Burbank Boulevard, Burbank, California 91506. Phone (800) 350-2978 or (818) 842-3040. Fax (818) 843-7423. Web site *http://world.std.com/~ssimon aioho.html.* AIOHO is an entrepreneurship program to help educate teen women on how to start their own business.

Association of Black Women Entrepreneurs, P.O. Box 49368, Los Angeles, California 90049. Phone (213) 624-8369. This national organization provides business and educational training, resources, a newsletter, and contacts.

Association of Small Business Development Centers, 1050 17th Street NW, Suite 810, Washington D.C. 20036. Phone (202) 887-5599. Fax (202) 223-8608. The development centers are located in all fifty states, plus Puerto Rico and the U.S. Virgin Islands. They provide business training and free consulting as well as programs with an emphasis on international trade.

Association for Women in Computing (AWC), 41 Sutter Street, Suite 1006, San Francisco, California 94104. Phone (415) 905-4663.

Business Women's Network (BWN), 1146 19th Street, 3rd Floor, Washington, D.C. 20036. Phone (800) 48WOMEN. Fax (202) 833-1808. The BWN offers a directory of 509 women's business organizations in the United States.

Center for Exhibition Industry Research, 4350 East West Highway, Suite 401, Bethesda, Maryland 20814. Phone (301) 907-7626. Fax (301) 907-0277. Web site *http://www.ceir.org.* CEIR is a neutral and independent umbrella organization representing the entire exhibition industry. It was organized eighteen years ago as the Trade Show Bureau by twelve industry associations who recognized the value of the exhibition medium. It operates on behalf of its members as the primary research, information, and promotional arm of the exhibition industry worldwide.

Chamber of Commerce of the United States, 1615 H Street NW, Washington, D.C. 20036. Phone (202) 659-6000. Fax (202) 463-5836. The Chamber provides directories for commerce and industry, business reports, clubs, organizations, and associations.

Child Care Action Campaign (CCAC), 330 7th Avenue, 17th Floor, New York, New York 10001. Phone (212) 239-0138. Fax (212) 268-6515. The CCAC is a national nonprofit coalition of individuals and organizations responding to the child care crisis in America.

The Committee of 200 (C200), 625 North Michigan Avenue, Suite 500, Chicago, Illinois, 60611. Phone (312) 751-3477. Fax (312) 943-9401. The Committee of 200 is an international organization of leading businesswomen, entrepreneurs, and senior executives of major corporations. C200 members own businesses with annual revenues over $10 million or manage corporate divisions with more than $50 million in annual revenue.

Direct Marketing Association (DMA), 1120 Avenue of the Americas, New York, New York 10036. Phone (212) 768-7277. Fax (212) 768-4547. A nonprofit trade organization representing direct marketers of all kinds, DMA offers conferences, seminars, and networking opportunities for people interested in the database marketing business.

Executive Women International, 515 South 700 East, Suite 2E, Salt Lake City, Utah 84102. Phone (801) 355-2800.

Federation of Organizations for Professional Women (FOWP), 1825 I Street NW, Suite 400, Washington D.C. 20006. Phone (202)

328-1415. The FOWP offers referral information to entrepreneurs through their bimonthly newsletter, *Alert;* career development seminars; and the *Women's Yellow Book,* a national directory of women's organizations.

Financial Women International (FWI), 7200 North Glebe Road, Suite 814, Arlington, Virginia 22203. Phone (703) 807-2007. Fax (703) 807-0111. FWI is a membership organization of nearly 10,000 women financial executives with more than 250 chapters across the country. It provides continuing education, self-study courses, and management and leadership training. It also offers subscriptions to *FWI Management Quarterly* and *Financial Women Today.*

Independent Small Business Employers of America, 520 South Pierce Street, Suite 224, Mason City, Iowa 50401. Phone (800) 728-3187 or (515) 424-3187. Fax (515) 424-1673. A membership organization that focuses on helping employers in their role as employers. It offers a hot line and a newsletter, *Smart Workplace Practices.*

Institute for Women's Policy Research (IWPR), 1400 20th Street NW, Suite 104, Washington, D.C. 20036. Phone (202) 785-5100. The IWPR is a nonprofit organization that offers a quarterly product mailing, *Research News Report,* which includes a collection of articles of research around the country and reports in four basic areas: education and training, health and domestic violence, work and family, and poverty and income.

The International Alliance (TIA), 8600 LaSalle Road, Suite 617, Baltimore, Maryland, 21286. Phone (410) 472-4221. TIA is a nonprofit umbrella association serving as a central forum for women's networks across the country. It provides its members numerous workshops, seminars, and educational programs, as well as products for groups and individuals to strengthen their leadership, management, and career development skills.

International Association of Business Communicators (IABC), One Hallidie Plaza, Suite 600, San Francisco, California 94102. Phone (415) 433-3400. Fax (415) 362-8762. Web site *http://www.iabc.com.* The IABC is a nonprofit organization with 12,500 members and 111 chapters across the U.S., Canada, U.K., Australia, Belgium, Hong Kong, Malaysia, Mexico, New Zealand, the Philippines, and South Africa. They sponsor seminars, workshops, and conferences about corporate communication, employee and internal communications, marketing communication, public relations, and government relations. Members receive their monthly magazine, *Communication World.*

International Franchise Association (IFA), 1350 New York Avenue NW, Suite 900, Washington, D.C. 20005. Phone (202) 628-8000. Fax (202) 628-0812. The IFA offers seminars and forums and is the leading source of information about franchising.

Life Plan Center, 5 Third Street, Suite 24, San Francisco, California 94103. Phone (415) 546-4499. Fax (415) 777-1396. Life Plan Center is a nonprofit organization dedicated to men and women over fifty who are in transition in their work and personal lives.

Minority Business Entrepreneur (MBE), 3528 Torrance Boulevard, Suite 101, Torrance, California 90503-4803. Phone (310) 540-9398. Fax (310) 792-8263. E-mail *mbewbe@ix.netcom.com.* Web site *http://www.mbemag.com.* National bimonthly magazine reaching 40,000 minority and women business owners and government/corporate purchasing/contracting agents.

Ms. Foundation for Women, 120 Wall Street, 33rd Floor, New York, New York 10003. Phone (212) 742-2300. Fax (212) 742-1653. E-mail *msfdn@interport.net.* Fax-on-demand service (800) 809-8206. The Ms. Foundation for Women is a national, multi-issue, public women's fund. It funds and assists women's self-help and organizing efforts. It also sponsors Take Our Daughters To Work Day.

National Association of Black Women Entrepreneurs (NABWB), c/o Marilyn French Hubbard, P.O. Box 1375, Detroit, Michigan 48231. Phone (810) 356-3686. Fax (810) 354-3793. The NABWB offers meetings and an annual conference.

National Association for Female Executives, Inc. (NAFE), 30 Irving Place, New York, New York 10003. Phone (212) 477-2200. Fax (212) 477-8215. NAFE has 200 chapters around the country with 200,000 members. It offers contacts, opportunities, information, and support for female executives and entrepreneurs. Membership includes NAFE's magazine *Executive Female,* their venture capital program, loans-by-mail, a career options test, and business publications.

National Association of Women Business Owners (NAWBO), 1100 Wayne Avenue, Suite 830, Silver Spring, Maryland 20910. Phone (301) 608-2590. Fax (301) 608-2596. NAWBO has sixty chapters across the country and offers a network of support, management and technical assistance, leadership skills, and business contacts and referrals.

National Association of Women in Construction (NAWIC), 327 South Adams Street, Fort Worth, Texas 76104. Phone (800) 552-3506 or (817) 877-5551. The NAWIC provides women in the construction industry with education in new construction techniques. It offers a bimonthly newsletter, *The Image.*

National Association of Women in Insurance (NAWI), P.O. Box 4410 Tulsa, Oklahoma 74159. Phone (800) 766-6249 or (918) 744-5195. Fax (918) 743-1968. NAWI is a professional networking and development organization for women in the insurance industry. It offers professional and leadership training and certification of individual members as Certified Professional Insurance Women. Membership benefits include subscriptions to *Today's Insurance Woman* and *Leadership News.*

National Association of Women Lawyers (NAWL), American Bar Center, 750 North Lake Shore Drive, Chicago, Illinois 60611. Phone (312) 988-6186. Fax (312) 988-6281. NAWL membership is restricted to attorneys, judges, and law students. The organization does not offer referrals but attracts a membership who wants to make a difference in society and improve the status of women in the legal system. They offer a quarterly magazine, *Women Lawyers Journal.*

National Business Association (NBA), 5151 Beltline Road, Suite 1150, Dallas, Texas 75240. Phone (800) 456-0440 or (214) 991-5381. Fax (214) 960-9149. The NBA offers a software program to anyone starting a business that includes how to put together a loan package in conjunction with the SBA. It offers group health insurance, more than 100 benefits, and a newsletter.

National Chamber of Commerce for Women, 10 Waterside Plaza, Suite 6H, New York, New York 10010. Phone (212) 685-3454.

National Education Center for Women in Business (NECWB), Seton Hill College, Greensburg, Pennsylvania 15601-1599. Phone (412) 830-4625 or (800) 632-9248. Fax (412) 834-7131. The NECWB offers research, education, and information to promote women and business ownership.

National Federation of Black Women Business Owners (NFBWB), 1500 Massachusetts Avenue, Suite 34, Washington, D.C. 20005. Phone (202) 833-3450. Fax (202) 331-7822. The NFBWB has chapters around the country and offers networking and business information.

National Federation of Business and Professional Women's Clubs, Inc. of the United States of America (BPW/USA), 2012 Massachusetts Avenue NW, Washington, D.C. 20036. Phone (202) 293-1100. Fax (202) 861-0298. The BPW has 70,000 members and chapters in every state as well as Puerto Rico and the U.S. Virgin Islands. The organization offers meetings, scholarships for women, seminars, and the BPW/USA bimonthly magazine, *National Business Woman.*

National Federation of Independent Businesses (NFIB), 600 Maryland Avenue SW, Suite 700, Washington, D.C. 20024. Phone (202) 554-9000. Fax (202) 554-0496. The NFIB is the nation's largest advocacy organization, representing small and independent businesses with a membership of 600,000 business owners.

National Foundation for Women Business Owners (NFWBO), 1100 Wayne Avenue, Suite 830, Silver Spring, Maryland 20910. Phone (301) 495-4975. Fax (301) 495-4979. The NFWBO is the premiere source of data and information on women-owned business in the U.S. It is the research, training, and education arm of the National Association of Women Business Owners (NAWBO).

National Organization for Women (NOW), National Headquarters, 1000 16th Street NW, Suite 700, Washington, D.C. 20036. Phone (202) 331-0066. Fax (202) 785-8576. NOW has chapters around the country and offers the bimonthly magazine *National NOW Times.*

Society of Women Engineers (SWE), 120 Wall Street, 11th Floor, New York, New York 10005. Phone (212) 509-9577. Fax (212) 509-0224. E-mail *71764,743@compuserve.com.* SWE is a nonprofit organization of men and women with equivalent engineering experience. It is a center for information on women in engineering and sponsors an annual convention and a student conference that includes technical workshops.

National Women's Economic Alliance Foundation (NWEAF), 1440 New York Avenue, NW, Suite 300 Washington, D.C. 20005. Phone (202) 393- 5257.

U.S. Small Business Administration: Office of Women's Business Ownership, 409 3rd Street SW, Washington D.C. 20416. Phone (202) 205-6673. *WEBMASTER www@www.sbaonline.sba.gov;* Web site *http://www.sba.gov/womeninbusiness* or *http://www.sba.gov.* The programs and resources available include: training programs, Women's Network for Entrepreneurial Training Mentoring Program, Interagency Committee on Women's Business Enterprise, Women's Prequalification Pilot Loan Program, Federal Procurement Pilot Program for Women-Owned Businesses, and Statistics on Women-Owned Businesses.

U.S. Small Business Administration: SBA Answer Desk, (800) UASK SBA. Call for answers to questions about the SBA and request *The Small Business Directory* of publications and videotapes for starting and managing a successful small business, which includes information for creating marketing and business plans, product development, financial management, management and planning, and personnel management.

Wellesley College Center for Research on Women, 106 Central Street, Wellesley, Massachusetts 02181-8201. Phone (617) 283-2500. Fax (617) 283-2504. A research center for women's issues.

The White House Office of Women's Initiatives and Outreach, The White House, 708 Jackson Place, Washington, D.C. 20503. Phone (202) 456-7300. Fax (202) 456-7311. This office is a liaison between public and private women's organizations and the Clinton Administration, working to voice women's concerns in the White House.

Women Construction Owners and Executives, USA, 1615 New Hampshire Avenue NW, Suite 402, Washington, D.C. 20009. Phone (202) 745-9263. Fax (202) 745-0026.

Women in Communications, Incorporated (WICI), 10605 Judicial Drive, Suite A-4, Fairfax, Virginia 22030. Phone (703) 359-9000. Fax (703) 359-0603. The WICI offers educational and networking opportunities to women in print and broadcast journalism, public relations, marketing, advertising, publishing, and technical writing. They sponsor an annual international conference, newsletter, and magazine, *The Professional Communicator.*

Women Employed, 22 West Monroe Street, Suite 1400, Chicago, Illinois 60603. Phone (312) 782-3902. Fax (312) 782-5249. Women Employed is a membership organization working to expand opportunities for women through service, education, and advocacy.

Women in Franchising (WIF), 53 West Jackson Street, Suite 205, Chicago, Illinois 60604. Phone (800) 222-4943. An educational, training, and consulting organization that provides information about buying a franchise or starting one from an existing business. It offers networking and workshops regionally.

Women Incorporated (WI), 1401 21st Street, Suite 310, Sacramento, California 95814. Phone (800) 930-3993 or (916) 448-8444. Fax (916) 448-8898. WI is a nonprofit organization created by and for women entrepreneurs that offers group health insurance, discounts on premiere products and services, and an access to a loan pool of $150,000,000.

Women in Information Processing (WIP), Lock Box 3973, Washington, D.C. 20016. Phone (202) 328-6161.

Women in Management (WIM), 30 North Michigan Avenue, Suite 508, Chicago, Illinois 60602. Phone (312) 263-3636. Fax (312) 372-8738. The WIM provides networking, professional development, and educational opportunities for women in management and leadership positions. It offers a newsletter, management conferences, and leadership training seminars.

Women's Action Alliance, Inc., 370 Lexington Avenue, Suite 603, New York, New York 10017. Phone (212) 532-8330. Fax (212) 779-2846. The Women's Action Alliance is a nonprofit organization dedicated to realizing the vision of self-determination for all women. It offers programs specifically geared toward women and girls.

Women's Bureau, U.S. Department of Labor Clearing House on Work and Family, 200 Constitution Avenue NW, Washington D.C. 20210. Phone (800) 827-2700. This bureau offers information and referrals about women's rights in the workplace.

Women's Business Development Center (WBDC), 8 South Michigan Avenue, Suite 400, Chicago, Illinois 60603. Phone (312) 853-3477. Fax (312) 853-0145. E-mail *WBDCCIED@aol.com.* The WBDC assists women starting or expanding their own businesses in the greater Chicago area. It also assists other organizations around the country to set up programs.

Women's Council of Realtors (WCR), 430 North Michigan Avenue, Chicago, Illinois 60611. Phone (312) 329-8483. The WCR is the only professional women's group of the National Association of Realtors. It offers professional development, leadership training, referral and relocation certification course, conferences, and a monthly magazine, *Communique.*

Women's Economic Round Table (WERT), 1633 Broadway, 4th Floor, New York, New York 10019. Phone (212) 492-4439. Fax (212) 492-4436. The Women's Economic Roundtable is a nonprofit membership organization that educates the public about national and international economic policies and issues.

Women's Work! The National Network for Women's Employment, 1625 K Street NW, Suite 300, Washington, D.C. 20006. Phone (800) 235-2732. Women's Work is a national nonprofit organization that offers programs at 1,300 sites around the country for career development.

Women's Work Force Network of Wider Opportunities for Women (WOW), and **National Commission on Working Women,** 815 15th Street NW, Washington, D.C. 20005. Phone (202) 638-3143. Fax (202) 638-4885. WOW offers business information exchange and leadership development.

YWCA, Many local YWCAs have programs helpful to women and their careers.

Consult your local library for further information about organizations in your area.

Index